PERFECT RED

PERFECT RED

THE LIFE OF PARASKEVA CLARK

JANE LIND

Cormorant Books

Canada Council
for the Arts
Conseil des Arts
du Canada

 ONTARIO ARTS COUNCIL
CONSEIL DES ARTS DE L'ONTARIO

The publisher gratefully acknowledges the support of the
Canada Council for the Arts and the Ontario Arts Council
for its publishing program. We acknowledge the financial support
of the Government of Canada through the Book Publishing
Industry Development Program (BPIDP) for our publishing activities.

Printed and bound in Canada

LIBRARY AND ARCHIVES CANADA CATALOGUING IN PUBLICATION

Lind, Jane
Perfect red : the life of Paraskeva Clark / Jane Lind.

Includes bibliographical references and index.

ISBN 978-1-897151-44-0

1. Clark, Paraskeva, 1898–1986. 2. Painters — Canada — Biography.

I. Title.

ND249.C494L55 2009   709.2   C2009-903868-4

Editor: Ruth Bradley-St.-Cyr
Cover design: Angel Guerra/Archetype
Front cover image: *Myself* (1933) by Paraskeva Clark.
Oil on canvas, 101.6 x 76.2 cm. National Gallery of Canada 18311.
Text design: Tannice Goddard/Soul Oasis Networking
Printer: Friesens

CORMORANT BOOKS INC.
215 SPADINA AVENUE, STUDIO 230, TORONTO, ONTARIO, CANADA M5T 2C7
www.cormorantbooks.com

 Mixed Sources
Cert no. SW-COC-001271
© 1996 FSC
FSC

For Tessa
And in memory of Natalie Luckyj (1945–2002)

Contents

PORTRAIT

When she, that soul of fire, appears,
O women of the North, among you,
It is a radiant challenge flung you,
Your dull conventions, worldly fears.
She spends herself as, bright and daring,
She rushes on against those bars,
How like a lawless comet flaring
Among the calculated stars!

— Alexander Pushkin, 1828
Treasury of Russian Verse, 1949

Introduction ⪢

In the southwest corner of Ontario's Algonquin Provincial Park, Canoe Lake, like a magnet, draws many Canadians to its bright blue waters surrounded by coniferous forests. Paraskeva Clark, too, felt that pull, so, on a summer day in 1950, she sat in a canoe while her oarsman paddled toward the Tom Thomson memorial in the southern part of the lake. Thomson, an artist who painted the splendours of Algonquin, drowned in the summer of 1917 at age thirty-nine. In this landscape painter, because of his love of Ontario's wilderness and his interpretation of it in his paintings — and because of the mystery surrounding his death — English Canadians have created an icon that even the Russian-born Paraskeva Clark could not resist.

When Paraskeva first arrived in Toronto in 1931, she roundly criticized and scoffed at the landscape painting of Thomson and his contemporaries, the Group of Seven. Having studied art in St. Petersburg, Russia, then having lived in Paris for eight years where she was exposed to modern art, Paraskeva could not believe that any nation would endorse a modern art movement based on landscape. And yet, despite her dogged determination to expose what she considered to be wrong-headed Canadian painting by ignorant artists, here she was, twenty years later, enveloped in that very landscape that had inspired the English–Canadian school of art she denounced. Despite herself, she was deeply moved by her visit to the Thomson cairn; she painted it twice, wanting other people to know about it and to understand what she perceived as the significance of the memorial for Canadians.

Something had changed in those twenty years: Paraskeva Clark had become caught up in the genre of Canadian landscape painting, becoming thoroughly Canadian herself. And yet — there is always an "and yet" in speaking of her — she remained critical of Canadian art, was still Russian, and would always be; herein lies the first of many contradictions I discovered as I explored her life and work.

Paraskeva chose to live in a culture completely alien to herself — another contradiction — when she married Philip Thomson Clark, an accountant from a family of United Empire Loyalist stock. Her complex person had been shaped in a working-class family surrounded by the continuous political upheaval and hardships leading to the 1917 Russian Revolution, whereas he was formed in one of Toronto's "good" families, indoctrinated in the proper behaviour of their quiet, staid society. In 1931, when the British accounted for eighty percent of the population, Paraskeva encountered a city of entrenched conservative values and attitudes, suspicious of people or ideas that did not fit into the established order — a city Wyndham Lewis called a "sanctimonious icebox."[1]

The vast difference between the two cultures presented many difficulties for Paraskeva Clark. From the day she arrived in Toronto until the day she died, she faced prejudice, not only because she was a woman, but because she was an immigrant. Even worse, she was a socialist. And if that were not enough, she had few inhibitions and spoke her mind without worrying what other people thought of her. How, then, could a daughter of a St. Petersburg peasant factory worker and a woman trained in traditional old-Russian flower-making feel at home among people born and bred in Toronto's propriety-obsessed Victorian culture? What about the contradiction of a Red Russian, a communist, whose birth family survived the violence of the 1917 Russian

Revolution, marrying a staunch capitalist? How was she to manoeuvre her way through this alien territory called middle-class Toronto? Here, the expectations for women and men were fixed. How did a woman blaze her own path when it was considered natural to deny personal ambition in favour of husband and children? What were the options for a dynamic, creative woman in the 1930s in Toronto? Could she have her own work, and what did having her own work mean? As she faced these questions and obstacles, Paraskeva had the audacity to develop her career in an environment that could swing back and forth between suspicion and acceptance.

Paraskeva gravitated toward the artists in Toronto immediately upon her arrival. It was only a year after she came that she took a first step into Toronto's art world by entering a self-portrait in an exhibition. From then on, her painting gained respect as she developed confidence in her ability as a painter and continued showing her work in Toronto and elsewhere.

I NEVER MET Paraskeva Clark, but in 1983, I saw her for the first time in *Portrait of the Artist as an Old Lady*, a documentary filmed near the end of her life.[2] From time to time during the next twenty years, the image of this small, uninhibited, spirited woman, with her scrappy enthusiasm for art in society, kept surfacing in my mind until I finally ordered the film from the National Film Board of Canada. Her sheer guts hooked me, and I became fascinated with her life story, which intersected with some of the most compelling political events of the twentieth century — the Russian Revolution of 1917, World War I, the Spanish Civil War, World War II, the Cold War — events that specifically influenced her life and art.

There are strong reasons for a book on Paraskeva Clark. Her story is a window opening onto a fertile period of Canadian art during the 1930s and 1940s when she became a catalyst among Toronto artists. Her life — a microcosm of a woman artist's struggle for self-fulfilment — becomes a macrocosm for the many female colleagues in similar circumstances, many of whom are still largely unknown to Canadians and ignored in Canadian art history.

PARASKEVA AVDEYEVNA PLISTIK was born in St. Petersburg in 1898 during a period of Russian history when upheaval and chaos were just a normal part of life. There, during her first twenty-five years, she experienced major disappointments and tragedies that determined the course of her life: her working-class parents could not afford the education she needed to go into acting, which was her passion; her mother died when Paraskeva was seventeen years old; her first husband drowned three months after the birth of their son, Benedict, in 1923. These life experiences during her childhood and youth, along with her discerning intelligence, shaped her personality and her outlook on life.

A diminutive woman with large hands, Paraskeva had intense blue-grey eyes, but did not seem small, for she had a forceful energy and personality that filled a large space. Her verve, her disputatious nature, and her uninhibited language disarmed Torontonians who expected women to be demure and quiet. Paraskeva was neither. Furthermore, people were unsure of the pronunciation of her given name, and even less sure about its spelling. However, her last name, "Clark," was as common as it was acceptable; these two names came to symbolize the contradictions she embodied.

Frequently, when people first met her, they assumed she was a White Russian who had escaped the Revolution to take refuge in the kindly atmosphere of Canada. Not so, she would say in her booming voice, "I am a Red Russian." That was the point when any conversation that might have begun often ended.

A common thread running through all parts of her life was her intensity. "Everything you love you have to work for," she said.[3] And she loved art. Because of this love and her painter's eye, over the years she created insightful portraits, still lifes, landscapes, and paintings about the social injustices of her time. As an influential artist in Toronto during the 1930s and 1940s, Paraskeva was included in many national and international shows of Canadian art.

Paraskeva was deeply affected both by the social framework erected for women, and by the political currents of history, beginning in St. Petersburg after the turn of the twentieth century. During the Depression, she challenged Canadian artists to paint the life around them, dry, dusty, and desperate. She took up the cause of Spain's nationalists during the Spanish Civil War. Throughout the years of World War II, she worked endlessly to promote support for the Soviet Union, especially for the city of Leningrad when it was under siege. She produced some of her strongest paintings during these years when world events compelled her to look outward and to act in the political realm.

As she participated in her community, she lived in total dedication to her husband and sons, but resented the time they took away from her work. Painter, wife, mother, social activist, she was always giving up the time of one for the other. The effort of integrating these aspects of her life threw her into turmoil. She complained bitterly, and blamed "god" for making women biologically responsible for giving birth and raising children. And yet, when it came to her sons, she had the tenacity of a mother tiger defending her young.

She drew on Tolstoy's characters to describe herself as a Russian, impulsive and self-confident; a Russian who will "bow low" with gratitude for being presented with a problem that seems beyond her strength.[4] This is how she saw herself, but at the same time, she also felt incapable in the face of the greatness and significance of Art.

She became a woman divided, full of many contradictions. Her desire to be Canadian while remaining Russian at heart gave rise to a conflict of her culture and personality with that of her husband: she, incapable of conforming to certain proprieties and he unable to be free of them; her strong belief in communism while he was a public servant in a bulwark of capitalism, the Ontario tax department; her need for his financial support and his willingness to give it, coupled with her own need for independence. These contradictions underlay Paraskeva's adult life.

When I spoke with Paraskeva's family members and friends, I frequently came away with the impression that this woman, for reasons known only to herself, withheld volumes about her life from them. Nevertheless, serious research unearthed a rich vein of information about her. Even though she left behind no known journals or diaries, we do have her handwritten lectures on art and a number of letters, which form an important part of the narrative of her life and provide some understanding of her thought processes.[5]

Of course, it is her many paintings and drawings, now in public museums as well as in many private collections, that make up a visual record of her interpretation of the world around her, and of herself in that world. Her portraits, her self-portraits, and her political works convey a directness of expression and skill in translating thought and observation into visual image. Her rural Canadian landscapes show a human presence; her paintings of woodlands evoke the interior of the bush; her still lifes provoke us to look at ordinary objects in a new way.

And yet, for all we know about Paraskeva Clark, there is still a sense that much about her remains a mystery. "No soul, no life, can be reduced to a biography ..."[6] said the great writer Octavio Paz, and this is especially true of Paraskeva Clark, a restless, complicated soul. I do not presume to portray the total person. Rather, I offer what I discovered of this artist and her life and times, and the images she gave us during her nearly eighty-eight years.

St. Petersburg Peasant Child

Into a red cluster
The rowan berries flamed.
The leaves were falling
I was born.[1]

Paraskeva Clark's name — Paraskeva Avdeyevna Plistik Allegri Clark — is a snapshot of her life. She was born in St. Petersburg, Russia, on a Friday, so her parents chose the Greek name meaning Friday. There was a saint of the same name and a church in Novgorod. Paraskeva was also named for her aunt, who ended up being called only "Pasha" or "Panya." For Paraskeva Clark, though she was no saint, her given name stuck.

Saint Paraskeva, also known as Paraskeva the Great Sufferer, was born in the third-century Roman Empire city of Iconium and over the years was attributed a number of powers and influences. She became the patron saint of female crafts, motherhood, and families. In Belarus, 28 October, Paraskeva Plistik's date of birth in 1898,[2] is also the feast day of Paraskeva the Great Sufferer. Had she been more superstitious, Clark could have attributed the many troubles in her life to her birth on this inauspicious-sounding day. Nowadays, St. Paraskeva's icon can be seen in the National Art Museum of the Republic of Belarus; she wears a red cape and a halo surrounds her head.

The icons of this saint bear no resemblance, however, to early photographs of Paraskeva Plistik. These photos, along with those of her family, rest in an old dismantled photo album, four faces looking out from their separate spots on the first page: a father, his son, and his two daughters. The lower right-hand corner of the page is scuffed and has a small hole where the photo of the mother must have been glued on and then pulled off. Who removed the photo and why? Many years later, Paraskeva, living in Toronto, would write to her father asking for a photo of her mother. He replied that he could not find one. It seems that no photo of Olga Fedorovna Plistik has survived.[3]

The father is Avdey Yakinovich Plistik. Zakhar Avdeyovich was his only son. His younger daughter was Palenka Avdeyevna; the older one, Paraskeva Avdeyevna. Her photo — a photo of one who would become an artist — stands out because of her large hat with the wide, filigree brim.

When the photo was taken of Paraskeva's father, he was probably in his late forties or perhaps even fifty. His coat — soiled, worn, and rumpled — tells his status: poor, working class, peasant. He wears a peaked cap typical of the time and has a goatee and ragged moustache. His sharp eyes peering through oval metal-rimmed glasses give him the look of a proletariat intellectual, discerning and bright. He also has an air of uncompromising dignity, despite his social class.

There is something stalwart about his children, as though they have a sense of their right to existence, even if their clothing is little better than Avdey's. Zakhar wears a cap similar to his father's, but his coat appears to be worn leather with brass buttons. Palenka's wrinkled striped shirt is a coarse cotton and she wears a tie, perhaps a school uniform. Paraskeva's expression is sober, almost glum. Her clothing gives the impression of attempted elegance, with her dramatic hat and a jacket revealing a low-cut blouse. She was probably in her late teens when the photo was taken, a young woman who had seen sophisticated clothing somewhere and tried, with what she had, to emulate good style. However, with her hat sitting too low on her head, her neckline lopsided, and her jacket ill fitting, she looks somewhat dumpy.

Zakhar and Palenka have their father's arched eyebrows, a physical feature that reminds one of Lenin, whereas Paraskeva's eyebrows are gently rounded.

All three of the children have full lips. Were the full lips and the curved eyebrows their mother's features?

We know little about Olga's origins, except that she was from St. Petersburg and had two sisters and two brothers. Her brother Vladimir was a sailor in the Russo-Japanese War, but her other brother was a factory worker.[4] Olga's sisters, also factory workers, were among the increasing numbers of Russian women working in manufacturing; between 1885 and 1899, the number of women in the workforce rose from thirty percent to forty-four percent. Opportunities for women in the professions were also expanding, particularly in medicine and education.[5] However, Olga was different from her brothers and sisters; she did not work in a factory but rather apprenticed with her middle-class godmother in the craft of making artificial flowers. Flower making was an old traditional Russian folk art, "scientifically done."[6]

Though Olga grew up in St. Petersburg, Avdey was a native of rural Russia, from the large Varvara and Yakina Plistik family who lived in the village of Zhabina in the district of Gorodok. Zhabina, five hundred kilometres south of St. Petersburg and about thirty-five kilometres northwest of the birthplace of artist Marc Chagall — Vitebsk — was in Belorussia, or White Russia, which the ambitious Catherine the Great annexed in 1772.[7] Belorussia was populated by peasants from a number of different ethnic backgrounds. The name "Plistik" apparently has Polish origins.[8]

Avdey was one of the thousands of peasants who flocked to the cities to look for work during the severe famine that swept Russia in the early 1890s. This famine was the first of a number of major national events that would influence Paraskeva's life. Because her father moved to St. Petersburg to survive the famine, she would grow up with the advantages of the city. At the same time, her frequent visits to her grandparents in the country gave her a love for the fields and forests of the Russian countryside and all her life she claimed to be, like her father, a peasant.

The peasants in Russia — like the large Plistik family — had been the bedrock of Russian civilization for centuries. Russia was a country of contradiction and excess, with extreme luxury and squalor, often side by side. Because the Russian people seemed capable of both great goodness and extreme cruelty, Catherine the Great was often baffled by the contradictions she saw in her people. She described the Russian soul as "limitless, now calm and sleeping, now swept by a raging wind."[9]

This "Russian soul" Avdey Plistik carried within himself when he headed for St. Petersburg in the 1890s, leaving behind the strikingly beautiful countryside of flax and wheat fields surrounding the peasant villages. In the area where the Plistiks lived, there were dark green forests of pine and cedar with white columns of birch, luring the peasants into the cool, damp darkness to hunt for mushrooms in the pungent forest earth. In the spring the peasants took sap from the birches to brew into a drink; black currant buds also made a good beverage.[10]

We do not know how Avdey met Olga but we know they married in St. Petersburg. Avdey worked in the Skorokhod shoe factory[11] and the couple lived in factory-worker housing nearby, at 45 Verejskaya Street where Paraskeva was born. She was baptized at the St. Petersburg Trinity Gavan Church when she was ten days old.[12]

At the time of Paraskeva's birth, Russia's last czar, Nicholas II, was in the early years of his rule. Known as the "Silver Age," this was a time of cultural revival based on the Old Russian traditions. A confluence of Russian writers, poets, artists, and philosophers gave their people — and the world — a taste through art of the richness of their culture. This cultural revival followed the abolishment of serfdom in 1861, which shook loose the whole of society, shattering the landed gentry-serf relationship. Serfs and peasants became landowners and merchants, or even teachers and doctors. With the rise of the bourgeoisie and intelligentsia — a new strata of society that patronized the arts — the world the Russians had long known became much more complicated. There was a surge in the number of common people, the *narod*, who learned to read and write in the late 1880s, and books were printed by the millions. The availability of books was a boon to Avdey Plistik, as he was among the increasing number of peasants who had become literate.

The year Paraskeva was born, bestselling author Maxim Gorky turned thirty and was writing his first novel, *Foma Gordeyev*. Gorky was already a celebrity, with his picture on postcards and cigarette boxes, and his clothes — the Russian blouse and high boots — became a costume everyone wanted to wear.[13]

Many writers of late nineteenth-century Russia were dissidents who opposed the czarist system. Because of censorship under the Romanovs, such writers as Anton Chekhov and Maxim Gorky found ways to criticize the regime through allusions and oblique references in fiction, which their readers understood. The revolutionaries who would seize power in 1917 learned much from these writers about the relevance of the arts to society. Contemporary cultural critics regard such writers as "precursors of the revolution."[14] Likewise, literary criticism in the early 1900s "served as a vehicle for political ideas, albeit in an Aesopian language that repaid careful reading between the lines."[15]

At the turn of the century, St. Petersburg had three museums showing magnificent collections of paintings and more than a dozen theatres where concerts, ballets, and operas took place. This theatre world held a special fascination for the young Paraskeva — a warm, dream-like glow in the dark grey St. Petersburg fog. This was the era when the great ballet impresario Sergei Diaghilev began his career in St. Petersburg. In the year of Paraskeva's birth, he received a special assignment to edit the *Annual Report of the Imperial Theatres*, and he organized an exhibition of Russian and Finnish painting. The same month Paraskeva was born, the first volume of *Mir Iskusstva* (World of Art) was published, a magazine "inspired by the idea of an art which existed in its own right, not subservient to a religious, political or social propaganda motive."[16] It was created by Diaghilev and the art historian and set designer Alexandre Benois, whose life would later touch that of Paraskeva.

In the sphere of politics in 1898, the Russian Social Democratic Labour Party was founded in secret by nine men who met in Minsk, declaring Marxist goals. Though they were subsequently arrested by police, these nine created the party that would end three hundred years of Romanov rule and execute Nicholas II in 1918.[17]

The 1890s had been a time of worker agitation, with Lenin educating workers as he went from factory to factory, gathering information on grievances and writing leaflets to explain workers' rights and the demands they could legitimately make for their own benefit. Strikes broke out from time to time — including at Skorokhod, where Avdey Plistik worked — but conditions did not usually change.[18] Marxist leaflets and booklets provided a philosophical explanation for the discontent and lack of resources of the peasants and factory workers. Many workers formed "Marxist circles" that encouraged an enthusiasm for self-education.[19] We do not know if Avdey was part of these circles, but he certainly would have known about them.

The Plistiks were among the thousands of people living in worker housing provided by factory owners. Their apartment, in one of a number of buildings clustered around a courtyard, was in the Moskovskaya district of the city between the Fontanka River and the Obvodny Canal. Not only was this Paraskeva's home, but she also went to school in one of the apartment buildings, one of the factory-operated schools controlled by the Ministry of Public Education for workers' children.

Paraskeva — as is true of everyone during their formative years — absorbed her childhood environment, her city of contrasts and extremes. The apartment buildings of her childhood enclosed a cobblestone courtyard where acrobats and travelling theatre troupes entertained the workers. The most popular entertainment of the time was the performance of the story of Petrushka. It was this courtyard setting that would appear in Paraskeva's signature painting *Petroushka* (1937) (Plate 19) about workers suffering at the hands of their capitalist employers.[20]

Just to the north, a short walk from the Plistiks' apartment, were the Central Baths near Gorokhovaya Street, one of the three broad avenues leading to the Admiralty, the other two being Nevsky and Voznesensky Prospekts. Paraskeva's childhood memories included going to the baths with her mother and sister. Many years later, the public baths would also become a subject for Paraskeva's paintings.

The building in which Paraskeva's family lived was relatively new, and in later years she took great care to explain that these apartment complexes were not slums. On each floor of the interior of the worker buildings was a long central corridor with doors leading into large rooms, one for each family group, with only a small kitchenette because each floor also included a large communal kitchen. The factory director's house, set in the middle of profuse gardens, which Paraskeva described as beautiful, was also built in the same area as worker housing.[21]

Paraskeva's memory of the area where the Plistiks lived contradicts other accounts of rough, crowded factory districts during the early twentieth century in St. Petersburg. A 1904 survey revealed that an average of sixteen people lived in a St. Petersburg apartment, with six to a room, and even higher numbers in the workers' districts.[22] Though it might seem to us that Paraskeva's family of five was crowded in one large room, by comparison to some other families, the Plistiks were fortunate. Fortunately, too, Russian women were known for their "domestic generosity," and their ability to create a feeling of security and coziness even in crowded conditions and poverty.[23]

However, the city's sanitary system was undeveloped — as were those of all Russian cities at the time — with polluted water, open sewers, and cows and pigs in the alleys. As new factory districts sprung up, the government was unable to cope with the influx. In many of the workers' districts, water had to be carried from pumps in the streets and required boiling. Even after cholera killed thirty thousand people in 1908–1909, the water and sewage treatment systems of St. Petersburg remained little changed.[24]

Given the conditions of Russian cities at that time, the story Paraskeva told her grandchildren is believable, that as a child, when she wanted to "go to the bathroom" in a back alley, to give herself enough time, she had to throw stones to ward off the pigs that roamed around looking for food and eating feces.[25] Despite these crude aspects of the city, Paraskeva remembered the area around the factory housing as beautiful, close to Nevsky Prospect with its panoramic view of beautiful architecture.

Built by Peter the Great on legends[26] and soggy land in 1703, St. Petersburg was the largest city in Russia when Paraskeva was a child, with a population of 1.267 million, including the suburbs.[27] To the south lay a sparsely populated area, marshy and wooded, and, to the east and north, hundreds of miles of wilderness began almost at the city gates.

Peter the Great built his city with straight, wide streets and waterways for transportation. Originally, there were more than a hundred islands making up the city, woven together — or separated, depending on one's point of view — by the great Neva River. A kilometre wide in places, the Neva flows from Lake Ladoga, branching into the four arms forming the delta where the city is situated, and weaving its way to the sea. Nowadays, sixty-five canals and rivers criss-cross the city with about four hundred ornamental bridges spanning the waterways.[28]

When Paraskeva was a child, only two permanent bridges connected the banks of the Neva, the Nicholas and the Alexander. Two others, built on boats, connected the islands in summer. More than twenty thousand canal and river boats were part of the transportation system and, on land, a 120-kilometre stretch of tracks for the hundreds of streetcars.[29] In winter, public sledges were used.

Nevsky Prospekt, sixty metres wide in some places, ran southeast across the city for four-and-a-half kilometres from the Admiralty to the Alexander Nevsky Monastery. By the early twentieth century, electric streetcars began replacing the horse-drawn ones on the Nevsky and other major streets. However, even by the beginning of the Great War, there were still some horse-drawn streetcars outside the downtown core.[30] Peddlers, with their horses and carts filled with all kinds of goods, travelled the sometimes rutted, muddy streets in warm weather and switched to sledges in winter.

As the capital of the empire of Czar Nicholas II, St. Petersburg was a city of extremes: a centre of wealth, nobility, and high society, as well as a place of abject poverty; a city of grand, ornate architecture and also of manufacturing, housing thousands of workers in close quarters in sharp contrast to the homes of nobility. Toward the centre of the city lived the wealthy with their lavish stores, expensive jewellers, and their all-important tea shops with samovars; off the great Nevsky Prospekt on the smaller streets lived the city's poor.

These extremes of St. Petersburg encompassed the wide gap in social status and privilege inherent in Russian society that gave rise to unrest in the early 1900s. However, Nicholas II was so entrenched in centuries-old czarist traditions that he could not see what was happening. As historian Orlando Figes points out, the nobility was cut off from the population by its wealth and governing status, and the intelligentsia were cut off "from official Russia by its politics, and from peasant Russia by its education."[31]

The city's extremes lay not only in its society, but also in its climate, from the long dark nights of winter to the late-June evenings when the white light of the midnight sun flooded the city, creating a feeling of enchantment.

At sixty degrees latitude, St. Petersburg is as far north as the mid-point of Hudson Bay and the town of Povungnituk, Quebec. Then, as now, during winter, daylight did not come until 10:30 in the morning and the city was gripped by an intense, damp, snowy cold, which could evoke moods of despair in its citizens. Blizzards whipped up with great force within a matter of hours and created huge snowdrifts everywhere among the green, yellow, and blue buildings of the city. The great Neva turned a silvery grey, frozen over from mid-November to mid-April, with the ice growing as thick as three feet; solid enough for the artificially lighted roadways created for sledges and pedestrians.

Set designer Alexandre Benois described such winters as "something grim, frightening, sinister ..." But the people, he says, by their stalwart nature, overcame winter to transform it into "something pleasing and magnificent."[32] The upper classes, of course, were not short of diversions. The theatres opened with elaborate performances of operas and ballets, there were dinner parties and balls, and Christmas and other holidays were celebrated with great feasts. However, those of the working class, like Paraskeva's family, could only watch from a distance the glamorous theatres and life of the noble circles.

The arrival of spring was high drama in St. Petersburg, no matter what your class. Igor Stravinsky loved winter's end because of "the violent Russian spring that seemed to begin in an hour and was like the whole earth cracking."[33] Usually by the middle of April, cannon shots from the Peter and Paul Fortress announced the breakup of the ice. Almost instantaneously the thawing earth had a pungent, sour smell as blades of grass began pushing up so fast you could almost see them growing. The spring flowers swelling into blossom were imprinted for life in Paraskeva Clark's memory. At the age of eighty she said, "I don't want to die — when I see the flowers come up in spring I talk to them."[34]

It was for the big spring holiday, Easter, that Olga worked all year long at making flowers. Each spring she went to city hall to arrange to rent a booth so she could sell her flowers during the week before Easter at the annual spring fair.

Easter was the high point of the Russian Orthodox year as well as a holiday to welcome spring. The extent and duration of the preparations for

Easter in Old Russia suggest an insatiable need for extravagant festivals to relieve the intense winter doldrums. By the twentieth century, the most extensive of these elaborate traditions had fallen away but enough remained to provide a market for Olga Plistik's flowers.

In Old Russia, peasants cut huge bundles of pussy willows, with some branches as large as trees, and brought them to the cities to sell.

On the Thursday before Palm Sunday, in the cities, a special market or Fast Fair took place, a cheerful and animated exhibition of toys and flowers. The Palm Market in St. Petersburg was full of every variety of branches, which were bought for children who carried them about the streets. Not satisfied with nature alone, to the bare branches the Russians added paper leaves, large and small, and gaily colored paper flowers. One branch would become the stem of a lily, another a gigantic bunch of tulips or a prodigious hyacinth. On some boughs were hung all sorts of fruit embossed on wax, birds and a little wax angel tied on with a blue ribbon.[35]

Many traditional flower-makers used paper, but Olga worked with cloth. She bought linens and velvets by the yard, and in their small apartment dyed them herself to achieve all the colours she wanted, including "perfect red."[36] For each type of flower — lilac, rose, nasturtium — she made paper patterns for the petals and cut the shapes from fabric. With wooden forms, a hot metal tool, and special presses, she worked over a rubber mat to create individual flower petals and assembled them into blossoms.

Paraskeva had a particular memory of her mother's lilacs since the flowers looked completely real to the young girl. Watching her mother make flowers was the beginning of Paraskeva's understanding of form and colour, the moulds contributing to her feeling for form, and the dyes, her sense of colour. At the same time, in those impressionable years she absorbed the idea that her mother had her own creative work, besides being a wife and mother. "I was a little girl and I was always hanging over her, behind her on her chair," Paraskeva recalled.[37]

If from her mother Paraskeva gained an aesthetic sense, her father's love for the Russian classics stimulated her intellectual development. She developed a strong curiosity, learned to love reading, and remained an avid reader all her life. Despite the limited family income, Avdey bought many books at second-hand bookstores. Space was precious in that small one-room apartment and when he had no other place for books, he stacked them under the bed.

With the money Paraskeva's mother made from selling flowers — Paraskeva speculated that it might have been more than her father earned — Avdey was able to buy a small grocery store in an apartment building close to where they lived. He also became the general caretaker there, looking after the building and the courtyard. Avdey was eager for his children to receive a good education. With their combined incomes, he and Olga managed to pay for secondary school for Paraskeva, four more years of education than was typical for a child in the Plistiks' position as city peasants. Her brother Zakhar finished school and became a locomotive driver on the railroad. We do not know what vocation Palenka pursued.[38]

When Paraskeva was a schoolgirl, her cousin Anastasia, the daughter of her father's sister Natalia, became her close friend and the two were "inseparable."[39] It seems that closeness between friends was more common than between parents and children in the Plistiks' working-class culture. As an adult, Paraskeva recalled, "in those days there was no such thing as 'close.' I was kind of revolted by sentimentality."[40]

At age ten, Paraskeva became ill with what she called something "like epilepsy on the leg." Her legs would shake as though they were vibrating with electricity and, when the agitation stopped, her limbs felt wooden and she could not walk without falling. Her father took her from one doctor to another, but no one knew what to do for the unusual ailment. In a neighbouring apartment lived a boy who had epilepsy, who had been treated in a special hospital by a neurological doctor. This doctor prescribed bromide for Paraskeva. She took the liquid three times a day for seven years, which could not have been pleasant given its distasteful odour. Gradually the number of episodes decreased until they discontinued altogether.

Many years later, Paraskeva read that bromide was given to German soldiers to dampen their sex drive in Paris during the war. She speculated that because of the bromide she lacked the sexiness she saw in other women. She would tell people that she was a romantic, "but I never was sexy"[41] — a statement many people disputed.

Avdey, like most peasants who worked in the city, maintained close ties with his family in the country. He frequently sent his children to spend time with their grandparents in the summer. Often accompanied by her younger brother and sister, Paraskeva went to St. Petersburg's Tsarskoye Selo Station, boarded the train bound for Vitebsk, and got off at the village of Neval, the stop closest to where her grandparents lived.[42] Even as a girl in her teens, she and her friend Elsa Brahmin still spent summer holidays with her Plistik grandparents in their log house.

In the peasant villages, houses faced each other on both sides of the road, with orchards and gardens stretching behind. These villages and small towns each had their own bathhouse. The schools for each district were located only in the larger towns. These towns all had a centre square from which the streets radiated, with the church as the dominant architectural feature.

The tenets of the Russian Orthodox Church permeated the life of the Russian people. Icons were everywhere, displayed by people of all classes, from peasants to nobility. A peasant house always had a place for an icon "in a place of honour in every living room — the upper angle of the walls."[43] Historically, the Russian people called the corner where they hung their icon the "red corner" because they were partial to the colour red — "in old Russian, the word for 'red' and 'beautiful' were the same."[44] Even shops and taverns had their icons, hanging over gateways and in roadside chapels. A photograph of a St. Petersburg grocery store around 1900 displaying a counter full of pears, apples, and other fruits shows an icon on an archway in the store between counters of produce.[45]

Wherever she went, Paraskeva would have seen the church's icons, both in the city and in the country when she visited her grandparents. As a child, she attended church classes on Sundays in a nearby apartment. Perhaps it was during those years that she learned the Russian Orthodox liturgy, because in later years she still knew it by memory. At an event at Massey College, she recited the whole thing to entertain her friends.[46]

THROUGHOUT PARASKEVA'S CHILDHOOD, political upheaval characterized life in St. Petersburg. Russia had slowly entered the industrial revolution but it was still a peasant society. The city's factory workers, restaurant waiters, doormen, and street vendors were all peasants, many of whom lived in poverty. Yet the wealthy and educated classes in the cities knew almost nothing about the lives of the peasants, in either the villages or the cities. In this "cultural gulf between the 'Two Russias' lay the roots of the social revolution and its tragic destiny"[47] — a revolution that would eventually influence the course of Paraskeva's life.

The upheaval of Bloody Sunday, 9 January 1905, occurred when Paraskeva was just six years old. G. A. Gapon — a priest who convinced workers that the czar loved them as his own children but their employers caused their problems — led a demonstration of 150,000 workers and their families. They carried religious icons and sang hymns along the wide streets in the winter sunshine, expecting their czar to greet them and listen to them like a kind father. However, Nicholas II was at Tsarskoye Selo outside of St. Petersburg and did not bother returning to the city to receive his "children." He asked that Father Gapon call off the march, because he wanted to avoid large crowds in the streets.

Father Gapon, with a portrait of the czar behind him, and the workers in a long column following, moved toward the Winter Palace. Despite the czar's request to cancel the march, the peasant workers were still confident their beloved "father" would receive them. Instead, the twelve thousand troops posted in the city charged the crowd, killing at least two hundred and wounding eight hundred more while thousands of students and onlookers poured into the streets.[48] Ever since, 9 January 1905 has been known as "Bloody Sunday," a day that changed forever how the workers regarded their czar. Paraskeva and her family apparently did not participate in the march, but they definitely experienced the consequences.

In the fall of that year, a national strike was called against the autocracy —

a strike that included thousands, from railway workers to actors in the Imperial Theatre. Such a widespread strike must have included Avdey. Certainly the Plistiks experienced the same hardships as everyone else, for stores were boarded up and such essential foods as milk, butter, and sugar were unavailable. From then on, as Paraskeva was growing up, workers' strikes and violence in the streets became commonplace with access to such essentials as food and fuel being cut off. The government of Nicholas II was unable to deal with the disappointment and anger following the betrayal of Bloody Sunday.

During this time, Paraskeva was in primary school, which included an art class once a week with a special teacher who had the students draw still lifes. In these classes, not surprisingly, Paraskeva showed that she had an aptitude for drawing. After four years of secondary school, Paraskeva was qualified to work in an office. She also had a basic grasp of French and German since these languages had been part of the school curriculum. What she really loved, however, did not come from her lessons at school. Paraskeva loved the theatre.

Perhaps it was because she observed the privileges of the noble class attending the theatre. Perhaps it was the excitement surrounding the arrival of the touring troupes in the apartment complex courtyard. Whatever the reason, Paraskeva decided she wanted to be an actor. When she reached her teenage years, she became obsessed with the idea. A friend told her about a theatre school, and that was what Paraskeva wanted. Nothing else. By then her father had the grocery store where she often she worked to help him out. Sometimes she would "swipe" money to go to the theatre. Two or three blocks before she arrived, she would find a taxi so she could "go in a grand manner to the theatre."[49] This little bit of elegance in her life was but a small taste of what Paraskeva would have observed only from the outside: the noble class in expensive clothes pouring in and out of theatres.

The filigree hat she wore for her photograph paled by comparison to what she saw the upper-class women wearing. By becoming an actor, she would free herself from the factory-worker existence — her dream of a better life would lead far beyond what her father had. Even though her mother's work was creative, Paraskeva envisioned a completely different life for herself on the stages of St. Petersburg.

The Faces of Love and Loss ⁓

And on the road two lovers sing a song:
They sing a joy that only lasts a day,
They sing the pain that lasts a whole life long.[1]

When a young girl is as determined and passionate as Paraskeva was, her dreams do not easily die. She was in her own theatre dream world, and could not have imagined the turn of events that was about to shatter the life of both her family and her country.

Paraskeva was almost sixteen years old when Nicholas II mobilized his army to fight Germany at the beginning of August in 1914. Anti-German sentiment in Russia escalated; German shops and offices were vandalized and the embassy was ransacked. Workers abandoned their strikes, and the streets of St. Petersburg filled with people cheering and shouting their support for the czar instead of demonstrating against him. He interpreted this nationalistic fervour as genuine loyalty in his subjects. How exhilarating for him, when he travelled to the Kremlin in Moscow to request God's blessing in the conflict, that a million wildly enthusiastic people filled the streets. In a burst of nationalistic zeal, Nicholas II changed the name of St. Petersburg to Petrograd on 31 August 1914.

Nicholas II needed this opportunity to bolster the imperial honour, but when the war dragged on and the government did not have what was required to keep its army functioning, his people's support wore thin. Furthermore, thousands of soldiers were killed, some became sick and died, many deserted; a year into the war only a third of the army was left.

Prices escalated quickly. A loaf of black bread in Moscow that cost 0.02 ½ roubles before the war began was 0.12 roubles three years later, an increase of 330 percent. A pair of men's shoes during the same period went from 20 roubles to 400. In Petrograd, food shortages were worse and prices even higher than in Moscow.[2] The winter of 1916–1917 was unusually severe. Blizzards and heavy snows caused even more breakdowns of the railways. In February that winter, the boilers of 1,200 locomotives froze and burst, leaving 57,000 railway cars motionless. As a result, there were shortages of coal and wood, and there was no flour available for making bread.[3] With these conditions, instead of helping Nicholas II, the war fuelled the revolution that would lead to his demise.

Russians were filled with grief and anxiety over the war. In this political climate of fear and uncertainty, when getting enough nourishment and fuel for warmth was almost impossible, Paraskeva's father and mother, like many other Russians, contracted pneumonia. With both parents seriously ill, Paraskeva, as the eldest, must have been worried and frightened. That her father began improving was some relief. However, watching her mother become more ill, and weaker by the day, was heartbreaking; the anticipation of a death can be as wrenching as the actual passing. Avdey recovered, but Olga, at age thirty-nine, did not survive. She left behind a family stunned by her absence. She also left behind her fabrics, her dyes, her tools, and the flowers she had made before she fell ill.

Years later in Toronto, when Paraskeva was an old woman, she still had some of these fabric pieces, according to Maja Miller Lees, a neighbour girl. Occasionally Paraskeva invited Maja into her studio and one day she showed her these flower-making materials saved from her mother's work. "I recall ... a trunk or wooden box." In it were "little bits of paper, drawings of flowers, and silks," Lees said. She still has a distinct memory of the colours — purples, mauves, whites, "incredibly delicate and exquisitely beautiful. I was so charmed by them, and I probably would have been eleven or twelve. I just thought this was the ultimate."[4] For Paraskeva, these fabric pieces were a tactile connection to her mother after her death.

Paraskeva, now only seventeen, took on the responsibility of dressing her mother's dead body. As was tradition then, the dead were kept at home, so Olga's casket stood in the Plistik apartment for several days. In her reminiscences, Paraskeva did not mention details about a funeral or burial. Nor did she speak about any additional responsibility as the oldest child in the family.

Day-to-day life was full of hardship for Paraskeva's family while the noble class continued their sumptuous living. Working-class people spent most of their time and energy searching for food and scrounging for fuel to heat their homes — there are countless stories of families tearing down fences and burning furniture to keep warm. It seems the Plistiks were among those who relied on the typical Russian stoicism as a means of coping with grief and the deprivation of the times.

Paraskeva had little to say about the privations she and her family experienced, or the violence in the streets, claiming to have been a young girl in her own world who didn't pay attention to what was happening. Perhaps this was a coping strategy since it is hardly possible to ignore hunger and the death of one's mother. Stories of others who lived in Petrograd at that time reveal the difficult circumstances she and her family experienced. One woman, then a girl the same age as Paraskeva, remembered that her mother went out as little as possible because people rioted and fought over any small food supply. Furthermore, a woman might walk for eight to ten miles to pick up her monthly potato rations only to discover that the clerk had written the wrong date on the potato chit and be told to come back when it was her turn. With the lack of adequate nutrition and warm clothing in winter, illness was more common than good health and great numbers of people died.[5]

By then Avdey no longer worked in the shoe factory; he was superintendent in a neighbouring building where he also ran his grocery store. It would have been very difficult, if not impossible, to stock the store during those times. Paraskeva's younger brother Zakhar and sister Palenka were still in school during the war, but Paraskeva had finished her basic schooling the year war broke out.

Whether it was because of a need to help support the family or for other reasons, Paraskeva took an office job in the Skorokhod factory the same year her mother died. There she met another young woman, Elsa Brahmin, an Estonian, who became her best friend. Elsa noticed that Paraskeva was continually drawing, often copying pictures in magazines. "Plissie,[6] you must study," Elsa told her friend, saying that Paraskeva should go to art school. At first Paraskeva was not interested — it was theatre school she wanted. However, with her mother's death, the family income was reduced considerably and Paraskeva began to realize that her father could never afford to pay for more schooling. Not having access to theatre school was her first personal experience of the kind of barriers the working class encountered in society.

That she was in the wrong strata of society to get what she wanted could well have been the seed of her strong socialist beliefs in later years. "In order to go to the state acting school, you had to have senior matric," Paraskeva recalled when she was more than eighty years old. "I couldn't go to gymnasium to get senior matric ..." The earnestness in her voice, even at that age, communicated how intense was her desire to become an actor.[7] She had even been bold enough to approach a great Moscow actor to find out what her chances would be, but he was very patronizing toward her and she felt repelled by the man.[8]

That experience finally led Paraskeva to explore other options. One day she went to the Petrograd Academy of Fine Arts to look at the art teachers' ads. There she discovered that the landscape painter Savely Seidenberg's studio was situated on the same streetcar line as the shoe factory where she worked. She realized she could take night courses and keep her day job. Because of Seidenberg's location, she could easily travel to her class after work, which was important to her.[9] The year after her mother's death, in the fall of 1916, she began to study painting with Seidenberg. Her night course was her first experience in a level of Russian society outside the peasant-worker environment, which was all she had known, except what she absorbed from her father's books and her forays into the theatre.

In Seidenberg's studio, she met new people and made new friends, including Ilya Yasha Raskin, a young, jovial, Jewish man from a wealthy family. Raskin, a cousin of her friend Elsa, became the first great love of Paraskeva's life. He soon left Petrograd for Berlin with his family. Paraskeva was not only disappointed, her heart was broken. When he left, she went with him to the train station; he hugged her and held her tight. "Plissa," he said, "Cover the hole in my heart."[10] From Berlin, he sent her a watercolour that she hung above her bed for many years. Raskin married another Russian woman in Berlin. Almost thirty years later, in 1945, Paraskeva received a letter from him — an old friend from Paris had given him Paraskeva's Canadian address.[11]

Seidenberg taught figure drawing as well as still life. For months, Paraskeva, as a beginning student, drew in charcoal from plaster heads, all the while feeling envious of the advanced students who worked from a model. Eventually she progressed to being able to paint and draw from a live model. In getting to know more advanced students, she experienced great excitement in her "first discussions on art and first resounding of such words as impressionists, post impressionists, cubists, Cézanne, Picasso, Braque, etc. Then the Revolution came."[12]

Leading up to the Russian Revolution that winter, artists, intoxicated with the excitement and optimism in the city, organized a parade called the "Carnival of the Arts." They rented buses and painted them in bright colours; painters, poets, writers, actors, and composers all piled into the buses and drove slowly down Nevsky Prospekt. With the spirit of revolution in the air, the present moment was all that mattered — doing "wild" things to wake up the bourgeois citizens of Petrograd, who couldn't stay away from the cafés where the artists performed in the same spirit as the Dadaists in Zurich. The painters Mikhail Larionov and Natalia Goncharova painted their faces, put seashells on their ears, and wore outlandish costumes to parade in the streets. The press reported all kinds of scandals in cafés, including performers fighting with the audience.[13]

Nevsky Prospekt had been, as early as 1905, "a sort of Speakers' Corner, a people's parliament on the street, where orators would stand on barrels or cling to lamp-posts, and huge crowds would instantly gather to listen to them and grab the leaflets which they handed out."[14] Often when crowds gathered, shooting occurred. All this excitement on the streets was accompanied by — or perhaps inspired by — severe hardship. Again, Paraskeva said little about it, except that the times were cold and hungry. Getting something as simple as a loaf of bread had become difficult, which, by some accounts, gave rise to the February Revolution.

On the eve of 1917, the average working woman in Petrograd was probably spending around forty hours per week in various queues for provisions. The bread queues in particular, became a sort of political forum or club, where rumours, information and views were exchanged. It was in these queues that the streets began to organize themselves for the coming revolution. The February Revolution was born in the bread queue ... when a group of women textile workers on the Vyborg side of Petrograd became impatient with waiting in line and went off to rally their menfolk in the neighbouring metal factories for a protest march to the centre of the city.[15]

The strikers, 150,000 strong, crossed the Liteiny Bridge that joined Vyborg to the centre of the city, and for the next several days, in mild, sunny weather, they continued their protest. Nevsky Prospekt — just two kilometres from Paraskeva's home — was crowded with not only the Vyborg metalworkers but also shopkeepers, students, and throngs of ordinary people who simply dropped their usual routines. Clashes with police alternated with demonstrators trying to win over the loyalty of soldiers and police from the czar to the side of the people. On 25 February 1917, near Kazan Cathedral, a young girl stepped away from the crowd and slowly approached the Cossacks who were blocking the demonstrators. As the crowd watched nervously, she drew from under her coat a bouquet of red roses. The officer on his horse leaned down, smiled, and accepted the flowers, and "the crowd burst into a thunderous 'Oorah!'"[16] The people had won. This February "bourgeois revolution" was followed by Lenin's "October Revolution" in November.[17]

This revolution was the second major national event that altered the course of Paraskeva's life, this time because of the resulting changes to education. In the spring of 1918, the new government closed not only the 174-year-old Petrograd Academy of Art, but also the artist teaching studios. The new government fired the teachers and declared the Academy's art collection to be state property. Paraskeva's studies were interrupted by this political upheaval.

In October 1918, the Academy reopened as the Petrograd Free Studios (Svomas), now under the jurisdiction of the Department of Fine Arts of the Commissariat for the People's Education, or IZO. Painter and writer Kuzma Petrov-Vodkin and set designer Alexandre Benois were among half a dozen artists elected to the Special Arts Council. Petrov-Vodkin, who eventually would become Paraskeva's teacher, was also a member of the commission given a mandate to reform the Academy of Arts after the Revolution. He became one of the most influential teachers of the institution.

Now, after the Revolution, students who had been in art school, and anyone else over the age of sixteen, could study for free; they were allowed to choose their professors and their working groups.[18] This big change meant that Paraskeva could quit her job and become a full-time art student; she also qualified to receive a government stipend.[19] She did not even have to pay streetcar fare because transportation was free after the Revolution. Most of the time, however, the streetcars were completely full and she had to walk to school anyway.[20] Given the situation in the city, chances are that she was often hungry on her long walks to the Academy. Furthermore, few street lamps were burning at night and indoors the lighting was sparse, perhaps just a kerosene lamp, restricting the viable working hours of artists, especially in winter.[21]

Each time Paraskeva arrived at the Academy, she passed underneath the inscription "For the Free Arts" carved over its imposing entrance. She remembered the school as a very beautiful place; it left an impression on her with its stately columns and, inside, the vaulted corridors, in which hung bas-reliefs. Off the corridors, doors opened into the classrooms and professors' apartments.[22]

Under the new regime, Paraskeva studied at first with Vasily Shukhayev, a relatively unknown painter and set designer.[23] His students worked at drawing and painting from the model, "one pose for a whole month. Composition problems were always too difficult for my technic [sic]," Paraskeva recalled. "Sometimes Mr Shoukhaeff [sic] would sit beside [me] and, with red chalk — two different rubbers and the magic touch of his thumb, would produce a marvellous, polished shoulder, saying afterwards — 'well you see how.' But it wasn't so easy — it did not appeal to me."[24]

During the time Paraskeva was studying at the Academy, the fallout from the Revolution brought about a great upheaval in all the arts. She was familiar with the many prominent artists, Vladamir Tatlin among them, who believed they were creating a revolutionary art — Cubism and Futurism — for the new regime. And she knew about the latest ideas on art.[25]

With many writers and artists claiming their art to be an integral part of the Revolution, the avant-garde movements thrived and the new era was celebrated in film, ballet, and theatre. The government declared that the art collections of the czars and the noble class now belonged to the people. A huge exhibition of more than three thousand of these works by three hundred prominent Soviet artists, called "First State Free Exhibition of Art Works in the Palace of Art" (Winter Palace), was held in April 1919.[26] It is possible that Paraskeva saw this exhibition.

The year after this large show, her teacher, Vasily Shukhayev, emigrated to Paris. Paraskeva had been discontent in his classes and welcomed the prospect of moving on to a different teacher, Kuzma Petrov-Vodkin, who was then a professor in the Higher Art School attached to the Academy of Arts.

Some other artists of the time who taught in the Free Schools — Kasimir Malevich, for example, who claimed to have invented a more "pure" form of cubism — are now much more widely known than Petrov-Vodkin. In fact, Paraskeva remembered that Malevich taught in a room across the hall from where she went to class.[27] She did not have direct contact with such artists as Malevich and Tatlin, but she absorbed the spirit of the academy's artistic community, throbbing with excitement and idealism, an atmosphere impossible to ignore because her teacher was a part of it. Paraskeva felt more comfortable with Petrov-Vodkin than she had with any of her other teachers.

Born in Khvalynsk on the Volga, as a child Petrov-Vodkin watched a neighbour bring to life Russian folk tales in brightly coloured drawings. Later, as a schoolboy, he became friends with an icon painter who lived nearby, and watched him work. When a sign painter visited the town, young Kuzma didn't miss his chance to observe how this artist worked as well. These different types of visual art left an impression on him, and he tried painting his own icons and landscapes.[28] By age seventeen, he had begun art school. When he encountered European painting in his studies in both St. Petersburg and

Moscow, he decided to travel to Europe. He visited Munich and a number of cities in Italy, but chose Paris as the place for the serious study of French art.

After returning to St. Petersburg in 1908, Petrov-Vodkin became friends with many of the Russian avant-garde painters and exhibited with the World of Art (*Mir Iskusstva*) Society. In this group, which mounted exhibitions of new and exciting art, Petrov-Vodkin was one of the major attractions for his *The Bathing of the Red Horse* (1912). This painting evoked a great deal of discussion and debate because its meaning seemed ambiguous: the massive, majestic red animal in the painting led one group of critics to link the work to the First World War; others saw in it a symbol of the Russian revolutionary spirit. The artist ridiculed both ideas.

Although he was friends with the "Blue Rose," a group of artists in Moscow who were symbolist painters, in his work he remained fiercely independent and formed his own unique theories. *Red Horse* was the culmination of the early period of his evolution as an artist, and it was after this work that he developed his personal philosophy of painting, what he called "the science of seeing," which was connected to his sense of the cosmos. He believed that "Motion is the main sign of existence," so he developed a painterly system to transform spatial concepts that broke with the laws of geometry. In other words, he wanted to convey a sense of overcoming gravity in an attempt at becoming part of the planetary system, or to have "cosmic involvement," as he put it.

In his landscapes, he often used a high horizon line that drooped at the edges, and many of his works are painted from the perspective of looking at the world from above. Sometimes his figures are set in landscapes that slope upward and away from us so that we feel we are floating in space. In his paintings of interiors, architectural elements are tilted instead of appearing as accurate vertical and horizontal lines.[29]

Petrov-Vodkin's ideas about spatial construction are evident in his still lifes. Like his landscapes, his interiors and still lifes convey a mysterious sense of space in relationship to the viewer. He places a table or a window at a skewed angle, throwing the viewer off balance. To create movement, the artist tilts the axes of objects, and the placement of objects within the space forces one to see them in a different way, to see their essence. With investing meaning in ordinary objects, Petrov-Vodkin revealed his attitude toward the world around him, that scarcity could be transcended by one's artistic vision.

When Paraskeva began studying with Petrov-Vodkin, painting still lifes had been his focus for several years. She was taken with his approach and she admired his paintings, sensing that the objects and portraits he painted had the warmth of the "emotion of life within." As she explained, "His somewhat austere, precise fine lead pencil or pen and ink drawing appealed much more to my character. His colour, restricted but brilliant and luminous enchanted me. It was not like anything I had been used to — not naturalistic nor realistic; it was classic in its simplicity ... I was very happy to be there at last."[30]

Not only was Paraskeva completely comfortable with her new teacher, she was happy that her friends from Shukhayev's class were there too. She discovered the hard work and discipline of good painting in Petrov-Vodkin's classroom. He used a traditional approach of having his students paint the cube, cone, and cylinder. "Another experiment involved the study of form and vibrancy," using only one colour to paint still life. And then there were the lessons on how to construct a head based on a form moving on its central axis, and seeing the smaller forms within the larger one. Paraskeva remembered, "For one month they painted the human head using basic geometric shapes" as a way of learning to "look beneath the skin for the real structure where he [Petrov-Vodkin] felt character is rooted."[31]

Paraskeva was excited by the study of colour and still life, to which Petrov-Vodkin brought his theories of space. She could relate to his way of depicting a visual perspective that was not an artificial architectural construction. "It seemed like getting new limbs to penetrate into space and to perceive the motion all around and to put it on canvas."[32]

Petrov-Vodkin, a humanist painter who integrated European influences of Matisse and Cézanne with his Russian experience, was a thinker, an intellectual, and from him Paraskeva gained some sense of the depth of an intellectual, thoughtful life, even though she might not have been conscious of this aspect of her education at the time. Besides learning from her teacher, Paraskeva also benefitted from the other students as she participated in "unforgettable conversations on art." Some of the students had studied with

Petrov-Vodkin for a number of years, had become his "disciples," and were "already good painters themselves, as well as perfect expounders [*sic*] of his teachings. In these two terms that I spent in this studio among these intelligent intence [*sic*] art students my soul and mind became forever imbued with the most advanced modern ideology in painting, with aspiration directed mainly to [the] School of Paris." According to a photograph taken circa 1920 of Petrov-Vodkin's "intelligent" students, the majority — thirteen of seventeen — were women.[33]

Paraskeva wrote about this part of her art school experience with enormous appreciation for what she learned. She felt that during the last half year she had become successful in her painting, a feeling confirmed by the compliments of her teacher and other students. "It was my best period as a young art student," she said. However, her account becomes melancholy and full of regret as she explains what happened next. "Then clouds of various complications in my personal life came to the foreground of it all — and being too young I allowed myself to be swept by life away from study, away from painting."[34]

Despite these "clouds" from her personal life, which we shall explore later, Paraskeva never lost what she gained from art school. In years to come, she would draw on her teacher's concept of tilting the usual verticals and horizontals, an artistic practice that becomes especially clear in her 1947 painting *Essentials of Life* (Plate 54). This use of the shifted axes in a picture is the major aspect of Petrov-Vodkin's work that most obviously influenced Paraskeva's painting. It was also Petrov-Vodkin's understanding of Cézanne that he passed on to her. And she, like her teacher, would become preoccupied with form. Petrov-Vodkin's "synthesis of intellect and imagination" suited Paraskeva's disposition, her hard-nosed approach to life couched in her strong creative drive.[35] Like her teacher, she possessed an unusually acute ability to observe visual fact, and for years to come she built on what she had gained in study with Petrov-Vodkin.

One of Petrov-Vodkin's still lifes, *A Herring* (1918), with its objects of ordinary life, symbolizes the necessities of life at a time when they were scarce: two potatoes, a hunk of bread, and a fish. Paraskeva's still life, *Essentials of Life* (1947) (Plate 54) — painted in Rosedale after World War II when she was far removed from the miseries of Petrograd — broadened and extended her teacher's ideas of life's necessities to include, besides a loaf of bread, a book, a flower, a candle, and butterflies, objects that symbolize the spiritual and aesthetic elements of life, with the book as the dominant image in the painting.

Though Petrov-Vodkin's *Red Horse* was painted before Paraskeva studied with him, she would have known about it. She painted her own *Bathing the Horse*, probably in 1938. An exhibition at the Art Gallery of Toronto in 1936, "The Art of Soviet Russia," could have been the catalyst for Paraskeva's horse painting,[36] unfortunately now lost, but it is more likely her teacher's *The Bathing of the Red Horse* would have been the stronger influence.

Petrov-Vodkin's 1922 *Portrait of Anna Akhmatova*, depicting the great Russian poet, is among his strongest portraits. It was painted the year after Akhmatova's husband, the poet Nicolay Gumilyov, was accused of partici-pating with a group of intellectuals plotting an uprising. They were arrested and executed without trial, an example of how the new regime, fearing fur-ther uprisings, terrorized artists and writers. Petrov-Vodkin knew Akhmatova well — they were both on the board of directors of House of Arts (or DISK — *Dom Iskusstv*, a literary centre in a building overlooking the Moika River). It opened in the fall of 1918 as a gathering place for all kinds of artists during this time of oppression of writers, poets, and scholars.[37] Petrov-Vodkin's painting captured Akhmatova's spiritual essence and the calm, deep sadness in her eyes.

The Akhmatova portrait illustrates the type of work that influenced Paraskeva's portraits of people in which she, too, captured the essence of the person; for example, her 1943 portrait of her close friend, the concert pianist Naomi Yanova. Michael Pantazzi, Curator of European Art at the National Gallery of Canada, pointed out that Petrov-Vodkin was the first of Paraskeva's teachers who, in addition to his work with students, was also a well-known artist at the time and had his own niche. He was a "supreme draftsman," preoccupied with the dynamic of form. However, according to Pantazzi, Petrov-Vodkin's training in draftsmanship sometimes stood in the way of his work as a painter. Pantazzi believes "painting came more naturally to her than to him. He was essentially a great draftsman and every now and then produced a great painting."[38]

Nevertheless, after having had two other teachers, by the time Paraskeva studied with Petrov-Vodkin, with her intelligence and understanding of art, she had an appreciation for his breadth of knowledge and skill. He was not only a good painter but he also played the violin, wrote books, plays, and autobiographical novels, and created holiday street decorations.

AS IN 1918 when the Revolution had opened the way for Paraskeva to attend art school full time, in 1920–1921, while she was studying with Petrov-Vodkin, another major political event resulted in an opportunity that would determine, in an even more dramatic and profound way, the direction of Paraskeva's life.

It happened like this. A famine of the same magnitude as the one in the early 1890s swept Russia, again the result of poor growing conditions and government incompetence. Thousands of people died of hunger; peasant revolts followed, along with workers' strikes in the cities. Electricity and fuel shortages plagued Petrograd. Paraskeva remembered that their apartment became so cold in winter that water froze in the sink and toilet. Rations were introduced, and some factories "were brought to a standstill while workers stood in line to receive their rations." Even the most privileged people were allowed only a thousand calories a day. The desperation and anger of the Russian people made Lenin nervous; the situation was all too similar to that leading up to the 1917 Revolution.[39]

At the same time, even though Germany and Russia were no longer at war, fighting within the country continued as the new Soviets battled the counter-revolutionaries. When the civil war ended, Lenin, in an attempt to be seen as capable of rectifying the situation, introduced his National Economic Policy during the Tenth Party Congress in March 1921, which was to be a "temporary concession to the market" as well as an effort to redefine the function of socialism in Russia. In this "concession," some private businesses were allowed to operate.

This change had a direct impact on Paraskeva because the theatres, in an attempt to find qualified staff, now recruited students to paint their dramatic decors. On the recommendation of an architect she had met, Paraskeva was hired by the Maly Petrograd State Academic Theatre to help paint set designs.

Here she worked under an Italian artist (whose wife was Russian), who had been associated with the Imperial Theatre as a stage designer and set painter for twenty-five years, Oreste Karlovic Allegri.

At the time, this must have seemed like a doorway into fulfilling her childhood dreams of a life in the theatre, particularly because after the Revolution theatre was no longer just for the noble class — theatre was for everyone. And yet, in later years she expressed regret at having abandoned painting when she was a young, impetuous student.

Allegri, who retained his Italian citizenship, had studied and then collaborated with the French artist and set designer Henryk Levogt, a neighbour of Alexandre Benois's parents. At one time Allegri had an enormous studio on Alexeyevskaya Street. This space, together with Allegri and all his assistants, was assigned by the authorities to Benois for certain productions. Allegri worked with Benois on many productions, among them the ballets *Le Pavillon d'Armide* and *Le Spectre de la Rose*.

From Paraskeva's description of the large studio where they worked, it is possible that it was the one mentioned by Benois in his memoirs.[40] Set design was a family business for both Allegri and Benois, and even though they frequently worked together, they also guarded their own turf, resulting in some tension. The sons of both Benois and Allegri worked as assistants — Nicholai Benois and Oreste Allegri, the latter named for his father.

In her new job, under the direction of the senior Allegri, Paraskeva was assigned to work primarily with Oreste the younger, an assignment that would change forever the course of her life. From the first time they met, their passion ignited and the two could not get enough of each other. Like characters in a novel, the fiery, determined Paraskeva and the handsome, dark-haired Oreste were inevitably swept into a great love affair. It was a romance of a poor working-class girl being carried away by a "prince" of the theatre world. They ended up spending most of their time together, not only in the studio at work but also in their free time. Within months, they were married.[41]

Before they married, Oreste had been living in a room adjoining the theatre. Now Paraskeva moved in too, and became acquainted with the other workers there, including the costume makers who lived on the next floor. Now her whole life was in the theatre.

By the middle of the summer, Paraskeva was pregnant, and their son Benedict was born the next year at the end of March. Oreste, who lovingly referred to his son in Italian — *"mon bambino"* — built and carved a beautiful wooden cradle for him.

During the hours when Paraskeva was working, the theatre costume designer, Madame Corchet, took care of the baby.[42] It seemed an ideal arrangement. Paraskeva had established her own life; she was earning a living while she spent her days with the man she loved.

To Paraskeva at age twenty-three, marrying into the respected Allegri family and working in theatre decor might have seemed a miraculous deliverance from her factory-worker beginnings into a higher class and a world of new possibilities.

Although she never publicly compared the two families, her personal photo collection tells of class differences between the Plistiks and the Allegris.[43] As we already know, the undated photos in Paraskeva's old family photo album unmistakably reveal her family's working-class status. The Allegri photos, however, portray a family that was clearly in the intelligentsia, meaning that Paraskeva married "up."

We do not know whether the Allegris thought that their son was marrying "down," but that might have been their first impression, which would no doubt have been overshadowed by Paraskeva's artistic ability, her personal flare, and her intelligence. The photos of Oreste and his mother convey a sense of well-being, even an aristocratic bearing, in sharp contrast to the Plistiks. In one photo, taken in Leningrad (c. 1920–1922) with soldiers in the background, Catherine Pavlova Allegri, a slim, attractive woman, is dressed in a well-cut suit, a skirt and double-breasted jacket, stylish hat, and boots. Oreste wears a tweed wool suit with knee-length pants, knee-length socks, and ankle boots.

We do not have pictures of the Plistik apartment, but pictures of the Allegri apartment in Petrograd tell us that they had elegant, beautiful furniture, and a lovely fireplace.

During those years after the Revolution, however, even people in the theatre world had difficulty supplying their basic needs of heat and food, but the Allegris had a way out. Like many other artists of the time, Paraskeva's in-laws left Petrograd and took up residence in their home in Chatou on the Seine, on the western outskirts of Paris. Given the political and economic situation in Petrograd, living conditions in Paris had great appeal. Furthermore, in Paris the opportunities for the Allegri family set-design business were greater. For these reasons, the Allegri family was planning that Oreste, Paraskeva, and the baby would also move to Paris in the summer of 1923 where they would all continue their work in theatre decor.

Before leaving, Paraskeva and Oreste wanted to spend some time with his sister Olga, a kleptomaniac who stole furniture and sold it, and for that reason lived in a psychiatric institution on the outskirts of the city. Oreste and Paraskeva invited Olga to have a picnic with them along the Neva. After lunch, Olga and Oreste went for a swim in a branch of the Neva while Paraskeva stayed with Ben on shore.

It was a July day and many people were swimming and enjoying the warm summer weather. Eventually Olga came back from swimming, but not Oreste. We do not know why Olga lost sight of Oreste, or why he did not return to shore when his sister did. Nor do we know whether any of the other swimmers noticed trouble in the water. As Paraskeva stood on the bank waiting for Oreste and looking out across the river, she started feeling anxious as the minutes slowly passed. Why did Oreste not return? She could not go looking for him because she could not swim. As she later remembered the scene, many people were standing around oblivious to Oreste's disappearance. Olga did not go looking for her brother.[44]

The longer Paraskeva stood on the bank of the Neva watching and waiting, the more desperate she became, and the more dismayed that no one tried to help. She eventually realized Oreste had drowned. In a state of shock, she took Ben home as the Neva claimed Oreste for the night. The next day, she stood holding her three-month-old baby, watching as Oreste's body was dragged from the water; then with her father at her side, Paraskeva officially identified the remains of her beloved Oreste. On their way home, they stopped in at a tavern for a beer.[45]

That her life could suddenly be so dramatically robbed of the person who shared her great happiness did not seem possible. Paraskeva was devastated, and she had no idea how to cope. She only knew that this drowning should not have happened, and she would never find out the reason that it did. Paraskeva felt sure that Oreste would not have drowned if somebody had tried to save him. She always carried inside herself the picture of how he came to his end, how far out he was in the water, that she could not reach him. She shouldered that burden all her life.[46] "Nobody helped him," she would say with great sadness over and over, even in old age. It was the second great loss of her youth; from this one she never recovered. The scarring of her soul from love and loss would have a ripple effect throughout her long life.

A Mother in Chatou⤳

For women it's no good …
Their heart is always taken with anxiety or something.[1]

The little room at the Maly Theatre that had been her home for more than a year no longer charmed Paraskeva after Oreste's death. She went to stay with Elsa Brahmin, her friend from the shoe factory.

Post-revolution Petrograd, in 1923, had little to offer a young widow with a three-month-old son. Nor was Paraskeva's father able to give much financial support. The Allegris, living and working in Paris, invited Paraskeva and Ben to live with them, and said they would pay for her trip. She had heard much about Paris from the Allegri family, and the previous plans for her and Oreste to move to Paris led her to believe that she could continue working in the Allegri set-design business. The Allegri home offered a security she desperately needed; she and Ben would not go hungry there. Furthermore, she had learned about the Paris art world as a student at the Petrograd Art Academy, and with that came an appreciation of French culture.

However, leaving Petrograd was a far-reaching decision. It would mean turning her back on her deep ties to Russia and saying goodbye to her father, sister, and brother. Given circumstances in the country, chances were that she would never see her family again.

Many in her situation would have thought the prospect of living in Paris instead of Petrograd the equivalent of entering Paradise. But according to her son Clive, Paraskeva never felt that way: "She wasn't of the culture that would say, 'Oh, isn't this great, I'm in Paris, there's lots of everything in Paris.' But on the other hand, I never heard her say 'When I got to Paris I really missed Leningrad.'"[2] He described Paraskeva as having "that Russian suffering soul," particularly rooted in their religion, for the Orthodox faith included the belief that "suffering is an important aspect of life."[3] As Maxim Gorky wrote in his autobiography, for Russians "suffering comes as a diversion ... In the monotony of everyday existence, grief comes as a holiday ... A scratch embellishes an empty face."[4] This characteristic, especially true of women, at least partially explains Paraskeva's reticence in speaking about the hardships of the St. Petersburg/Petrograd years.

In 1923 when Paraskeva decided to leave Russia, she knew what she owed to the Revolution: her exit from the life of the oppressed factory-worker into the world of the artist. That in itself would have deterred her from talking about the adversities of the upheaval once it was behind her. In later years, Paraskeva repeatedly told people that she did not "escape" Russia, which was true, at least not in the sense of the many fleeing the Revolution. Still, to say that she did not leave because of the regime or the deprivations is somewhat of a quibble. It was precisely because of the political and economic situation at the time that Paris had a better market for the Allegris' work than did Petrograd, and she would have known that.

As was true of many Russians, including the St. Petersburg poet Anna Akhmatova — who never went into exile during the many years she was harassed by government officials — Russia, particularly St. Petersburg, was riveted into Paraskeva's soul. A woman with her own sense of pride, at heart she remained a Russian all her life and fiercely defended her country. This is the real reason she never would admit that she left because of the extreme conditions at the time, even though she did not actually escape.[5] Nevertheless, she did not take long to accept the Allegris' invitation and move to Paris in the summer of 1923.

IN THE MIDST of her grief, Paraskeva had to focus on the arduous preparations for leaving Petrograd. The process of getting papers for herself and Ben before they could leave Soviet Russia was complicated. She had been given Italian citizenship when she married, according to a Soviet law passed two years before, stating that Russian women would take on their husband's citizenship. But now she needed an official document saying that she wanted to take back her Russian citizenship to be given a Russian passport.[6] This kind of official document could take months, given the bureaucracy, and in recounting the story of this period of her life, Paraskeva spoke of the process as a long ordeal. However, less than a month had passed from the day of Oreste's death until the date of the document giving her back her Russian citizenship, leading one to wonder whether someone intervened on her behalf. But she still had to wait for her passport.

Another step in the preparations to leave Russia was obtaining an Italian passport for Ben. Because of his father's nationality, Ben was Italian, which created a problem; Petrograd had no Italian consulate. Paraskeva would have to travel with six-month-old Ben by train from Petrograd to Riga, Latvia, to the Italian consulate there. Fortunately for her, the Russian language had been used for years for administrative matters in Riga, which made the process easier. While she was waiting for her papers, she made a sketch called *Memories of Leningrad* (Plate 55), a sad picture of a lonely mother sitting at night with her child in her lap, an open book in front of her on the table. Ben's cradle that his father had made is in the background. Later, she would complete several more self-portraits from the sketch.

Getting her papers and preparing to leave Petrograd took between two and three months. When Paraskeva's documents finally were ready, she gathered a few of her belongings, packed diapers for Ben, and also put into her bag the sad sketch and one small canvas, *Tomb of Allegri*, a painting she made while she waited for her papers. This is her earliest dated painting to have survived.[7]

With the papers she was given in Petrograd, she obtained the Italian passport for Ben in Riga. There she boarded the train to Berlin where she took a rest stop with her mother-in-law's friend and then continued on by train to Paris. In later years she would speak about how disoriented she felt — she must have still been in a state of shock. In her bewilderment, she took almost any advice, good or bad. When she wanted to send a telegram to the Allegris to tell them when she would arrive, a woman on the train told her to write the Russian words in French, which she did and later thought that was "very stupid,"[8] the telegram being hard to understand.

After travelling for a week, Paraskeva reached the Gare du Nord in Paris. No one was there to meet her, so she sat down to wait until she finally realized she would have to find her own way to the Allegris' home, fourteen kilometres west of Paris. "I sat, sat and sat, and finally I went to the street and got a taxi and the taxi went to a different place, and another taxi ..."[9] Her story sounded like that of a person dazed and overwhelmed, not knowing where she was going.

She finally arrived by taxi at the Allegris' home in Chatou just as Catherine, her mother-in-law, was leaving for the Saturday-morning market. "Oreste!" she exclaimed when, for the first time, she saw her beautiful dark-haired grandson; he looked so much like his father when he was Ben's age.

The lovely village of Chatou on the Seine must have seemed like Eden after so many years in a city ravaged by revolutionary uprisings and war. Living in the Allegri's handsome house, twenty minutes by train from central Paris, was Paraskeva's first extended experience of middle-class life, a spacious, well-furnished place compared to a one-room apartment in St. Petersburg worker housing, or a room in the Maly Theatre. Her 1930 tempera and watercolour, *Overlooking a Garden* (Plate 6), was likely painted from the window of her third-storey bedroom, and provides a glimpse of the lush environment into which Paraskeva was received.

Living with her in-laws provided the security this young widow so desperately needed; they treated her with generosity and dearly loved their grandson. Despite her need for security, Paraskeva was also by nature a fiercely independent woman, and she had no intention of becoming dependent on the Allegris, which would have been humiliating. She wanted to "command respect," she said,[10] and began taking care of the housekeeping. She suggested that Catherine let go Mme Foucard, the cleaning woman. Catherine agreed. It was an arrangement that allowed Paraskeva to look after Ben and contribute to the household at the same time.

All the beauty and security of her new home could not make up for being separated from her own family and country, nor could it erase the grief of losing Oreste. She became depressed and bored. Her father wrote to her in 1924, saying he had warned her that she would feel this way, and now it was too late for her to cry about it. He seemed to be advocating the stoicism that must have gotten him through the pain and hardship of his own life.

After telling her he was glad she did not have to worry about feeding herself, he advised her to get married again, and said that living among foreigners meant that she was just surviving, and not really living.[11] Although Avdey Plistik thought Paraskeva was too emotional, he was proud of her because Monsieur Allegri held a high opinion of her. Olga Allegri, who was still in Petrograd, would report to the Plistiks about what she heard from the family in Paris. But letters from home did little to make Paraskeva feel better or dispel her sadness.

Around the time of the letter from her father, her father- and mother-in-law went to London to see the British Empire Exhibition. While her in-laws were away, Paraskeva was extremely lonely with her own memories; she painted another version of the sad sketch — obviously a portrait of herself holding her son — she had made the previous year in Petrograd.[12] Included in the scene again is the cradle Oreste had made for Ben.[13] Perhaps Paraskeva's loneliness and sadness was intensified by a letter from her sister saying she and her father had visited her mother's grave. They had also been to Oreste's grave, and planted a tree and two shrubs there.[14]

It is possible that the Allegris visited the Canadian pavilion at Wembley where the Canadian government exhibited the country's resources to attract British immigrants. This pavilion also introduced Canadian art to the world, featuring an exhibition of paintings managed by the National Gallery of Canada and selected by a group of artists.[15] Among the artists in the exhibition were Emily Coonan, Lawren Harris, Kathleen M. Morris, and Tom Thomson. British critics had nothing but high praise for the paintings of Canadian landscapes.[16]

From our vantage point, it seems that fate was doing an ironic dance around Paraskeva, with an introduction to Canada so close she could almost have touched it had she accompanied her in-laws to Wembley. Instead, she stayed home and made a painting that would be shown years later in Canada.

Before going to Paris, Paraskeva could not have predicted what her life would be like living with Oreste's family without him. "They were very good to me," she said, but if the 1924 photographs are any indication, she was unhappy during those years.[17]

In one photo, Paraskeva is seated, holding Ben, whose chubby hands are folded over each other. One of her large hands is held around Ben's arm, the other is held protectively over his legs. So far she had kept herself and her son alive but she must have wondered how she would find her own way in the future without dependence on the Allegris. No wonder her face, registering the tragedy she had endured, is extremely sad in that photo. A Christmas photo from the end of the same year shows Paraskeva ill at ease. Paul, Oreste's younger brother, has a perturbed expression on his face. On the table, a bowl of oranges is a fitting symbol of the plenty available to Paraskeva. In another photo with the Christmas tree, Catherine Allegri, wearing a knit dress, holds her arm around Paraskeva's waist; Paraskeva's hand is on her mother-in-law's shoulder. Ben, who would have been about twenty months old, holds a large, plush toy.

In contrast to Paraskeva's plenty, the news from her family would have given her reason for feeling depressed. Her sister Palenka was often unhappy and could not find work. She obviously missed her older sister a great deal. When Paraskeva sent photos of herself and Ben, Palenka wrote back commenting on Paraskeva's beautiful clothes and how youthful and attractive she looked; everyone to whom Palenka showed the photos said she looked like a real Parisienne. Though Paraskeva would have enjoyed being seen as elegant, at the same time she could not have avoided feeling guilty for enjoying beautiful clothes and other pleasures while her sister was stuck dressing in whatever she could scrounge together.

The letters from her family conveyed their unhappiness, poverty, and monotony. Her father again urged her to return home. If Paraskeva's family's letters are an accurate indication of the mood then in the Soviet Union, people must have been dispirited and in a dreadful state of depression.

Paris was the complete opposite. Frenetic, crowded, and a magnet for artists and writers, it was the centre of Western culture in the 1920s, a city of night-life in cafés, and Diaghilev's *Ballets Russes*. The city attracted American literary expatriates who patronized Sylvia Beach's famous bookstore, Shakespeare and Company, known for publishing the first edition of James Joyce's *Ulysses*. Paris "offered the climate, the ambience, the importance of the recognition of the new for the artist." Foreign writers and artists gathered here where "French intelligence seemed to be all around one in this city with its open beauty, its elegance, and that splendid indifference of the French citizen at the next table to your private life."[18]

In 1925, with the jazz age having arrived in Paris, one could see the American entertainer Josephine Baker at the Théâtre des Champs-Élysées in La Revue Nègre or attend Collette's performance of her own *La Vagabonde*.[19] As for visual art, that same year the first major exhibition of surrealist work was hung at the Galerie Pierre, a show that included Paul Klee, Hans Arp, Man Ray, and Joan Miró; of course, there were also exhibitions by Picasso. And Paris was the fashion capital of the world, with Coco Chanel at the peak of her popularity introducing "the little black dress."[20]

On the rue Dantzig in a housing project called La Ruche lived, not American, but Eastern European émigrés. La Ruche was one of the most original of the marginal artist-studio villages at the time. The ambience here was Russian, with social life revolving around the samovar and endless cups of tea. "Ambulant peddlers" went door to door "selling pumpernickel bread and sausages with horseradish," and when the artists had money, there was vodka and slivovitz. Elsewhere in Paris, Russian aristocrats who had escaped the reprisals of the Revolution became headwaiters, doormen, and taxi drivers; beautiful Russian women became fashion models and "Russian princesses were in demand as governesses."[21]

Ironically, Paraskeva, a young and charming Russian woman, was living a life that might have been seen as similar to that of a governess, had the child in her care not been her own. With no choice but to accept her identity as a widow and a mother, she lived, for the most part, removed from the exciting life of the city in one of its quiet suburbs. This period must have given rise to the intensity of her lifelong complaint that the order of human existence was unjust — "god" having made women to endure such physical trials as menstruation and responsibility for childbearing and child rearing. Here she was, a young woman who cared deeply about the arts, landed in the Paris of the twenties with its rich culture and excitement, and for six years, her life consisted primarily of looking after the Allegri household and taking care of Ben.

It was some compensation that she was occasionally included in the Allegris' business, helping with painting theatre decor and meeting artists who were friends of the family. Still, when she worked in the family business, exciting though it might have seemed, she was in the service of her in-laws, just as much as she was when she polished stair railings and brass knobs in their house.

From time to time, Oreste Allegri worked again, as he had in Petrograd, with the eminent set designer Alexandre Benois. Among Benois's many commissions in Paris in the 1920s were *Giselle*, in collaboration with Diaghilev, and Rimsky-Korsakov's *Le Coq d'Or*.[22] It is highly possible that Paraskeva worked on these and other Benois productions with the Allegris. She also met painters in Paris, including her former teacher Shukhayev, as well as artists in the world of ballet. Sometimes she was given theatre tickets.

One evening when she went to the theatre with her brother-in-law Paul, their seats happened to be beside Pablo Picasso's. Picasso knew the Allegri family because he had worked on a set in the elder Allegri's studio on the Left Bank of the Seine. Paul introduced Paraskeva to Picasso. This encounter was the greatest thrill of her life. Years later, she would delight in telling about having chatted with him, this great artist whose work she had admired since she was a student in Petrograd. It seemed she felt a personal connection with him because his wife, dancer Olga Khokhlova, was Russian.

Paul, seven years younger than Paraskeva, still lived at home and they saw each other every day. Paul fell in love with her; they became lovers and Paul wanted to marry her. "He was after me all the time," she recalled many years later. She said little more about him, other than that he was a "good" man, and he adored Ben.[23] We do not know how long Paul and Paraskeva were lovers, but his feeling for her was intense; fifteen years later, he wrote her a letter addressing her as "Bieletchka," apparently his own affectionate name for her. He told her in this 1945 letter that it took years for his strong feeling for her to die down, but now those emotions were replaced with memories and brief bursts of joy.[24]

Paraskeva never talked much about all those years with the Allegris, and we do not know how she got along with them, but her need for independence — and the conflicting need for security — became clear in decisions she would make. She decided to learn English and took lessons from an English woman, Bernice Bleakman, who lived on the same street. Paraskeva thought English was such a strange-sounding language that her curiosity about it drove her to those lessons.[25]

However, she had another practical reason for learning English. From the signs "*On parle anglais*" (We speak English) in shop windows, Paraskeva knew that fluency in English would be an advantage if she wanted to work in the elegant shops catering to tourists. With so many English-speaking tourists in Paris — according to one estimate, forty thousand Americans were in Paris in 1927 — learning English was a smart move.[26]

Many years later she recalled her life in Chatou, saying, "In Paris I worked very little [on painting], by myself — just [a] few hours now and then, stolen from house work. But my mind, my eyes, were painting all the time. My ideas on painting grew in meditations, in seeing occasionally exhibitions of painting particularly russian [*sic*] artists."[27] However, when she saw the art around her, particularly the work of Picasso and Cézanne, she was filled with such awe that she felt intimidated and was reluctant to show other people her own work.[28]

Her 1927 *Landscape in Chatou* (Plate 3) is a watercolour reminiscent of Cézanne. She also painted self-portraits during her years in Chatou (1925 and 1929–1930), which show the influence of her studies with Petrov-Vodkin when his students spent a month drawing and analyzing the structure of a face.

In her carefully painted self-portrait — from 1925, just two years after she left Russia, and signed "Paraskeva Allegri" — the right side of her face particularly expresses pain and sadness and in her eyes she captured the sense of loss she experienced. She portrayed herself as the broad-faced peasant, who, in the Russian manner, endured stoically the hardships life brought her. This is one of her smallest self-portraits (Plate 4), a jewel hanging, when I last saw it, next to a James Tissot painting called *The Shop Girl* at the Art Gallery of Ontario in Toronto.

A "sense of enclosure" results from the tightly framed image, a technique also used by Petrov-Vodkin in his 1918 *Self-Portrait*.[29] Her expression is intense but at the same time vulnerable; the contour of the face with the strong lips conveys a spirit of determination. In this sense, the self-portrait is a true rendering of Paraskeva's emotional state at the time.

After Paraskeva had lived with the Allegris for a number of years, one of their friends, a painter and interior designer, saw her painting — we don't know if he saw her painting set designs or if she was working on her own painting. He must have sensed her need for life outside the Allegri household, for he told her: "I must get you a job so you will meet somebody."[30] He put her in touch with an interior design shop.

Much as she loved Ben and wanted to devote herself to him, Paraskeva needed the independence a job would give her. When Ben was school-aged, Paraskeva signed him up for boarding school at the Collège St-Germain. He came home on weekends, but five days a week Paraskeva was free from motherhood and began working in downtown Paris at a new job, which became another turning point in her life.

It was 1929, the same year that Diaghilev died, when Paraskeva began working at DIM, Décoration Intérieure Moderne, located at 19 place de la Madeleine near the Saint-Lazare train station. DIM was a gallery and shop that sold Venetian glass by Venini, as well as small sculptures and other objets d'art. To get to work, she took the train from Chatou-Croissy. Perhaps the importance she attributed to the freedom of her new job can be seen in what might seem a small detail: she saved some train tickets as souvenirs.[31] In the large hall of the Gare Saint-Lazare were many tables and chairs where people sat to relax and have a drink. One can imagine her sitting at one of these tables for some time and space away from Ben and the Allegris, thinking about her life, a glass of beer in her hand — in this train station, she developed her life-long love of beer.

Besides keeping some of the train tickets all her life, Paraskeva also kept copies of the 1930 issues of the French design magazine *Ce Temps Ci*, with the DIM ads.[32] The shop's clientele were tourists, interior designers, and others interested in the arts, which meant that she met interesting people outside the Allegri circle, and earned her own money separately from her in-laws' business. DIM gave her a measure of independence; it was an opening into the broader world of Paris, and a door into a new phase of her life.

Two Canadians in Paris⤳

In a summer season when soft was the sun
I clothed me in a cloak, as I a shepherd was
and went wide in this world,
wonders to hear.[1]

Among the many North Americans who descended on Paris in 1929 were two Canadians from Toronto, Philip Clark and Murray Adaskin, who were spending the summer in France.[2]

Philip was the son of Harold Thompson Clark, a Toronto dentist of United Empire Loyalist stock. His mother was the pianist Marguerite Greene, the daughter of Cordelia Greene, a medical doctor from New York State. Tall and slim with almond-shaped eyes, Philip stood nearly a head taller than Murray, who had dark curly hair. They both grew a moustache and wore similar glasses; there the likeness ended.

Murray came from a Jewish family of scribes near Tiflis in White Russia. His parents were born in the same village. Before they immigrated to Canada, they lived in Riga, Latvia — about five hundred kilometres southwest of St. Petersburg. Murray was born in downtown Toronto in a "shack" on Elizabeth Street.[3]

Philip and Murray, a musician, had met more than ten years earlier when Philip, who also loved music, was a teenager studying piano at the Toronto Conservatory of Music. Over the years, their paths crossed in Toronto's small music world where everyone knew each other. In fact, Philip's father, Harold Clark, was a close friend of Dr. Stephen Augustus Vogt, the founder of the Toronto Mendelssohn Choir and the director of the Toronto Conservatory of Music. After Vogt's wife died, he was a frequent dinner guest at the Clarks' house, where he played their Steinway.

Like Murray, an accomplished violinist and composer, Philip had wanted to pursue a career as a concert pianist but had some doubts due to the mistaken idea that a concert pianist's success hinged on perfection. Furthermore, his father did not like Philip's career choice because he thought a musician's income was too low for the life he envisioned for his son. The two made an agreement that if Paul Wells, the piano teacher, felt Philip had enough talent to become a concert pianist, he could count on his father's backing.

Philip suspected that his father talked to Wells privately and told him what he should say to Philip. Wells told his young student that he did not have what it takes to become a concert pianist, and then painted a rather far-fetched scenario of Philip's career path in music in another Canadian or American city somewhere as a director of a conservatory, something that did not appeal to Philip in the least. Philip discontinued studying music when he was eighteen.

The next winter, Hart House opened as a student centre for men at the University of Toronto. Murray and Philip often met there because Murray's brother Harry played in the Hart House String Quartet, and Philip attended the performances. Philip also went swimming there, used the gymnasium track, and frequently attended theatre performances there after discovering that he loved theatre. He even had a walk-on part in the production called *The Chester Mysteries*. With acting in this play and "hanging around" Hart House, he became friends with some of the actors who were members of the Arts and Letters Club.

These Hart House contacts early in his life opened up opportunities in the Arts and Letters Club, which became a central part of his life later on, and fuelled his interest in the arts, leading to his friendship with musicians and painters. Of course, Philip's early interest in theatre and the arts, and becoming friends with artists, would benefit not only him, but also his future wife.

Having abandoned the idea of studying music, Philip concentrated instead on completing his senior matriculation. In 1917, he registered in the Commerce and Finance program at University College at the University of Toronto. Three years into the program, Philip, after several tries, was unable to pass the required Latin course, so he left the university and became an apprentice-accountant with Clarkson, Gordon & Dilworth in 1921. That same year he also began his studies for certification as a chartered accountant.

By the late twenties, Philip had completed the Intermediate Chartered Accountant Course and was a senior audit clerk, auditing the books of several stockbrokers. In his auditing work, he had access to the account of Augustus Vogt and discovered that this musician was successful at working the stock market. Philip had managed to save two hundred dollars to invest, and following Vogt's lead in buying and selling, by the spring of 1929 Philip's investment had grown to twenty-five hundred dollars — an admirable pot of money for the late twenties — opening up the possibility of travel.

By then Philip and Murray, despite their very different personalities, had become close friends. One day Murray revealed that he wanted to spend a summer studying violin in Europe but he had no money. That seemed strange to Philip because Murray was director of music at a stock company theatre, Toronto's Empire Theatre on Temperance Street, and played the overtures each evening and the music between the acts. He earned twice as much as Philip, who had been able to save as much as forty dollars a month. Philip told Murray to open an account and deposit thirty dollars a week without touching it. Before long, Murray had saved enough to go to Europe for three months as a student. Murray and the violinist Adolph Koldofsky had planned to travel together, but Koldofsky changed his mind at the last minute. Murray did not want to travel to Europe alone, so he asked Philip to go with him.

At first, Philip did not want to consider the idea. He was preparing for his final exams at the Chartered Accountant Institute, and furthermore, had a full-time job. Murray used his persuasive powers to convince Philip that he could take his accounting books along and prepare for his exams in Europe while Murray practised violin and took lessons. Following his friend's advice, Philip asked for and was given a three-month leave without pay from Clarkson, Gordon & Dilworth.

Murray was relieved. "I was so glad," he said. "I didn't know how to exchange Canadian funds, or American funds for, say, pounds and shillings. And then when we got to France it was francs! So I simply gave him all my money. Philip was meticulous."⁴ Together, they had fifteen hundred dollars in travellers' cheques. Philip and Murray boarded the *Westerland* on the Red Star Line in New York at the beginning of June 1929. A week later, they landed in Antwerp, Belgium. Adaskin had a letter of introduction to the renowned violinist, Eugène Ysaÿe in Brussels. When they arrived at Ysaÿe's residence, they learned that he was in a nursing home because of a leg amputation and it would not be possible to study with him; the two set off for Paris. After making several inquiries, unsuccessfully, for other teachers in Paris whose names were familiar to Murray, he finally signed on with a violin teacher at the Paris Conservatory, Marcel Chailley.

Philip and Murray found a suitably large room with a bath at the Hôtel des Saints-Pères on the fifth floor. Their room, including one daily meal, cost them only $2.60 a day. By comparison to other North Americans who were in Paris that summer — among them the Canadian novelist Morley Callaghan with his bride Loretto — Philip and Murray were the absolute models of discipline. They had a strict daily routine of work for three hours in the morning and two hours in the afternoon with Philip studying his accounting books and Murray practising violin and taking his lessons.⁵ In the evenings, they explored the city. It's hard to imagine what they did because Philip, in his memoirs, does not mention going to any of the popular nightspots for artists, writers, and intellectuals such as La Coupole and Les Deux Magots where Callaghan met Ernest Hemingway and Scott Fitzgerald.

One night during their third week in Paris they went to a performance of Debussy's *Pelléas et Mélisande* at the Opéra-comique. During an intermission, Philip spotted a tall, lanky man he felt sure was from Toronto. He was right. Douglas Duncan, whose name would become synonymous with Toronto's Picture Loan Society, and who would become a friend of Paraskeva's, was in Paris studying the fine art of bookbinding. He invited his two fellow

Torontonians to his flat on boulevard Montparnasse for tea. A few days later an envelope arrived addressed to Adaskin with tickets enclosed for a performance of Wagner's *Der Götterdämmerung* at the Théâtre Marigny on the Champs-Élysées.[6]

From time to time Philip and Murray visited the American Express office to cash their travellers' cheques and to pick up their mail. Sometimes they explored the area along the way. On one of these excursions, they wandered down the boulevard Haussmann to the place de la Madeleine where a beautiful church stood in an area of elegant shops. They came upon a window full of Venetian blown glass, vases, and chandeliers. In the centre of the window display stood a beautiful, small wooden sculpture, a seated nude with her arms circling her knees. This sculpture seemed a suitable gift for Murray's brother Harry. Wondering if they could afford it, they entered the store to ask the price.

Immediately, Murray and Philip were struck by the dark-haired, petite, attractive woman, so charming and self-assured, who was looking after the shop. In broken English, she told them the sculpture, called *Zlata*, was carved by a Russian sculptor. It cost one thousand francs, or forty Canadian dollars, an amount Philip and Murray could afford.

"You're Russian, aren't you?" Murray said as soon as he heard her speak: "And she pulled herself up to her full five foot three and said, 'How do you know that?' I said, 'Almost every violin teacher I ever had came from Russia and they, as well as my parents speak English the way you do.'"[7] With this, the saleswoman scrutinized these two Canadians with her sharp eyes. They seemed different from American men who had come into the shop. Something about these two made an impression on her; the one, short, curly haired, effusive; and the other tall, restrained, with something intriguing about his eyes.

Murray and Philip, completely taken with this woman, chatted with her as long as they dared, put a deposit of one hundred francs on the sculpture, and said they would return in a few days to pay the balance and to pick it up. Then they left the store.

Outside, Murray commented on how interesting the woman was, and Philip acknowledged that he liked her and also thought her fascinating. "Philip," said Murray, "it's time you got married and that is the girl for you."

Philip was blunt: "You're nuts! She might be a nice girl but why should I get mixed up with a girl in a shop?" Certainly Philip's upbringing precluded the possibility of making a proposition to a woman in a Paris shop, and if he were to pursue her he would need a way to find out if she was "worthy" of him.

Murray, detecting Philip's interest in the woman, suggested that Philip go back alone to pick up the sculpture and invite the woman to dinner. If she accepted, in the two men's puritanical way of thinking, she was not the kind of woman Philip should pursue. If she refused, she must be respectable. Murray's idea was that he would contact Lillian Sparling, another Toronto violinist also studying with Chailley, and the four of them would have dinner together.

Later, Philip wrote an emotionless account of the encounter in the store, a reflection of his repressed Victorian upbringing. He said little about her in his story of that summer in Paris, just mentioning "the girl's lack of English."[8] However, it seems she had ignited feelings he could not ignore. He returned to pick up the sculpture, and as Murray suggested, invited the woman to dinner. The two had difficulty understanding each other because her English was limited and Philip's French was little better. With the help of a French-English dictionary, she explained she could not accept a dinner invitation because she was *"une veuve"* — she did not know the English word for "widow" — with a young son. But at least Philip found out her name, Madame Allegri.

According to Murray, in his reminiscences years later, when Madame Allegri turned down the dinner invitation, Philip came out of the shop dancing because he was so happy. In Philip's mind, turning down the dinner invitation meant the woman's virtue had been tried and she had passed this first test.[9] But Paraskeva was simply setting her own boundaries, and these happened to coincide with Philip's ideas of a good woman. He knew nothing about her; years later, to his dismay, he would learn that being a "proper" woman was not her idea of how she wanted to live.

Philip and Murray were about to leave Paris for Seignelay, a small village seventy miles south of Paris, because Murray's teacher was going there to his summer residence. There are differences in the two men's stories about what happened next, significant because of what the accounts tell us about Philip's undemonstrative manner. Each said the other took the initiative. According to Murray, Philip had the presence of mind to tell Madame Allegri that they were going to Seignelay for the summer and asked if they could write to each other. "He said she could write in English and he would correct it and he would write in French and she could correct that for him."[10]

Philip's story is that after they arrived in Seignelay, they found accommodation in the village and again settled into their routines. Then Murray suggested they write a flirtatious letter to Madame Allegri, and they were pleased when she replied in an equally flirtatious letter in French. Philip remembered two more exchanges during the next four weeks, whereas Murray described letters going "back and forth from Paris to Seignelay and from Seignelay to Paris. It was wonderful."[11]

Clearly, Philip's story is more muted than Murray's and, regardless of which way the correspondence actually developed, when they returned to Paris, Philip went alone to Maison DIM and invited Madame Allegri to go for a walk. With permission from the shop's manager, Madame Allegri accepted and the two walked for an hour to the *Jardin des Tuileries*. By then Philip's French had improved enough that they could communicate comfortably, though from time to time she supplied a French word for which Philip was searching. When they came to the Café Weber on rue Royale, Philip tried to persuade Madame Allegri to have a coffee with him, but she declined and they returned to the shop. Philip left her there and they said goodbye. Philip and Murray returned to Toronto. Immediately Philip wrote a letter to Madame Allegri, using the address of Maison DIM. He was pleased that she replied.

Shortly after his return, Philip read a newspaper article that predicted a stock market crash. His small investment had increased during the summer, and he decided to take the advice of the author of the article. He sold his stocks and in October when many people lost all their savings, Philip had fifteen hundred dollars in the bank. At the age of thirty, he was still living with his parents, and often after a late night out, like a guilty teenager, he crept up the stairs as quietly as possible, trying not to wake his dad. But one night his father told him if he could not get home before midnight, he should live elsewhere. That winter he began sharing Murray's apartment at 40 Huntley Street in Toronto.

By then Murray had already begun buying paintings and decorating his apartment to suit his own personality and tastes. Photos of the apartment show a Chinese-patterned tapestry hanging on the wall above a table that held two large candlesticks. In the centre of the table stood the small wooden sculpture that Murray and Philip had purchased from Paraskeva. In a photo of another part of the apartment, a Lawren Harris iceberg painting hangs on the wall above Philip, who is sitting on a couch wearing a good tweed suit. Living with Murray introduced Philip to the pleasures of the visual arts, and provided him with a richer environment than the gloomy atmosphere of his parents' place.

Philip was still working for Clarkson, Gordon & Dilworth, the company that had given him a leave for his summer in Europe. He knew that when he acquired his accounting degree, he would be entitled to a higher salary. The company, not willing to pay him more, offered him a job in Mexico City. Philip, not wanting to go, asked for such a high salary that he knew he would be rejected. But at the end of June 1930, when he was offered a bonus of two months' salary if he left the position, he accepted and had six hundred dollars extra in his pocket. After a short vacation in Bermuda, he accepted a position with George A. Touche & Company at $225 a month.

Around that time, Philip had another stroke of luck. Because Murray had progressed so well in his violin playing after studying in Europe, his brother Harry Adaskin also wanted to spend a summer in Europe studying with Marcel Chailley, accompanied by his wife Frances, and they asked Philip to take over their flat. In comparison to the plight of many Torontonians and others across the country who had no work and not enough to feed their families, the Depression affected Philip hardly at all. He was being paid well and he had few expenses, so he was able to save money.

Philip, feeling pleased about his financial success, was also successful in his correspondence with Madame Allegri, for the first two letters had turned into a regular correspondence criss-crossing the Atlantic between Toronto and Paris. Philip must have sensed that she was genuinely interested in him. As in France, Philip continued to correct Madame Allegri's English in her letters. Also, Philip had put her in touch with Harry and Frances Adaskin that summer; Frances helped Paraskeva with writing letters to Philip. He seemed determined that she learn English. By that time, Philip had definite ideas about the outcome he wanted from his correspondence with Madame Allegri, whom he now called "Paraskeva." What a loss that these letters have not survived!

What has survived is a photo album Philip sent to Paraskeva, probably early in 1931. He must have put some thought into the album he chose; it has a beautiful handmade cover, umber with magenta geometric patterns on it. The album includes many photos of Philip in a variety of poses, always wearing a good suit. The Toronto skyline is there, as is Niagara Falls. The Clarks on excursions and picnics, including a Muskoka scene with their boat, give the impression of a family of leisure. And then there is the photo of the view from the Clark cottage on a large lake surrounded by forest. By that time, Philip must have known enough about Paraskeva to be sure that such a scene would appeal to her. Sending this album to her in Paris was one way of familiarizing Paraskeva with his world, once he had decided he wanted her to become part of it.

In the meantime, life at the Allegri house in Chatou had taken a predictable turn. Paul and Paraskeva continued their affair and they even planned to get married. Although Paraskeva was ambivalent, Paul was quite determined, and his parents accepted the idea. One would think that another Allegri marriage would have given Paraskeva security and a comfortable life, but she did not love Paul. Even though she went along with the marriage plans, she was reluctant: "I didn't feel like it," she said years later.[12]

For Paraskeva, marriage to Paul would have translated into being tied into the Allegris' set design business for life, which may have felt by then more like a prison than an opportunity, despite the familial fondness. Her own independence would have been subsumed in the family business. We will never know for sure if this was the real reason she refused marriage to her brother-in-law, or if she simply did not love him.

Philip's proposal of marriage meant Paraskeva had an alternative to Paul, which included adventure as well as security. She wrote a letter to her father to tell him that she planned to marry a Canadian chartered accountant and live in Toronto. Her father replied from Leningrad in a letter, "Don't go. There you'll be like a grain of sand in the ocean."[13] Figuring into her father's advice would have been the knowledge that Canada was much farther from St. Petersburg. Paraskeva ignored her father's admonition as she weighed her options, perceiving Canada as a country rich with opportunity, available to her through this man, steady and dependable, and somewhat shy. She must have known, too, that with his somewhat restrained temperament she had the dominant personality in the relationship, which would have appealed to her.

Philip was head and shoulders taller than Paraskeva. He was different from her own family, different from the Allegris and other people she knew in Paris. What she did not know was the extent to which he was different from people she knew, and how dissimilar the two of them were.

With all she had experienced, she was emotionally bruised. However, she was caught by a traditional notion of romance and a feeling of enchantment at the idea of slipping away from Paul, boarding a ship, and sailing off to an unexplored country. Marrying Philip would bring her countless new experiences. She had already survived so much that had seemed impossible to endure, so what did she have to lose?

We do not know whether she "fell in love" in the traditional sense; however, she made her choice despite whatever uncertainty there may have been in her feelings for Philip. What she did know was that Philip was both reliable and responsible. A 1931 photo shows her leaning into Philip, who has his arm around her, surely symbolic of how the two felt. And yet, having met Philip only a few times and corresponding for just two years, she knew very little about him.

Had he sent her a copy of his diary along with the photo album, she would have learned much more about him, even reading his account of only ten days of his life. The diary is written in a stilted, controlled style and reveals the stranglehold of Victorian-like society on him and on the formation of his personality. He had a very clear opinion of how people, especially women, should behave and he expressed disapproval when they did not fit that picture. He commented on his sister Virginia's behaviour, and wondered what people thought of her because she talked a lot and "allowed her little hat to sit on top of her head" when they were visiting friends near Hamilton. He gives the impression of a man for whom others' opinions of him and his sister held a great deal of importance.[14]

When a father squashes his son's creative drive, as Harold Clark did Philip's passion for music, the son learns to straitjacket himself in other ways as well, something that becomes clear in Philip's diary, for it is the writing of a man drained of emotion. He was a man of his time, and many men in that era did not allow themselves free expression. Neither in Philip's diary, nor in his "Memoires" does he ever mention having any interest in women or dating. In those days, men with Philip's upbringing simply would not have written of such things.

It is clear, however, that he had what was needed to be an accountant, and he was very good at saving money. If he wanted to marry Paraskeva and bring her to Toronto, the decent thing to do would be to pay the fare for her and Ben. A return fare between Canada and Great Britain in 1931 cost $175 for third-class tourist accommodation.[15] Philip's savings from the two years since he had returned from Europe were more than adequate to cover the travel for himself and for Paraskeva and Ben. Even if he had not had enough, Philip would not have considered asking for money from his father because Harold was disappointed in his older son, favouring his younger son Ralph. When Philip moved out on his own, he was determined to show his father he was competent at managing his own affairs, which he did well.

By the end of that winter, Philip must have told his family of his intentions, for his father sent Paraskeva a letter in which he acknowledged that she would be encountering new people in a new country that he described as one of the best in the world. "I think you are very courageous," he said. "But my own desire is that you and Phil shall be very happy." He said he often thinks of her as he walks to work, and has had in mind writing to her "for many moons."

The purpose of his letter was to welcome her into the family. "Mrs. Clark," he said, is a "fine stirling [*sic*] woman." Ralph he described as "a thorough lover boy. There is very little I could wish to change in him." Virginia and Philip, he said, were both "of the temperamental type," implying that Harold Clark wished he could change them.

This letter, dated 6 April 1931, for all its overtures of acceptance, also revealed for Paraskeva how her future father-in-law perceived what her relationship would be to his son — a helper. Paraskeva was encountering the attitude that women and men were not equal partners; a "husband" was the one who "established" the home and a "wife" was a woman who deferred to her husband, who had no personal desires for her own fulfilment, only desires for the welfare of her family. Harold's letter clearly reveals these attitudes:

> There is nothing, to my mind, that Phil needs quite so much as to be married to a good and wholesome woman, which I am sure you are. Philip is a good boy and, I think, clever above average and is capable of going a long way. I am sure you will be a valuable help to him in many ways. I am glad he is at last founding a home. It is the only way to live. And you are equipping the home with a fine little boy who should brighten the lives of both of you.[16]

Paraskeva probably chuckled at the idea that she was a "wholesome" woman and surely Harold would not have used that word had he known of her affair with her brother-in-law. This letter might have led Paraskeva to wonder whether she was jumping out of one family web only to be caught by another. Perhaps leaving the Allegris behind was an attempt to escape the constant reminders of her aborted dream of life with Oreste; but it was not something she could forget. Throughout her life, she would talk to her friends about the loss she carried.

However, with Philip Thompson Clark towering over her at her door in Chatou that day in May 1931, Paraskeva knew with certainty that she had a real opportunity for security and a new life — she agreed to marry him and live with him in Canada. The photographs of Paraskeva then show a much happier woman than those from the early years in Chatou.

The same month Philip arrived, Paraskeva received a letter from her father asking her to return to Russia. Apparently, she had told him that life in Leningrad was awful, but he objected to her criticism, saying it was not like that anymore because rebuilding was going on all over the city.[17] However, she was not about to return to Russia, given her prospects for a new life in Canada.

When Philip arrived to take Paraskeva and Ben to Canada, he must have been alarmed at the seriousness of his rival, Paul Allegri. By chance, he had met Paul two years earlier on one of his visits to Paraskeva at DIM, so he knew something of the competition.[18] Given the situation, he realized that the sooner Paraskeva left Chatou, the better. However, French law governing marriage would have required too long a wait for a licence. Philip consulted the Canadian consulate and was advised to establish domicile in England for two weeks and arrange to have the marriage there.

Philip quickly went shopping and bought suitcases for Paraskeva, then left for England and arranged to rent a room from Deirdre Doyle, an actress in London whom he had met in Toronto when she played Eliza Doolittle at the Empire Theatre as a member of the Maurice Cockburn–Barry Jones Shaw Repertory Company.[19]

Paraskeva packed the essentials for her and Ben in the suitcases Philip had bought. It seems puzzling that Paraskeva's mother-in-law helped her, but while the two Allegri men were out one day, Paraskeva left with Ben and took the Cherbourg boat to meet Philip in England. The elopement was complete and one can only imagine the scene in the Allegri household when the men returned to find Paraskeva and Ben gone.

For Ben, this sudden rupture of the only home life he had known since infancy could only have been traumatic. He had no father, but had formed attachments to his grandfather and uncle. Now he would have a new step-father, a man who was taking him and his mother to a country where he could not understand what people said. He must have wondered what would happen to him, and whether he would ever see his grandparents again.

In London, Deirdre Doyle and her sister were the witnesses to the marriage of Philip Thompson Clark and Paraskeva Plistik Allegri at the Kensington Registry on the ninth day of June 1931. Listening to his mother's vows in English during the ceremony gave eight-year-old Ben the giggles. Afterward, the two sisters celebrated the couple with a breakfast party; Paraskeva and Philip spent their wedding night in a large hotel near Regent's Park.

A bonus to the timing for their elopement to London was a show of Picasso's work. "Thirty Years of Pablo Picasso" was showing at London's Lefevre Gallery, an exhibition Paraskeva would not have wanted to miss. She still had the catalogue of the show among her books at the end of her life.

Before they could leave for Canada, Paraskeva and Ben had to have a medical examination.[20] Then, after obtaining a British passport for Paraskeva as Philip's wife, the Clarks were ready to sail away to Canada on the *Empress of France*.[21] Ben's dominant recollection of the voyage was that "the sea was huge and really light"; the voyage was sunny, with no rain or storms, according to Ben.[22]

ONE WONDERS IF the romantic adventure of Paraskeva's elopement still filled her with excitement, or whether apprehension had begun overriding the whirl of the previous weeks. What were her thoughts? Did she think back over the years behind her? What did she picture of the life ahead of her?

She was now married and committed to being the wife of a traditional Torontonian. The new Mrs. Clark was a tough, strong-minded woman who had weathered extreme personal difficulties. She had survived not only physical and political turmoil in St. Petersburg; as a teenager she had lived through the loss of her mother and at age twenty-five, the death of her husband. She had protected and cared for Ben while, through her resourcefulness, supporting herself and avoiding becoming a burden to her in-laws. She almost married her first husband's brother.

By contrast, Philip Clark with his middle-class Canadian reliability — his ability to support her and Ben — would have seemed almost a mirage as he suddenly appeared that day in front of her small figure among the Venini glass pieces, with the possibility of a welcome security after her life of upheaval.

Of course, Paraskeva knew the marriage was a trade-off because it would mean devotion to running a household, giving rise to the question of how painting would fit into that scenario. However, she claimed not to think of being an artist until she was living in Canada, which is hard to believe.

When they first met, Philip had no idea that Paraskeva was trained as an artist. A year into their correspondence he still had not known. About a year before he declared his intention to marry her, she found a clever way of revealing this other part of herself. She sent him a self-portrait (Plate 5).[23]

Like the 1925 oil, this portrait, too, is tightly framed. A big difference is that her face has a pleasant expression, just short of a smile, albeit a somewhat sceptical expression and her eyes are sharp and clear; she painted the same determined mouth. She wrote directly on the painting in French that this was not really a portrait of the artist by the artist, but a small sketch with a little touch of colour, which she wanted to send to him anyway because it looks a bit like her. It's difficult to draw myself, she said, just as it is to photograph me because the lines of my face are all at the limit between beauty and ugliness. In her later self-portraits, she would show qualities in herself other than the two extremes of "beauty" and "ugliness." Philip knew enough about art to see that this portrait was not the work of an untrained amateur, despite her inscription.

Until receiving this watercolour, Philip had known Paraskeva only as a charming "salesgirl" with good taste, a Russian widow with a young son, completely unlike any middle-class, conventional woman he might have found in Toronto. The obvious question is, given Philip's family and his own conventional attitudes, why did he marry Paraskeva? There is no simple answer. That he "fell in love" with her is not an entirely satisfactory explanation in the face of their completely diverse backgrounds and extremely opposite personalities. However, it is not unusual that in a new, exciting environment like Paris a person's emotions are stirred in ways that perhaps would not occur in home territory.

He decided she was a risk he was willing to take even though she seemed to be the kind of improperly behaving woman he had written of in his diary; she would not easily fit into the mould of his traditional family and its class-conscious society. People have speculated about why he took that risk, some concluding that as a stolid chartered accountant this was his "streak" of doing something to break out of his conventionality. As a kind, altruistic man it is not out of the realm of possibility that one of Philip's motives would have been simply to help Paraskeva, for he would have had compassion for her, seeing that she needed the security he could offer. Whatever the layers of reasons were, like thousands of people who make inexplicable choices for "love," Philip and Paraskeva were now married.

During the month Philip spent with Paraskeva in Paris and London, he would have learned something about her knowledge and love of art, especially if he went to the London Picasso exhibition with her. A genuine love of art was something the two shared. Perhaps Philip told her of the many artists in Toronto that he knew. During that month, he may have also had a glimpse of other parts of Paraskeva, her impetuous, unbridled Russian nature.

Philip knew that Paraskeva, as an "exotic" wife, would give him a distinction in Toronto, a certain cachet among his musician and artist friends. He could introduce her to Toronto's art world and offer her a chance to become a respected artist among artists. It would be interesting to have heard the conversation between Philip and Paraskeva as the ship approached Quebec, whether they talked over the idea of spending some time in Montreal looking at art before going on to Toronto, or whether he made the decision himself, thinking it the best way to introduce his new wife to Canada. However it happened, after the trio arrived in Quebec City on the thirtieth of June, they stopped off in Montreal to visit the art museums and galleries there before boarding a train for Toronto.

On the train from Montreal to Toronto, Paraskeva, now with her new last name, would have had time to ponder the finality of her decision while the train rocked back and forth as she glimpsed for the first time the Ontario landscape, Lake Ontario, and then the city of Toronto. She knew only five people in all of Canada: her son, her new husband, Murray, and the other Adaskins, Harry and Frances.

With her years of grief and adversity behind her, at the moment she could take comfort in the romance of having found a man whom she enthralled. Still, this measure of security would not dilute her unconstrained nature. At the time, she would not have known that these two contradictory elements would storm about within her in years to come — her conventional marriage versus her unconventional self. Her marriage to Philip Clark tied together two contradictory cultures and intensified her inner contradictions. She, who had wanted all her life to be an actor, would discover in Toronto the stage to play out her life as a woman of an independent mind. The Russian peasant had landed.

The Shock of the Clarks⤳

... oh for a half-hour of Europe after this sanctimonious icebox.[1]

Toronto's Union Station was Paraskeva Clark's introduction to the city, a temple-like building officially opened in 1927 when railways ruled the country's transportation world. Through this building, with its Missouri Zumbro stone walls, Bedford limestone pillars, and Tennessee marble floors, immigrants from many countries passed — many less fortunate than Paraskeva and Ben — in search of a new home. They looked up to see light pouring through the four-storey-high arched windows, and if they spent enough time they could find the names of some of Canada's cities and towns — places linked by the railway — inscribed in stone.

On the Wednesday that Paraskeva arrived at Union Station with Philip, the city was in the middle of a heat wave, the kind of hot, humid day that drove people to the shores of Lake Ontario; families flocked to Sunnyside Beach and Hanlan's Point with their picnic baskets and bathing suits. It was Dominion Day 1931 and the city of 600,000 was celebrating Canada's sixty-fourth birthday. The twenty-ninth annual Open-Air Horse Parade was also taking place at Queen's Park and in the streets adjacent to the Clark home. However, the Montreal train pulled into Union Station too late to see the horses as Philip took Paraskeva and Ben to Willcocks Street to meet his family.

One can imagine the apprehension and excitement in the Clark household that day. Now the site of New College of the University of Toronto just north of Spadina Crescent, 44 Willcocks was a solid brick house with an ivy-covered front, part of a middle-class neighbourhood of Victorian homes. For a newly landed Russian who had just spent eight years in Paris, the street seemed as strange to her eyes as the sounds of the English language to her ears. And she had never before encountered people like the Clarks. Even after fifty years of living in the city and claiming it as her own through her many long walks, Paraskeva still talked about how strange the new culture had seemed when she first came to Canada.[2]

As Paraskeva entered the front door where Harold and Harriet Clark politely received her, she saw for the first time the interior of a typical Toronto Victorian house, somewhat dark, with a stairway leading directly from the front hall to the second floor. Off the hallway to the right was the living room with its Steinway grand piano, so fine that just by looking at it one could imagine an evening of splendid music. The dining room, with its great bay window, led into a large farmhouse-style kitchen that ran the width of the rear of the house. As the Steinway did for the living room, a shiny enamelled-steel Moffat electric stove put heart into the kitchen, a stove that after so many years is still used — with occasional repairs — in the Clark family cottage.

The heavy, dark, Victorian furniture throughout the house had little appeal for Paraskeva — she would avoid this type of furniture when she and Philip eventually furnished their own house on Roxborough Drive.[3] She could see how the heavy draperies muted the light that might have brightened the rooms. Ornately patterned area rugs lay here and there on the floors. On the walls hung historic prints and photos — no original paintings. Upstairs, the house had three bedrooms on the second floor, and two on the third floor.

For their part, Harold and Harriet, knowing very little about Paraskeva, would have noticed that she wore a finely tailored, elegant dress and beautiful shoes. Her red lipstick dismayed them, as all makeup was forbidden in their family with its history of strict Presbyterianism, an attitude common at the time in Toronto's more strict religious circles.[4] They heard her heavy Russian accent and her less than acceptable English, but at least they could understand her. However, they could hardly communicate with eight-year-old Ben because he knew little English. He, too, wore well-made clothes, and to their relief, he was quiet and polite.

One of the third-floor rooms was given to Philip and Paraskeva. So here she was, part of the household of another set of in-laws. It seems only natural that Paraskeva would have compared the Clarks' family life with that of the Allegris. Though Harold and Hattie were not as strict as Harold's Presbyterian ancestors, they maintained the old "children should be seen and not heard" attitude. At the Clark house, you had to sit up straight at the table, eat everything on your plate, and behave, meaning be quiet.[5] Breakfast, lunch, and dinner: three times a day Paraskeva and Ben experienced the Clarks' proprieties at meals for nearly two weeks.

Paraskeva knew little — if anything — about the Clark family history, which would have gone a long way in explaining their behaviour. Harold's grandparents, Justus Clark and Elizabeth Dunning, came to Canada out of loyalty to Britain instead of remaining in the United States after the American Revolution. They were typical of strict Presbyterians, requiring family members to repeat the catechism and keep the blinds drawn on Sundays.[6]

Philip's father Harold was born north of Toronto in the village of Newtonbrook, now part of Willowdale, where his father Egbert Asahel Clark was a schoolteacher until his doctor advised him to quit because of his severe asthma and the family moved into the city of Toronto. Like his father, Harold became a junior public school teacher, and later a principal of Duke Street School in Toronto. He began studying dentistry while he was teaching, and became a dental surgeon in 1894.

Philip's mother, Marguerite Greene, embodied mystery for the Clarks. She was an adopted daughter of Dr. Cordelia Greene who was in charge of a sanatorium for middle-aged women in northwestern New York State. Marguerite's gift as a pianist is one of the reasons Harold was drawn to her.

Marguerite had been abandoned as a baby on the steps of the sanatorium. She was dressed in silk and wore a gold brooch with "Marguerite" engraved on it. No one ever found out who her parents were, but the baby's clothes indicated a family of wealth. Because of her facial features, there was speculation that at least one of her parents was Asiatic, possibly Japanese — Philip inherited traces of these facial features around his eyes.

Philip might not have been conscious that there was a parallel between his father's marriage and his own, but he could have been justified in feeling that his father could not fault him for marrying Paraskeva when Harold himself had chosen a wife whose background was anything but typically Torontonian.

After Philip's sister Virginia was born in 1908, Marguerite died of septicemia. Philip remembered his mother's body lying in her coffin, a doily over her face to cover the suffering that Harold felt was visible. When Harold removed the doily for eight-year-old Philip to see his mother's face, it made an enormous impression on him.

The next year Harriet Stevens, the daughter of his grandfather's friends, came for a visit. Later, Harold told Philip that he wanted to marry Harriet and asked for his oldest son's permission. Philip agreed reluctantly with one condition: that his father and Harriet have no children, because he had heard of cruel stepmothers favouring their own children and wanted to avoid the miserable experiences portrayed in stories. Two years later, Harold Clark married Harriet, the woman his first wife had said he should marry if something ever happened to her.

Philip grew up with a stepmother after age eight, just as Ben would grow up with Philip as his stepfather after age eight. Philip, born in 1899, was the oldest in his family, but Harold preferred Philip's younger brother Ralph, who lectured at the university, and "had the right connections and he was dogmatic and boring." Also, Ralph was athletic and Philip was not. Furthermore, Philip had monocular vision and even though he was "an accomplished pianist, very talented ... he wasn't the son that Harold wanted."[7]

Philip's 1927 diary shows that he did not like much of what he saw in his family. He said they were a dull lot in a house with a heavy atmosphere. "Impossible to work up any enthusiasm around here," Philip wrote one evening, "so went over to Miss Williams. She though old is a character whose company is most stimulating. Wouldn't we all be much happier if we had the courage of our convictions and expressed them," he muses. "So many people are just bumps on logs. Miss Williams isn't a bump on a log — far from it. She gave me whisky & ginger ale. Dewars Scotch. We talked about tenors & string quartettes & marriage. She doesn't talk much about herself. I wonder why she didn't marry."[8]

Even though he did not like how dull his family was, he also had contradictory feelings about how people should behave and speak. He liked his sister Virginia's enthusiasm for things, but he also thought she talked more than was appropriate. When a "Mrs. M." had dinner with the Clarks, he warned Virginia not to talk too much. "V. didn't like not talking but she managed alright [*sic*]." When he was a guest at the home of his friend Lester Turnbull in Dundas, near Hamilton, he commented that a woman named Daisy came into the conversation too much.[9]

With his choice of a wife, Philip was breaking out of the dull life he described. She was anything but a "bump on a log," a woman who *did* have the courage of her convictions and had no hesitancy in expressing them, a characteristic that in the end made him uncomfortable. How ironic that Philip, who objected to women having their say, chose to marry a woman whose nature prevented her from holding back her own comments in any situation!

Philip also wrote in detail about his job at Lever Brothers, about setting up accounts and reconciling financial statements; where he had lunch and what kind of sandwich he ate. He chided himself for not spending more time studying for his exam, and said, "This diary may help me to settle down."[10] It seems his training for the meticulous work of accounting pervaded the rest of his life, doing things just so and expecting others to do the same.

Paraskeva learned very quickly that Philip's father had wanted his son to choose a woman of a proper lineage. Harold "was absolutely distressed," Paraskeva recalled.[11] "I was scared as hell of him," she said. "He was severe and very unsentimental but somehow he accepted me."[12] She once told Harold, "I shall make the name of Clark famous!"[13]

However, Harold and Hattie were "reasonable people," Clive Clark said. "They weren't the type that said you're out of here and we don't want to see you anymore."[14] Even so, until that first meeting, Harold knew nothing about

Paraskeva's Russian personality, what it meant that she was an artist, nor did he know his daughter-in-law was a woman with a sense of style and elegance. When he met her, he must have swallowed down his distaste for her stylish appearance; he handled his displeasure by delegating to his daughter Virginia the task of bringing Paraskeva into line. Virginia told Paraskeva to take off the red on her lips because that was not allowed in their family.[15]

Many, many years later, Virginia wrote a letter to Paraskeva referring back to this incident. "I can assure you," Virginia said, "the only reason for my saying them [those things] in the first place was to protect you from Daddy's eagle eye. It must have been a very trying experience for you to come into such a narrow minded household."[16] Indeed! Paraskeva would have felt annoyed with Virginia and, at the same time, it would have struck her as ludicrous, something to simply ignore, but the lipstick incident gave her additional information about her new husband's family.

According to old family photos, the Clarks were generally well dressed. Apparently, society and family decorum dictated what is now considered formal clothing, even when they were at their cottage or lounging about. In a photo of Philip reading in the Clarks' living room, he is wearing a suit and tie; and photos of his father at his cottage in Milford Bay show him dressed, for example, in a dress shirt with a bow tie or a suit even when he was at work in the boathouse.

Paraskeva discovered that the atmosphere in the Clark household was not unusual in early-thirties Toronto; 44 Willcocks Street was for her the centre of a shock that radiated outward into the rest of the city. She would have agreed with Anna Jameson's description one hundred years earlier of Toronto's "conventionalism in its most oppressive and ridiculous forms ... they live under the principle of fear — they are all afraid of each other, afraid to be themselves ..."[17] Jameson's observations from so long ago still seemed to apply, for much of Paraskeva's discomfort in Toronto arose from being surrounded by people who were dismayed because she insisted on being who she was instead of conforming.

Toronto had a reputation of being stodgy, particularly among Montrealers and Europeans, of having a "heavy-handed code of public behaviour" that restrained activities. At one point in the city's history, there was a bylaw stating that no one was allowed to sell anything by "crying, hallooing, or creating any other discordant noise," nor ringing a bell or blowing a horn. However, later on pedlars were allowed to "moderately cry their wares."[18] Supporters of this kind of control were interested in peace and quiet, a reasonable desire, especially in a country that prized, above all, "peace, order and good government."[19] Sundays were kept especially quiet, with only church doors open — work and play were considered inappropriate.

Even libraries were not exempt from the city's strict decorum. "We do not buy books we consider immoral," one librarian said in the late twenties.[20] Even books sold by the Methodist Book Room were not exempt; in 1912, the Toronto Public Library's head librarian, George H. Locke, had banned two of their books.[21]

Before World War II, most of the immigrants who settled in Toronto came from England, Scotland, and Ireland, and at one time almost a third of the city's population was born in Britain.[22] No wonder, since the country's official policy, even in the 1930s, favoured immigrants from the British Isles. Unofficially, racism helped to keep Toronto British. For example, advertisements for domestics at the beginning of the twentieth century might claim, "Anglo-Saxons were superior in moral character to other races" and therefore more desirable as employees.[23]

An immigrant from outside the British Isles was something of an oddity in Toronto in 1931, a reality that is hard to imagine in a city now considered one of the most multicultural in the world,[24] a diversity that is a point of pride. Film director Ted Kotcheff, born in Toronto's Cabbagetown and the son of Bulgarian immigrants, described 1930s Toronto as "a xenophobic town" because his family felt unwanted. There was little understanding between the Eastern Europeans and the established Torontonians, who seemed to respond with fear to the unfamiliar. Paraskeva discovered that the gulf between a woman from Leningrad and the Clarks' culture was almost impossible to cross.

A "Woman's Point of View" feature — the women's page — in a 1937 Toronto newspaper describes how Torontonians kept their distance from a stranger, waiting to find out "whether a newcomer is going to be taken up before they make a friendly move toward that person."[25] The article goes on to say that people are afraid to do anything that "some one else who is socially prominent isn't being or doing." This attitude was not only foreign to Paraskeva, but she would have been inclined to deal with it all by thinking "to hell with them."

In spite of itself, Toronto at that time benefited enormously from what immigrants offered in enriching the city's cultural life. For example, the Hambourgs, who emigrated from Russia, started the Hambourg Conservatory (1911–1951) and created a nucleus from which musical groups evolved, among them the Hart House String Quartet. Murray Adaskin's brother, Harry, was one of the members of that group. The Hambourg Conservatory was also a centre where musicians, visual artists, and writers gathered to share their interest in the arts.

The Adaskin brothers, whose family too were immigrants, also became part of the cultural life of the city. Murray, initially Philip's friend, along with his wife, singer Frances James, became close friends of both Philip and Paraskeva during the 1930s. (Murray and Harry Adaskin each married a woman named "Frances.") Murray was first violinist in the Toronto Symphony Orchestra in the early thirties, and later, violinist in the Royal York Hotel Trio.

Besides the rich culture of music in Toronto, the city also had its arts clubs, which in the early twentieth century sprang up in cities across the country. Toronto's Arts & Letters Club, founded in 1908 by a group including art critic Augustus Bridle, provided a meeting place for men who enjoyed the arts, as well as for male artists.[26] This organization, which offered Philip a place to make friends with artists when he joined (many years later he became the group's treasurer), placed emphasis on Canadian art, unlike many of the

> private cultural organizations ... content to remain exclusive enclaves complacently encouraging traditional British culture, which they believed to be infinitely better than that produced by the New-Canadian or ethno-cultural groups in their midst, the modernist forms appearing abroad, and the popular forms entering from the United States. They were the preservers and keepers of the established and familiar, and very much content to be so.[27]

Salons were held in private homes, which included musical performances and readings. Philip had belonged to a music club in the 1920s, and according to his diary, he and his friends spent many evenings playing music: Mozart, Bach, and Schumann.

In the early thirties, Toronto also could boast that it had the largest hotel in the British Empire, the Royal York, as well as the tallest building, the Bank of Commerce.[28] In the context of North America, these buildings were deserving of the pride Torontonians felt. But to the eyes of anyone who grew up with the antiquity and grand architecture of Europe or Russia, these buildings lacked character and dignity.

Canada was just in the beginning stage of establishing itself legally as a sovereign nation. In 1931, as Philip and Paraskeva were being married in London, the British government was working on the Statute of Westminster, which would establish Canada's legal independence from Britain. The same week Paraskeva first stepped onto Canada's shores, the House of Commons in Ottawa approved the statute, and it was ratified five months later in the British Parliament. Because Paraskeva arrived in Canada before this statute was passed, she became a British subject as her husband was. At that time there was no such thing as a Canadian citizen — if you lived in Canada you were British, and a woman was automatically given her husband's citizenship.

Even though Canada, by the end of 1931, was legally no longer tied to Great Britain, the emotional and cultural ties remained. The City of Toronto particularly, because of its history, was a cultural repository of British life and traditions. This was the city and country that received Paraskeva, and we can be sure that having their Russian daughter-in-law stay with them was no easier for Harold and Hattie than it was for Paraskeva and Ben.

After nearly two weeks of living at 44 Willcocks, Philip and Paraskeva found their own third-floor apartment at 52 Admiral Road. Very quickly, Philip found a job as office manager at Canada Gypsum. Now he was becoming settled, with his own home, wife, and family. Paraskeva, with her European sensuality and mischievousness, gave Philip a reach outside of Toronto's proper middle class, sometimes called "FOOF" — Fine Old Ontario Family.

In later years, Paraskeva would complain that Philip was not poetic, or romantic. When her son stated that in general chartered accountants are not very poetic, Paraskeva complained that she had not known that when she married him.[29] Nor had she known anything, in 1931, about how an accountant might compensate for a lack of poetry, in his "strong streak" of breaking out.[30]

Just a month after she arrived in Toronto, her photo appeared in the "Society Notes" of *The Mail and Empire*, under the heading "Charming Torontonian," wearing a hat and a dress with a V-neckline emphasized by a necklace. The caption reads, "Mrs Philip Clark, who before her recent marriage was Mlle. Paraskeva Allegri of Paris and Leningrad."[31] Having been from Paris and Leningrad was enough to make her exotic in Toronto.

Philip was proud of his "Charming Torontonian." On a birthday card, he wrote to her, "Speaking of wives, some wives are clever, some wives are sexy, some wives are barrels of fun, and I've got some wife who happens to be all these things rolled into one."[32] However, in 1931, Philip did not know exactly what all the "things rolled into one" were, something Paraskeva would soon reveal.

Welcome to Toronto
as Hinterland✑

*Having the good luck of meeting among my new friends some
painters who after seeing my work encouraged me to exhibit I
started my painting career in Canada.[1]*

Paraskeva's first painting after her arrival in Toronto was a still life that has
the viewer looking down on three bulging yellow and red pears clustered
together, and a pairing of two other pieces of fruit that could be apples or
peaches, also red and yellow. They lie beside a small white bowl holding purple
grapes, which are all reflected on the dark green tray underneath them. The
selection of fruit suggests she might have painted the oil in the fall, the season
when these fruits would have been plentiful in the Toronto area.

It is not surprising that Paraskeva ventured into her painting career in
Toronto with this oil she called simply *Fruit* (Plate 9); a high regard for the
genre of still life was characteristic of artists in Russia during the first fifteen
to twenty years of the twentieth century. Furthermore, her teacher Petrov-
Vodkin painted many still lifes, but his are unique for their viewpoint —
the perspective in most of them is from above. And many of his still lifes
portray a table or other flat objects at a diagonal in relation to the edge of the
painting.[2] As he said about this genre:

The still life represents one of the painter's intimate conversations with nature. Here neither the narrative nor the psychological aspect obscure the spatial definition of the object. What sort of an object this may be, where it may be, and where I, who see this object, stand — these are all points that constitute the basic principles of the still life. And therein too lies the great joy of cognition experienced by the viewer who sees the still life.[3]

Now, ten years later, she emulated her teacher. The tray in *Fruit* sits at an angle across the corners of a small table covered with a cloth, pale blue with yellow stripes that pick up the yellow of the fruit.

Fruit was painted at the Clarks' first apartment, a small place on the third floor of a red brick house on Admiral Road, a pleasant tree-lined street with large houses, just seven blocks from Toronto's Yonge–Bloor city centre. With such a convenient location, Paraskeva could walk to do household errands and grocery shopping, but streetcars were also available for only seven cents a ride.

After growing up in a one-room apartment, Paraskeva learned about taking care of a large house with the Allegris in Paris, but this was not at all the same. This was her own apartment, her first one with her new husband, and she thought it "very romantic."[4] Setting up the apartment while she was making the transition to a new culture and expanding her understanding of English could not have been easy. And yet, despite — or perhaps because of — the strange environment and new routines, she enjoyed looking after their place. And there was the excitement of painting along with doing the housework.

Paraskeva also had to oversee Ben and get him settled into his first school, Huron Street Public School, which was just two blocks from the Admiral Road apartment. Ben spoke only French and, at first, he was unhappy among English-speaking classmates. The transition was difficult for him in a school full of children unaccustomed to someone who could not speak English well.

Ben must have missed the only family he had known, the Allegris. They wrote letters back and forth fairly frequently during the first several years after Paraskeva and Ben left Paris. Letters from Oreste Allegri, Ben's grandfather, communicate genuine warmth for both Ben and Paraskeva. When Ben sent the Allegris his drawings, his grandfather wrote to thank and praise him for his beautiful pictures.[5]

It seems Philip and Paraskeva did not agree on matters relating to Ben. Paraskeva even wrote a letter to her former lover Paul Allegri complaining that Philip was inflexible. Clive and Mary Clark acknowledge that writing that kind of letter would have been characteristic of Paraskeva.[6]

In a reply addressed to Philip, Paul Allegri reminded Philip that there would always be a difference of "race," meaning between Philip and Ben, and that Philip should be flexible enough to allow for individuality. Paul also thanked Philip for what he was doing for Ben, and acknowledged that Ben had better circumstances for his life in Toronto than he would have had in Paris.[7] That Paraskeva would have written to complain about Philip to her former lover, and that Paul would have presumed to dispense advice must have irked Philip; this was only the beginning of the friction over Ben throughout the years.

Paraskeva's behaviour — Philip would have considered her letter to Paul mischievous and inconsiderate — must have been hard for Philip to take, especially since he was genuinely trying to be a good father for Ben. Neither Paraskeva nor Ben was conditioned in the same ways that Philip had been, and for eight years, she had been making her own decisions regarding her son. It is not surprising that, given his upbringing, Philip might not have been flexible enough in his approach, and he undoubtedly had difficulty understanding both Ben and Paraskeva; and they would have had a hard time understanding Philip.

For Philip, part of being a good father was carrying out his responsibility to support the family well, which he was doing. His position as office manager at Canada Gypsum was not his idea of the best he could do, however, so in 1933 he became an Assessor in the Income Tax Division of the Department of National Revenue. That year he also moved his family to another apartment in the same building where Murray and Fran Adaskin lived on Lonsdale Road, just west of Avenue Road.

Being near the Adaskins must have helped Paraskeva since she knew few people in the city. The Adaskins and the Clarks developed a deep friendship, a bond so strong that Paraskeva came to feel they were like family. Furthermore, if it hadn't been for Murray, it is unlikely that she and Philip would have met. At that time, Murray was playing in the first violin section of the Toronto Symphony and his wife Frances James was a professional singer. They introduced Paraskeva to their friends, many of whom were professionals in Toronto's classical music world. With her somewhat limited use of English, making friends was not easy for Paraskeva in this totally new environment. She joined L'Alliance Française, an organization promoting the French language and culture, as a way of finding other people with whom she could speak French.

Somehow, soon after her arrival in Toronto, she met Douglas Duncan, whom Philip and Murray had encountered in Paris when they had gone to the theatre. Duncan had left Toronto for Paris in 1925 for post-graduate work at the Université de Paris but soon gave up academe and spent his time soaking up French culture by attending theatre and films. He met the eminent bookbinder, Agnes St. John, studied with her, and also became a master binder.

Though they had never met in Paris, the years Paraskeva and Duncan lived there had overlapped. Now in Toronto, Paraskeva found in Duncan someone who knew French culture, understood both European and Canadian art, and helped her ease into the community of artists in the city. He would become her "good fortune," and "the climate that was beneficial to my taking roots in Canadian soil."[8]

By then Philip knew with certainty that Paraskeva was an artist. Through his membership at the Arts & Letters Club, he knew the prominent Toronto artists and, with great pride, introduced his wife to them. Sometimes Paraskeva ventured out to the Art Gallery of Toronto on Sunday afternoons. It was there that she first met the artist A.Y. Jackson who, as a strong member of the Group of Seven, was a leader among Toronto's artists.

Six months after Paraskeva arrived in Toronto, she saw an exhibition of the Group of Seven's northern Ontario wilderness paintings for the first time, though she likely had seen individual works by these artists before during visits to the Art Gallery of Toronto. That December 1931 show, called "An Exhibition of Seascapes and Water-Fronts by Contemporary Artists and an Exhibition by the Group of Seven," featured primarily paintings of lakes, mountains, trees, rocks, and snow. This was the last exhibition of these seven male artists as a group, who by then wore the persona of men in flannel shirts whacking through the bush in northern Ontario with the purpose of creating a "national art" rooted in Canada's good earth. Works of other artists from Victoria, Vancouver, Winnipeg, Toronto, Oshawa, Ottawa, Montreal, and other smaller centres were also included, but paintings of the Group dominated the show.[9]

Paraskeva would have been pleased to see that of the thirty-two artists in the show, fourteen were women. On the walls were five paintings by Emily Carr, whom Paraskeva would meet not long afterward. A painting that stood out among all the landscapes and the few figural works was Prudence Heward's then recently painted oil, *Girl Under a Tree*, which Lawren Harris praised as the best nude ever painted in Canada.[10] Paraskeva would definitely have noticed this painting of a woman with a somewhat androgynous body; the background seemed influenced by the work of Cézanne, whom Paraskeva admired, and it was different from the other paintings in the show.

Of course, as she looked at the paintings on the walls of the Art Gallery of Toronto, she compared the work to what she had seen in Europe. Paraskeva discovered the strong grip landscape painting had in Canada, something that continued into the next decade. "She could not fathom the idea of a modern art movement devoted exclusively to landscape painting, the style of which she felt was overly design oriented."[11] She did not yet know enough about Canada to understand the strong force of the physical geography in the Canadian psyche as the reason for the preoccupation of these artists searching for a Canadian identity, with the goal of creating an art for the people of Canada.

Her observation that the paintings were "design oriented" was true. Most of the Group of Seven painters were commercial artists who painted in their spare time, though a few of them had studied in Europe. Grip Studio in Toronto where they worked was "the technical birthplace" of the Group and their "*spiritual* birthplace was the lake district of northern Ontario."[12]

Paraskeva concluded that the Group's men were "attached to the rocks," rather than having a good philosophy of painting.[13] The Group's "philosophy" was more a creed than a principle of inquiry: It was a belief in a Canadian nationalism — a yearning for a truly Canadian art — romanticized on board and canvas to express the emotions the artists experienced about the landscape, which is what being "attached to the rocks" meant to them. The Group's pre-occupation with the definition of art in political and geographical terms hindered their ability to see and respond to "what was actually happening on the surface of the canvas — and ultimately inhibited an appreciation of Canadian art in any but those ways. Judgment came to be based on 'Canadianism' of a painting rather than its inherent pictorial qualities ..."[14]

As an outsider with European training, Paraskeva could look at a Canadian painting that might have been considered to be among the best and conclude that the artist did not understand the principles of form and colour. There was more behind her criticism of Canadian art. To her, Toronto was a hinterland in the world of art, and Canada an anomaly. She could barely conceive of a country of just over ten million people, a nation so young, whose cultural history was as thin as it was young, hardly comparable to that of her own country of origin, except that Russia, too, was a northern country stretched over a vast territory. In a 1929 article, the artist Bertram Brooker pointed out that Canada is "*not yet* a people!" but a geographically disparate place with a history of what the French and English did to the Aboriginal people, and what they — French and English foreigners — did to each other, who also remain foreigners to each other.[15] Brooker was among the few who paid attention to the country's history before European settlers arrived. "Canadian" art at that time meant European-Canadian art or British-Canadian.

In his article, Brooker had also made a case for claiming Canada as *our* homeland where artists could create an art that is our own. However, a later letter to a friend shows that he was aware of the way that Canadian nationalism could hobble artists. He worried that the "utterances of the old Group" would continue to influence the Canadian Group of Painters.[16]

What creating "our own" art meant, with a self-consciousness and its mythologies based in landscape, was something Paraskeva would come to discover as she read about Canadian art and attended exhibitions — it was her nature to learn as much as possible about her new environment. She would find out that through the early Canadian paintings she could gain an understanding of the evolution of Canadian culture from the time of the first European settlers, "of hunting and of peasant-farming ... settlers and burghers alike, till the end of the epoch of Kane and Krieghoff in the 1860's."[17]

Industrialization in its opening era was also reflected in Canadian painting, as was the portrayal of a rustic simplicity, the farmers and *habitants*, followed by the impact of Impressionism, with an endless number of paintings of snow. In contrast to the style of European landscapes of a more intimate scale, the monumental quality of the 1920s landscapes was also characterized by a lack of evidence of human presence, which Paraskeva would eventually criticize with fervour.

Over the years, when she spoke about Canadian painting she developed something of a mantra that reflected what she thought. "Landscapes, landscapes, landscapes," she complained, emphatically cutting the air with her hand. "Nothing but the bloody Group of Seven."[18] And yet, ironically, she, too, would paint landscapes in her effort to claim Canada as her own, and as a way of finding the similarities between her two northern countries as she struggled to find her place here and put down roots.

If we look beneath the surface of the relationship between Canada's art and politics and economics, we discover that Paraskeva's criticism had a basis in her philosophy of socialism whereas the general endorsement of the Group of Seven's paintings of the Precambrian Shield as a national art was integrated into the capitalist system. The Group rose to its height when mining and lumbering fed the expansion of the Canadian economy. As one study revealed, "The coincidence of a surge in the export of natural resources and the selective promotion of wilderness landscapes is compelling."[19] A nationalist art, based on northern Ontario, merging with the purposes of a capitalist system did not satisfy artists who saw themselves as having a role in restoring the social fabric of their 1930s society.

Paraskeva was interested in these matters: the connection between the social climate and painting. The big stock market crash occurred just a few months after Philip and Paraskeva met in Paris when William Lyon McKenzie King was prime minister of Canada. King, who had a hobby of collecting stones from famous buildings to build "ruins" at his summer home, instituted policies that choked the country's economy. One writer described him as having "the spiritualist tendencies of the Romanoffs."[20] During the first half of the thirties, the millionaire lawyer R. B. Bennett of "Bennett Buggy" fame was in power, until King was voted back again in the fall of 1935.

Many people in Canada, including some of Paraskeva's artist friends, questioned the basics of Canadian capitalist society. One result of the general discontent in the country was the formation of a new party in 1932, the Cooperative Commonwealth Federation (CCF). The purpose of this social democratic party was to remedy the inequities of society by establishing a universal health care system and other programs that would provide a humane network of support to fulfil the needs of Canadians, needs that became obvious during the Depression. Still, Paraskeva did not think much of the CCF, believing that communism offered a better solution for societal ills.

In the 1930s, thousands of single young men were unemployed, and under Bennett, work camps were set up, usually in wild, undeveloped areas of the country under the jurisdiction of the Department of National Defence. Here the unemployed men lived and worked for twenty cents a day, paid by the government. As Bennett's Conservatives were worried about revolutionary action among the disgruntled unemployed, the men in the camps who complained were labelled as "Reds," and ended up with RCMP files.

In fact, "Reds" were present in Canada. The Communist Party of Canada had begun in secret meetings in 1921 in a barn near Guelph, Ontario. The party was illegal under the War Measures Act of 1918 and remained underground for a time but organized a legal party, the Workers' Party of Canada. However, in 1931 Prime Minister Bennett used Section 98 of the Criminal Code to outlaw the party again. Tim Buck, who had become leader, along with seven other communists accused of attempting to overthrow the country's institutions and destroy social order by use of violence, were given a five-year jail sentence in November 1931. Widespread criticism resulted in Buck's release in the summer of 1934, two and a half years into his sentence in the Kingston Penitentiary. This was the same year that public pressure forced the government to repeal Section 98 of the Criminal Code. When Buck returned to Toronto from Kingston, four thousand people welcomed him at Union Station, and when he gave a speech at Maple Leaf Gardens, seventeen thousand came to hear him.[21] We do not know whether Paraskeva went to Maple Leaf Gardens that evening. However, when she was interviewed nearly fifty years later for a film on her life and work, she claimed, "Tim Buck was my best friend,"[22] probably an exaggeration.

Even though she talked about herself as "Red" and in support of Tim Buck and workers in general, Paraskeva did not join workers' organizations, nor did she ever join the Communist Party of Canada, because she worried that political activity could put her and her family in jeopardy — that people knew she was Russian would have made her feel somewhat nervous. She focused on her painting and looking after her family. She was fortunate that she did not have financial pressures and did not personally suffer from the Depression because Philip had a decent job and supported her.

The timing of her arrival in Toronto was an advantage to her for the temper of the Depression era brought about changes among Toronto artists: social issues were beginning to break into the hold that landscape painting had. Until then, cultural groups and artists had overlooked "issues of social or economic inequity."[23] Another benefit of the time of her arrival was the number of women among Toronto's professional artists; it often comes as a surprise that between the two World Wars many of Canada's professional artists, both painters and sculptors, were women.[24] Furthermore, many of the female artists were not strictly bound by the Group of Seven approach to landscape painting, and contributed to the general expansion of subject matter into portraiture and other figurative work.

And yet, despite the number of women artists, they had historically been barred from the art associations. The Royal Canadian Academy allowed women to join, but their attendance at business meetings was not required and they were not allowed to hold administrative positions. It was not until 1933 that a woman, Marion Long, was elected a full academician. Until then, nineteen women had been voted associates of the Royal Canadian Academy, a lesser rank. The Ontario Society of Artists had a similar policy when it began but, in 1924, Mary Wrinch Reid was elected to an executive position.[25]

Among the women who were professional artists, with whom Paraskeva became friends, were Yvonne McKague, a teacher at the Ontario College of Art and a founding member of the Canadian Group of Painters, sculptor Elizabeth Wyn Wood, and painter Isabel McLaughlin. The sculptors Frances Loring and Florence Wyle — dubbed "the girls" and the "Loring-Wyles" — by then were established in an old church, which they converted into their studio and home on Glenrose Avenue, a street in Moore Park that was at the end of the streetcar line and considered far from Toronto's city centre. In their home full of sculptures, cats, and dogs, Loring and Wyle hosted dinners and parties for artists, musicians, and photographers.

The home of Bobs Coghill Haworth and Peter Haworth — both employed at Central Technical School, she an art teacher and he the head of the art department — became another place where artists gathered for dinners, and Paraskeva developed a particular fondness for and friendship with the Haworths. As well, Lawren and Bess Harris invited artists to tea. It was at one of those teas that Emily Carr and Paraskeva met; a brief reference in Carr's journal stated simply that she went to tea with "a little Russian lady artist."[26] For her part, Paraskeva thought Emily Carr was just an old woman Lawren Harris was promoting who looked like a dumpy housewife, "not even a lady."[27]

Of particular interest to Paraskeva was a small nucleus of artists whose sympathies lay with the labour movement because of their affinity with workers. These men and women, aware of their social responsibility, believed that art played a vital role in the advancement of society. Of course, Paraskeva had absorbed these ideas when she was an art student after the Russian Revolution; so among these artists — Bertram Brooker, Charles Comfort, Pegi Nicol, Carl Schaefer — she found a philosophy of art compatible to her own, which made her feel more at home.[28] As she had been at the centre where big changes occurred in art in Leningrad, so now, again, in Toronto in the thirties, she was at the centre where new things were happening in art, albeit on a smaller scale.[29]

Eventually becoming a key figure in this group and the most outspoken, Paraskeva was a catalyst among her colleagues in "the progress of socially-conscious Canadian modernism."[30] She could happily discuss and argue about politics, social issues, and art for hours on end with these artists. Their landscapes of cultivated fields and farm houses — the work of Carl Schaefer, for example — portrayed a human presence rather than the mythical uninhabited wilderness. The Dominion of Canada was a nation "fast on the rise as an autonomous country dealing with major economic and political upheavals," and these artists' paintings of the civilized landscape were "meta-phorical expressions" of this "socio-political reality."[31]

Other artists, too, both in Toronto and Montreal and in other parts of the country, were influenced by the social upheaval, resulting in a more humanistic approach to their work. Some painted domestic scenes as well as the human figure, and attempted to portray the real life of Canadians, among them New Brunswick artist Miller Brittain. In Montreal, where the theme of ordinary urban life had become important, were Fritz Brandtner and Edwin Holgate.

In this environment of a readiness to take Canadian art in a different direction, the Toronto artists welcomed the Russian painter, described in Montreal's *Vie des Arts* as a bird of paradise with brilliant plumage (*une sorte d'oiseau de paradis au brillant plumage*).[32] She brought a burst of energy and vitality into the "stifling atmosphere of those art societies which no longer represent the creative movement of art in this country."[33]

Paraskeva's arrival in Toronto coincided with another development among Toronto painters, the formation of a new group following the dissolution of the Group of Seven. After the December 1931 show, A.Y. Jackson announced that the Group was disbanding and joining in with a larger group of artists.[34] In March 1933, the men from the Group invited a number of younger artists to a meeting at Lawren Harris's home on Ava Crescent in Toronto to discuss the idea of a new group. It seems significant that the meeting was held at Harris's home because the force of his ideas about art and artists has often been overlooked in the stories of the Group of Seven and their leadership. A.Y. Jackson described Harris as a man for whom "art was almost a mission. He believed that a country that ignored the arts left no record of itself worth preserving. He deplored our neglect of the artist in Canada, and believed that we, a young, vigorous people should put the same spirit of adventure into the cultivation of the arts."[35]

Now, in a new era for the Group, Harris's influence — the importance of "spirit" in art — was still strong, as was that of the other Group members. Even so, after an evening of arguments and differences over the purposes and parameters of this new society, the Canadian Group of Painters (CGP) was wrestled into being.[36] It seems the younger artists were intent on going beyond the nationalistic landscape art of the Group of Seven to create an art with "a more common language of expression."[37] The artists present were certainly not unified in formulating one definitive ideology, but they did form an association that functioned for many years. Nevertheless, the men of the Group of Seven continued as an integral force.

For English-speaking Canadians, Toronto was the centre of Canadian art, the cultural heart of the country. As Michael Tooby, who curated a show in the early nineties called "The True North 1896–1939" pointed out, the sense of nationhood resides in the centre that establishes itself as predominate. However, as soon as an urban centre cultivates "a vision of the surrounding landscape as the national identity, reaction from another centre is bound to emerge."[38] That other centre was Montreal. Though some Montreal artists joined the Toronto-centred Canadian Group of Painters, Montrealers did not see the painting of the Group of Seven as the defining images of Canadian nationalism.

In many ways Paraskeva had more in common with the Montreal artists than with those in Toronto and she articulated the difference in the two centres: she felt that Europeans came to Toronto "to make dollars, they really don't care. Art takes centuries to grow up in countries." In Montreal, she detected the "Latin spirit, ancient inborn," based on the human spirit instead of economics.[39] She, of course, favoured the diversity of Montreal's painting, which included artists strong in figurative work.

Montreal's Beaver Hall Group had come together in 1920, an association that included a core of women who were professional painters, some of whom Paraskeva would come to admire. In reviewing a 1930 show at the National Gallery, the critic Blodwen Davies said that the women "revealed themselves as experimenters of vision and courage."[40]

The artist John Lyman, who after eighteen years in France had returned to Montreal in the fall of the same year Paraskeva came, was critical of the Group of Seven's idea that a Canadian art was intertwined with exploring and painting northern Ontario. He thought of that kind of "self-conscious nationalism" in Canadian art as "bordering on artistic xenophobia."[41]

One of the aspects of Toronto that made Paraskeva think of the city as backward was that few galleries existed where the dozens of painters and sculptors could show their work; how then could the city be the centre of a nationalist art? Roberts Gallery, Mellors Gallery, and the Galleries of

Paraskeva, probably when she was in her teens. Library and Archives Canada e002712778.

Avdey Yakinovich Plistik, Paraskeva's father. Library and Archives Canada e002712775.

Zakhar, Paraskeva's brother. Library and Archives Canada e002712777.

Palenka, Paraskeva's sister. Library and Archives Canada e002712776.

Skorokhad Shoe Factory (in the 1950s), where Avdey Plistik worked in the early 1900s. When Paraskeva was a teenager, she also worked here in an office. Courtesy School of Slavonic & East European Studies Library, University College, London.

Oreste Allegri, c. 1922 or 1923, probably in his room at the Maly Theatre. Library and Archives Canada e006580512.

Catherine and Oreste Allegri, 1920s in Chatou. Library and Archives Canada e006580516.

Christmas in Chatou, probably 1923: Catherine Allegri, Ben, Paraskeva, and Paul Allegri. Library and Archives Canada e006580513.

Paraskeva Allegri holding Ben, late 1923 in Chatou. Paraskeva's face shows the pain she experienced losing her husband earlier that year. Her arms and hands protectively encircle her son. Library and Archives Canada e006580515.

Philip Clark and Murray Adaskin on a ship en route to France, 1929. Library and Archives Canada e006580503.

Philip and Paraskeva, c. 1929. Photo courtesy of Dorothea Larsen Adaskin.

Philip and Paraskeva, with Ben, 1931. Library and Archives Canada e006078601.

Murray's apartment at 40 Huntley Street, Toronto, which he shared for a time with Philip in 1930. *Zlata* can be seen on the table. Library and Archives Canada e006580564.

The Clark home is the house on the far left at 44 Willcocks Street, Toronto. The house is no longer there. Library and Archives Canada e006580506.

The interior of the Clark home. Courtesy of Clive and Mary Clark.

Philip as a teenager reading, at 44 Willcocks Street. Library and Archives Canada e002712781.

The Clark Family, c. 1935 at 44 Willcocks Street, Toronto. L to R: Ben Allegri, Earnest Moogk, Harriet Clark, Harold Clark, Paraskeva holding Clive, Ralph Clark, Philip Clark. On floor: Virginia Clark Moogh with Marguerite. Library and Archives Canada e0060788598.

Paraskeva's self portrait collage she contributed to Charles Comfort's sketchbook when he was working on his mural in the Toronto Stock Exchange. Library and Archives Canada C139718.

Paraskeva did not hesitate to wear "shocking" gowns for special occasions in the early thirties. Courtesy Clive and Mary Clark.

Paraskeva painting outdoors, 1936. Courtesy Clive and Mary Clark.

Dr. Norman Bethune, Madrid, 1937. Library and Archives Canada e006980511.

Paraskeva's friend, the art critic Graham McInnes. Courtesy of Simon McInnes.

New Year's Eve party, 1930s Front Row: Elizabeth Wyn Wood, Parskeva Clark, Will Ogilvie. Second Row: Doris Davies, Charles Comfort. Back: (unidentified), Emmanuel Hahn, Louise Comfort, Gordon Davies. Photo taken by Charles Comfort, late thirties, Leica Camera. Library and Archives Canada e006078602.

Paraskeva holding a Picasso catalogue, standing in front of her portrait of Philip, c.1939. Library and Archives Canada e002712783.

J.S. McLean, 1948. Yousuf Karsh, Ottawa. Courtesy of the McLean Foundation.

Paraskeva in one of her hats, 1938. Many years later, she was amused when she recalled the hats she had worn in those days. Charles Comfort photo, cat.38/5-1, The National Gallery of Canada Library and Archives, Ottawa, Record #74815.

Jack Nichols, Arthur Lismer, Martin Baldwin, Paraskeva Clark at the 1941 Conference of Canadian Artists at Queen's University, Kingston, Ontario. Photo credit: Hagan Sise, courtesy of The National Gallery Archives.

Clive, Ben, and Paraskeva in the garden at 56 Roxborough Drive c. 1943. Courtesy Clive and Mary Clark.

Second Congress of Russian Canadians 1944. Paraskeva is the woman directly below the "X" on the group photo. Library and Archives Canada e006078604.

Paraskeva with other members of the Congress. She was in charge of the arts and culture photos displayed at the conference. Library and Archives Canada e006078596.

Ben Clark, Philip Clark, Paraskeva Clark with friends Leonid Altsev and Olga Altsev at 56 Roxborough Drive in 1945. Library and Archives Canada e006580508.

Murray Adaskin at the Piano, 1953. Library and Archives Canada a215155. Photo credit: Gordon Sisson.

Harry McCurry, Director of the National Gallery of Canada from 1939 to 1955. Paraskeva was fond of McCurry because he encouraged her, and during World War II he commissioned her to paint the work women were doing in the war. Library and Archives Canada e006078606.

Paraskeva with Colonel Nikolai Zabotin, a Soviet attaché in charge of collecting intelligence who stayed with the Clarks when he was in Toronto in 1945. Library and Archives Canada e002712780.

H. Walker, Philip Clark, Paraskeva Clark, The Honourable Dana Porter, and Dorothy Porter at the opening of the 1949 exhibition of the Canadian Society of Painters in Water Colour, during the year that Paraskeva was president of the society. Photo: Art Gallery of Ontario.

Paraskeva in her studio with her painting of a blind woman on a Toronto streetcar (untraced) c. 1949. Library and Archives Canada e002712782.

Paraskeva and Alice Sutton, probably 1950s, in Alice's farmhouse kitchen. Courtesy of Murray and Dorothea Adaskin.

Ben and Paraskeva, October 1958, after Ben's second severe illness. This is one photo in which Paraskeva's worry about Ben was evident. Ben's lip was scarred because he bit his lip during one of his treatments and the doctors did a poor job of stitching the wound. Courtesy Clive and Mary Clark.

A.Y. Jackson, Paraskeva Clark, and Jack Nichols at the 1953 Canadian Group of Painters Exhibition opening. Photo: Art Gallery of Ontario.

Paraskeva's studio, showing her tools on the table. Note the hammer and sickle hanging on the wall under the window. Library and Archives Canada e006580509.

Paraskeva and A.Y. Jackson, late 1950s. Courtesy of Clive and Mary Clark.

Paraskeva and Carl Schaefer dancing, late 1950s. Courtesy of Clive and Mary Clark.

The Clive and Mary Clark family in 1965, Toronto: Mary holding Panya, Jennifer, Joel and Clive. Courtesy of Clive and Mary Clark.

Paraskeva and Philip outside their house at 56 Roxborough Drive, September 1977. Courtesy Dorothea Larsen Adaskin.

Paraskeva standing outside the house at 56 Roxborough, July 1979. Paraskeva had large hands in comparison to the rest of her body. Photo credit: Kind permission of David Saltmarche, courtesy Joan Murray.

Louis Muhlstock, Carl Schaefer, Paraskeva Clark, André Bieler, Yvonne McKague Housser, Isabel McLaughlin at the opening of *Canadian Painting in the Thirties* at the Art Gallery of Ontario in 1975. Photo: Art Gallery of Ontario.

Paraskeva giving a speech in the late seventies. According to Clive, her son, she is probably saying "You have to have guts." Photo credit: Kind permission of David Saltmarche, courtesy Robert McLaughlin Gallery, Oshawa.

Though many people thought of Paraskeva as disagreeable, she had a great ability to laugh and express her joy. Photo credit: Kind permission of David Saltmarche, courtesy of Joan Murray.

J. Merritt Malloney were the only private galleries in Toronto at that time. The associations — Ontario Society of Artists, Canadian Society of Graphic Arts, Canadian Society of Painters in Water Colour, Canadian Group of Painters, the Royal Canadian Academy — showed primarily at the Art Gallery of Toronto when they held their annual exhibitions.

As the Arts & Letters Club was open only to men, Paraskeva could not accompany Philip during the many hours he spent there mingling with artists. Nevertheless, she had met artists at social gatherings, and at one of Lawren Harris's tea parties she was surprised to meet the daughter of Sir Edmund Walker (a founder of the Art Gallery of Toronto), Dorothy Buhler, who had been a client at Maison DIM where she worked in Paris.[42]

Through meeting Toronto artists, Paraskeva was invited to exhibit a work in the November Royal Canadian Academy show at the Art Gallery of Toronto a little more than a year after she arrived in Canada. She showed her 1931–1932 *Self Portrait* (Plate 7), an unusual pose in which she is looking over her left shoulder with a sober, guarded expression against a somewhat abstract background that appears to include pine trees and a horizon line.

Later, Paraskeva wrote on the back:

Painted in winter of 1931–32/Toronto — invited by Many [sic] Hahn to Exhibit in Academy/was accepted by jury and thus it became a 'foot/in the door' into the Temple of Canadian Art.[43]

Ironically, the first exhibition of the newly formed Canadian Group of Painters in the summer of 1933 was in Atlantic City, New Jersey, funded by the American corporation, H. J. Heinz.[44] In November, the twenty-eight members of the Group had their Canadian debut at the Art Gallery of Toronto, and Paraskeva was among the twenty-five non-member artists invited to exhibit. Many of these later became members; non-member artists had to show their work for two years in the Group shows before they were invited to join in the third year. Paraskeva was elected a member in 1936.

The same month that the Canadian Group of Painters was formed, Paraskeva showed a new painting, *Portrait of Philip* (1933) (Plate 8), in the Annual Exhibition of the Ontario Society of Artists at the Art Gallery of Toronto. Had she thought through a strategy of showing a portrait of her husband who was well known in the arts community before she introduced herself in a striking self-portrait the same year? She presented Philip from the point of view of looking down on him seated in a chair with his hands invisible and part of his feet outside the canvas. He appears to be a diffident, still figure, a sharp contrast to the way she painted herself — animated and exuding warmth and confidence in her new self-portrait with her hands prominent in the painting. She called it *Myself*, a dramatic work that has become one of her signature paintings, now in the collection of the National Gallery of Canada.

Myself (1933) (Plate 11), was a strong statement of introduction in the 1933 Canadian Group of Painters exhibition,[45] as though declaring dramatically, "I am here! Not only am I here, but I am my own person, a woman of style and elegance to be reckoned with." She presented herself with the door closed behind her as though she had just entered the room and announced, "I'm pregnant." She was three months pregnant when she painted this portrait, though at the time it was still a secret.

In 1930s Toronto, pregnancy was not discussed, nor did images of pregnant women appear in the media, "and women in the months prior to birth were normally expected to disguise their condition as much as possible and not to draw attention to themselves by any more public display of their person than was absolutely necessary."[46] Her painting broke this taboo, which people would discover when she exhibited the portrait about five months after the birth of her son Clive.

Not only did she thumb her nose at the socially unacceptable portrayal of herself while pregnant, but she also broke class lines; she was a peasant who was having a child with an upper middle-class husband, for a second time. The Clarks received congratulatory notes from their artist friends when Clive was born. Charles Comfort, whose vague language reflects the mores of the time, wrote:

During the past few months I have felt that something of this sort was about to happen. Now that it is all so happily over and we are to benefit to the extent of another human who will radiate among us some

of your own charming self; allow me to congratulate you. I will follow
the lads [*sic*] career with great interest.[47]

The "all" that Comfort referred to was no more than a simple birth, an
event now treated by the medical profession as completely normal with
minimal medical attention necessary in most circumstances. In the 1930s, a
mother was kept flat in bed for five or six days in hospital after giving birth.[48]
To remain in bed so long would have been a trial for Paraskeva. The entire
hospital stay was twelve to fourteen days, which at least postponed the
laborious routine of washing diapers.

However, all that was still ahead of her when she painted this self-portrait
early in 1933, which she signed in bold block letters, unlike her signature in
most of her other paintings, reflecting her concept of herself in this painting.
The contrast between this new oil and the self-portraits of 1925 and 1931–
1932 is striking. In the first, she presented herself as the broad-faced peasant.
The second carries the same air, but is more refined. Despite her claim all
her life that she was a peasant, the 1933 painting leaves behind Paraskeva the
peasant, and instead presents the artist as a woman — a society lady — who
exudes elegance and a sense of pleasure in herself.

In letters from St. Petersburg, her sister commented on how slim and well
she looked in the photos Paraskeva sent her, and that is exactly how she
painted herself. Certainly, her dress is not that of a woman of the working
class. In those days, people commented on Paraskeva's flair for style, the way
she wore her hats and her elegant dresses.

On two different occasions, Murray Adaskin recalled what she wore at an
exhibition in which some of her work was shown. It was a gown she had
purchased in the French Room in Simpson's department store, not only cut
low in the back, but also curved down in the front almost to her navel. "And
of course everyone nearly died."[49] Perhaps Murray's memory of the gown is an
exaggeration, but Paraskeva would have loved the effect on proper Torontonians. An undated old clipping described her at a van Gogh exhibition at
the Art Gallery of Toronto: "Tiny Russian Paraskeva Clark, who ... is the wife
of Philip Clark, wore one of the loveliest gowns of the evening in a deep rich

emerald shade with a fish train, long pointed sleeves and graceful back drapes, which crossed below the bodice and passed over her shoulders."[50] Mentioning her husband told everyone that Philip was the reason she could afford the gown.

Paraskeva's self-portrait tells us how she saw herself, and how she wanted the world to see her. Many people who viewed her self-portrait before meeting the artist were surprised to learn that she was tiny, not the seemingly tall woman they saw in the painting. "I think she kind of wished she'd take up more space than she did. And she had a great amount of confidence in the way she moved," Mary MacLachlan recalled. MacLachlan, who interviewed Paraskeva a number of times, also said she felt that the self-portraits give an accurate sense of the largeness of Paraskeva's persona.[51]

This 1933 portrait portrays a woman who is confident and self-possessed, with a vibrant presence and sense of purpose, a statuesque woman with blue-grey eyes. Despite her physical size, she was a woman of a forceful character and the portrait was a statement that she deserved this kind of representation. Art historian Marsha Meskimmon's perception that artists' self-portraits give others a "route to knowing the creative personality through the image" is certainly true for this painting.[52]

Looking at the self-portrait, one's eyes go directly to the face, and then follow the pale tones in the low neckline, and down to the torso and the hands, which become a dominant part of the painting — Paraskeva did have large hands. The painting is unified by the tilt of the figure and the slanted architectural elements. Although the use of this kind of architectural framing device reflects the influence of Petrov-Vodkin, Paraskeva turned onto a different path from that of her teacher when she chose black for the painting. She loved black, and Petrov-Vodkin never used it, she said.[53] At the same time, she strove for luminosity in her work, wanting the "magic of light," as she declared in a 1977 video.[54] In the video, her hands are as expressive as her compelling voice; indeed, they were the same strong hands of *Myself*.

Meskimmon links Paraskeva to the Russian avant-garde, "whose formal revisions of Byzantine icons and Russian folk art combined with adaptations of French modernist form carried particular nationalist and socialist tendencies." Meskimmon describes the 1933 self-portrait as bridging the European avant-garde and the realistic Canadian tradition, saying that Paraskeva becomes "part of the socially elite Canadian circle as well as a woman modernist."[55] This reading of Paraskeva Clark illustrates a basic contradiction in her life, being a proponent of the Russian system — and socialism — and becoming part of the Toronto artists' circle and its middle-class society based on capitalism.

Nevertheless, the self-confidence radiating from the painting was a quality extending far beyond the canvas, and characterized Paraskeva's whole life at that time. In the spring of 1933, she exhibited not only with the Ontario Society of Artists, but also sent a still life to Montreal for the 50th Spring Exhibition of the Art Association of Montreal. The Clarks spent that summer at the family cottage in Muskoka where she painted two landscapes: *Muskoka* and *View from Huckleberry Rock*. At the end of the summer, she exhibited in "Canadian Paintings" at the Canadian National Exhibition in Toronto.[56] The energy to produce and show new work, besides caring for her infant son and Ben, now ten years old, tells a completely different story than the one in the sad self-portrait, *Memories of Leningrad* nearly ten years earlier. Her life had changed dramatically.

No wonder that in later years as she looked back at the early thirties, she commented that in coming to Canada she regained her "freedom in the use of my time. I started to paint again — still life, self-portrait — and was joy-fully surprised that I could do as well as I did after practically 10 years without doing any painting."[57]

After the success of her 1933 self-portrait, Paraskeva painted the portrait of her friend, Naomi Adaskin, a concert pianist who used the professional name Naomi Yanova, the feminine form of her mother's name, who came from a Russian family from a disputed part of Poland and Germany. Yanova was married to Murray Adaskin's younger brother, John, and she and Paraskeva became good friends — another Toronto friend linked to Russia.

As when she painted herself, in *Portrait of Naomi Yanova* (1934) (Plate 12), also a three-quarter length figure, Paraskeva achieved a sense of drama. She also used architectural elements in the background, including a slate-topped coffee table built for Paraskeva and Philip by Murray and John's father on which rests a clear glass bowl holding delphinium blossoms. The curve of the outer rim of the bowl intersects and refracts ever so slightly a part of the edge of the table.

The burgundy velvet dress brings a richness and texture to the painting, creating a contrast with the pale, smooth skin of the face. The tilt of the form of the flower leads one to focus on the dark eyes of the petite figure, and as the viewer walks around the room, those piercing eyes seem to follow wherever one goes. According to Yanova's daughter, the artist's portrayal is accurate. "She captured ... the essence of being of my mother, not just her outward looks, but her soul," said Susan Adaskin.[58] As did Petrov-Vodkin, Paraskeva in this portrait portrayed the inner structure of the face to evoke the interior life.

That was a good year for Paraskeva. In 1934, she and her friend Pegi Nicol were among the artists hired by the French architect and designer, René Cera, who was on staff at Eaton's College Street department store. Cera designed the art deco concourse of this opulent building that opened at the corner of College and Yonge in 1930. Eventually, this was just one of many family-owned Eaton's stores across the country. Eaton's was so well loved by Canadians that when, in a new economic environment of big box stores, the company went bankrupt in 1999 and closed its doors, the event was greeted with sadness, and even tears.

Eaton's College Street was truly unique at the time for housing a department store in the same building as the street-level lending library and the second-floor art gallery. Not only did the store enhance the cultural climate of the city but it sold everything one could imagine, from groceries delivered in wooden crates, to screws, to lipstick, to teas specially blended by the store's own tea taster.

The seventh floor was known for its Round Room Restaurant, which featured a round fountain and large murals by Natacha Carlu, as well as a grand foyer and an art deco auditorium designed by Jacques and Natacha Carlu. With seating for more than a thousand people, the auditorium featured a ninety-stop Casavant Organ and was a favourite venue of artists and entertainers, the likes of Duke Ellington, and Serge Rachmaninoff. Glenn Gould made more than thirty recordings in this auditorium because of its fine acoustics. The retail spaces were decorated with great flair and imagination. For example, the fifth-floor furniture showrooms at one time included "a mock-up of Marie Antoinette's Versailles boudoir."[59]

Cera, who wore a beret, had a "gravelly voice, earthy manner, heavy Picasso-like face and a 'wicked eye,'" was "Debonair, cocksure, and energetic" and made the Eaton building a great showpiece; window shopping along College Street was its own kind of entertainment and was extremely popular. Landscape architect Humphrey Carver reported that the building became "... the art gallery of Toronto in the 1930s with Cera. In the windows were beautiful compositions, the work of painters, women's clothes, and pretty, rich coloured things. They were superb."[60] At Christmas particularly, Eaton's was the heart of Toronto. People would make a special trip downtown to see the store windows before Christmas, and for the Santa Claus parade, hosted by the store.[61]

Cera had "persuaded" Paraskeva to do a "panel imitating the painting on tiles for a bathroom." This was her first job for him in 1933; following this commission, she decorated three or four windows a year for five years.[62] Working on the windows was similar to painting theatre decor, the work she had done with the Allegris, and caused her to reminisce about her life. "It turned my thoughts back to my work in my student days, so entirely forsaken."[63] She gained a great deal of satisfaction in the work for Cera, and learned much about composition, something she felt she had not known before. In later years, she said painting those window panels gave her the "nerve" to use what she learned in her painting, particularly in *Petroushka* (1937).

Paraskeva was happy for the opportunity to work with Cera, as he was familiar with Maison DIM, the interior design shop where she had worked in Paris. She shared with him "an understanding of modern European art which Paraskeva missed in her new Canadian colleagues."[64] She must have felt a close bond with Cera, who arrived in Toronto two years before she did, because she gave him a gift of one of her paintings, *In a Public Bath* (1934). When Paolo Venini, famous for his *objets d'art* in glass, visited Cera, Paraskeva was thrilled to meet him and talk in French about Paris — in her job in Paris, she had sold Venini glass, and she brought one of his pieces with her when she came to Canada.

Several of her working drawings that survived are in a Japanese style, likely created for the same background screen that Pegi Nichol worked on.[65] One drawing in that series of three windows is Chagall-like, with a red goat leaping from one side of a canyon to another (Plate 13).

According to Pegi Nichol, painting for Cera did not yield very good pay and, according to Paraskeva, could even be dangerous. "Once I was nearly killed in that corner window [at Yonge and College]," she recalled many years later. "We were putting the work up and suddenly the ladder fell right beside me."[66] Still, for Paraskeva, the work gave her an opportunity to practice her painting and drawing skills, a context for meeting people in the community, and contact and recognition among other artists. Finding a place and becoming accepted into the Toronto community of artists was important for her if she was to make a contribution to Canadian art, which was an ambition that, despite herself, began growing within her.

Like many female artists, Paraskeva lived a divided life: she was a housewife as well as a painter, and some of her paintings reflect these two worlds. Her *Still Life with Apples and Grapes* (1935) is an exquisitely rendered composition in which the large bowl anchors the painting and sits in contrast with an aloe vera plant and a small bowl with half a pear on opposite sides. Like the tray in *Fruit* from four years earlier, the table sits at an angle to the rest of the painting. It is a still life recording her pleasure in an aesthetic experience in her own home, as well as claiming the validity of her interior environment as subject matter.

Her domestic responsibilities demanded her time, especially when the Clarks moved, as they did every few years. In 1935, Philip joined the Ontario tax department and, once again, the family moved, this time to Ferndale Avenue, a quiet street only a block long, just east of Yonge Street at St. Clair. Both parts of her life carried the challenge of learning new ways. Being accustomed to difficulties, she tackled both aspects with a sense of adventure, but it was the respect from other artists that made her feel her paintings had something to offer.

Gaining the respect of her colleagues was rewarding but being recognized by critics made her feel even more accepted. In November, she showed a painting at the Art Gallery of Toronto in a special exhibition when new rooms were opened. European paintings were featured, along with contemporary Canadian works. Paraskeva's *In a Public Bath* was among these, and was mentioned in *Saturday Night* magazine as evidence that "there need be no fear for the future of Canadian Art." Among the other artists mentioned in the review were two of Paraskeva's friends, Pegi Nicol and Carl Schaefer.[67]

The author of the review was Graham McInnes, a new critic in town who had come to Toronto from Australia via England. He came to find his father — Bach singer James Campbell McInnes, who lived in Toronto — and it was through him that McInnes was hired as a writer, first briefly at *The Mail and Empire* and then at *Saturday Night*. McInnes very quickly gained an understanding of Canadian art. In his first article on art, he described what he saw in Canadian landscape painting: academic work that squashed creative impulses; painting expressing a Canadian spirit, but which was becoming formulaic; and the work of artists who were "experimenters."[68] As his later columns show, he tried to find something broader than simply technical skill when he looked at art: evidence of intelligence and an aesthetic appeal. He had a genuine appreciation for artists whose work showed all three of these characteristics, and expressed disappointment when he could find nothing but technical skill.

Despite her acceptance in Toronto's art world, and all the new friends she made, Paraskeva missed Paris and the French language. Apparently, Philip and Paraskeva invited Oreste Allegri to visit them. In April of 1934, he wrote them a letter lamenting how difficult his life was, full of worries and debts, and he didn't have enough calm to undertake a journey to Canada. Hearing how miserable the Allegri family was must have given Paraskeva some assurance that leaving them was the right decision.

Still, establishing herself in Toronto came with a personal price, as she juggled a host of contradictions: she became financially dependent on her husband, enjoying the security of being Philip Clark's wife but eventually railing against the obligations a woman took on in marriage; she loved to paint but felt impelled to give much of her time to being a model housekeeper; she espoused communism but lived the life of a capitalist; she fervently adopted Canada as her country, and was grateful for the opportunities given her, but in her heart she remained Russian.

Of course, it is human nature to be full of contradictions, but in Paraskeva Clark, the contradictions were sharper than most, and gradually, as her life in Toronto evolved, these contradictions caused her considerable inner turmoil, which bubbled over in combat with Philip and in arguing and picking fights with her friends. She began developing a reputation for deliberately irritating other people.

She was not the only Russian émigré who "announced rather than discussed, proclaimed rather than communicated, dictated rather than conversed." In that regard she was like Tatiana Yakovleva du Plessix Liberman, the hat designer for Saks Fifth Avenue in New York under the name of "Tatiana of Saks," who also suffered during her years in Russia, but chose, for the most part, to say little about it.[69] Some of Paraskeva's friends had enough of a sense of humour and a genuine affection for her that they were not offended, but disagreements could cause a break in friendship. Painter Gordon MacNamara remembered that when he asked Paraskeva to be more tactful in speaking about others she became furious with him. "I got a slice of her Slavic temper," he said. "I don't think I associated with her very much after that."[70]

Charles and Louise Comfort met Paraskeva as soon as she arrived in 1931 and spoke of her fondly. When Comfort was working on his eight-panel mural in the Toronto Stock Exchange, he laid out a sketchbook — or guest book — in which his friends could draw and write their comments. Paraskeva drew herself partly hidden by a Sandeman's Armada Sherry label affixed on the page, a somewhat humorous sketch, in watercolour and pencil, dated "4:31 P.M. March 12th, 1935." In Russian, she wrote her three identities: Paraskeva Clark, also Paraskeva Plistik, also Paraskeva Allegri.[71] These are the identities of a woman divided.

Some artists, like A. Y. Jackson, were frightened of her and even though they admired Paraskeva's competent work and courage, they kept their guard intact around her and learned, because they respected her knowledge of art, how to talk with her in ways that avoided having her walking off in a huff. She had been welcomed into the circle of artists, and in spite of herself and her denunciation of Canadian art, she settled into the artistic hinterland of Toronto.

A "Raw, Sappy Life"

... there is not much sign that Canadian artists
have been moved by the phenomenon of a civilization
dissolving before their eyes.[1]

Paraskeva had an exhilarating start to 1936. In January, she showed her paintings in the Galleries of J. Merritt Malloney. In the brief review of the show, "Rody Kenny Courtice, Isabel McLaughlin, Kathleen Daly, Yvonne McKague and Paraskeva Clark," she received high praise. "Here is an artist who thinks and feels plastically, who has a deep and quick sensibility, and has applied to it the most stringent discipline from within. This has given her an authority which moulds her vivid conceptual faculty and establishes once and for all the complete identity of form with color and the complete coincidence of feeling with form," wrote the new critic in town, Graham McInnes.[2]

Although McInnes described all of these artists as "gifted," he felt that Paraskeva's paintings were the most compelling and held one's attention. He discovered that she was extremely sensitive to her environment and had "an ability to externalize it in authoritative creative work ..."

The paintings McInnes cited were landscapes.[3] However, he later pointed out what distinguished Paraskeva's from those of other humanist artists; she was among the vanguard of Toronto artists who were changing the direction of Canadian painting away from imitations of wilderness scenes of the Group of Seven. These younger artists, McInnes said, portrayed "the land as it looks after Canadians have tilled it, lived by it and died in it — the land which has left its mark on a people and has in turn been marked by them."[4]

Paraskeva's sensitivity to her environment went beyond the physical landscape and increasingly included an awareness of social issues as the Great Depression continued to take its toll. It was both a dreary time and a fortuitous time for her to begin life in Canada, as the political situation aroused her sense of social justice. A well-known incident in Estevan, Saskatchewan was often cited as being characteristic of the times. Five hundred striking coal miners, who wanted an eight-hour working day at a $5.40 daily minimum wage and union recognition, held a demonstration. They were attacked by armed RCMP officers and three men were killed. Similar incidents occurred in a number of cities when workers demonstrated. Women accompanied their jobless men to the docks in Toronto to plead for jobs to feed hungry children. Even after weeks of faithfully showing up when ships came in, men still could not find work.[5] These were the kinds of stories Paraskeva encountered in the daily newspapers. She believed artists must become immersed in the "mud and sweat" of life, that they should not be left alone in a garret to paint apples.[6]

Consequently, in the summer of 1936, when Paraskeva learned of the Spanish Civil War, she paid attention. Radio reports coming from Madrid and Barcelona were confusing when the news of Francisco Franco's attack first broke in Toronto. However, it was clear that there was fighting in Madrid and the democratically elected government was in danger of being overthrown. The Popular Front government, a coalition of socialists, anarchists, and communists, had the support of Spain's working class and intellectuals. Franco's support came from rich landowners, business people, and the Catholic Church. Germany and Italy came to the aid of Franco, and the Soviet Union supplied arms to the Republican cause.

Although the Soviet Union appeared to be helping the Republican side — the International Brigades were under Red Army commanders — Stalin infiltrated the country with his own agents in an attempt "to consolidate the image of the Soviet Union as the only point of reference for all Communist parties around the world."[7] He gradually took over the Spanish Communist Party. As in the purges in the Soviet Union, Stalin secretly did away with certain people, particularly Marxists and others pushing for a real revolution. At the time, this aspect of the war in Spain was not known to Paraskeva and others who sided with the communists, just as the Terror in the Soviet Union was not known by many in the West. In fact, Stalin's regime appeared decent in comparison to the threat of Hitler's in Germany,[8] explaining why many people on the left supported Stalin.

On the surface, Paraskeva, like many others, saw the fundamentals of this war as simple: a confrontation between democracy and fascism, a matter of right and wrong. She, of course, sided with the people of Spain. Eventually it became obvious that Spain was a larger battleground, where powerful nations were struggling for the supremacy of their own ideologies, with the people of Spain innocent victims and the soldiers pawns of powerful factions.

Paraskeva followed the events in Spain closely. In a climate when Canada's social problems were worse than ever, she still believed people should unite to fight against Franco in Spain. If the cause could succeed in Spain, perhaps radical change could also occur in Canada. This was the thinking behind the formation of an International Brigade that gathered in Spain to help the citizen's army formed by the Popular Front government. Many Canadians, including poor and unemployed men who had been in the work camps, volunteered to fight in Spain.

When the Canadian Committee to Aid Spanish Democracy formed soon after the beginning of the war, Paraskeva participated. The purpose of the committee was to inform Canadians as events unfolded, to raise money for medical supplies, and to rally support for the volunteer fighters. It was in the middle of October 1936, after meeting with members of this committee and gaining its support, that Dr. Norman Bethune resigned from his positions in Montreal so that he would be free to set up a mobile blood transfusion unit in Spain. The week following his resignation, he went to Toronto.

His Toronto visit coincided with that of four emissaries of Spanish loyalists — supported by the Canadian Committee to Aid Spanish Democracy and the Canadian League Against War and Fascism — touring Canada and the

United States. When they arrived at Toronto's Union Station, Paraskeva was among the several hundred enthusiastic Torontonians there to greet them. A newspaper photograph shows her shaking hands with Senora Isabel de Palencia.

The Spanish emissaries' Toronto visit included a rally at the Arena Gardens attended by five thousand people. At the rally, Bethune, introduced as "our ambassador to Spain," delivered a passionate request for money to buy boxes of anti-tetanus and anti-typhoid serum to take with him to Spain. This kind of rally would have fed the fervour already evident among men thinking of volunteering. It was during the latter part of 1936 that Canadian volunteers began leaving for Spain. The total during the following months would reach more than thirteen hundred, some claiming there were as many as fifteen hundred. The Canadians who went to Spain eventually formed their own battalion, which included other internationals. They called themselves the "Mac-Paps," a shortened form for the Mackenzie-Papineau Battalion named for the two heroes of the failed 1837 Upper and Lower Canada rebellions against Britain's rule, William Lyon Mackenzie and Louis-Joseph Papineau.

When a second organization was formed to help the cause in Spain, called "Friends of the Mac-Paps," Paraskeva contributed to both groups, her donations ranging from three dollars to sixty in a two-year period during the war.[9] That she made donations at all is significant. Being dependent on Philip, she had little money of her own at that time and frugality guided her spending. Paraskeva also wrote to her friend, businessman J. Stanley McLean, asking him for donations, and he, too, contributed.

Aside from her political philosophy, on a personal level Paraskeva had a special interest in the Spanish Civil War because of Bethune. Pegi Nicol had introduced Paraskeva to "Beth" about four months before the war began. Pegi, a small, vivacious woman with an impish look and pug nose, had been moving back and forth between Ottawa and Montreal, until she heard that René Cera needed artists for his design work at Eaton's. She had arrived in 1934 and was disappointed by the city's sleepiness, finding it, as Paraskeva did, too conservative and dull. "I feel no stimulation for art here," she wrote to her friend, Montreal artist Marian Scott.[10] Pegi thought there was no one in Toronto who could make up for the people she left behind in Montreal, which is why she was happy when Bethune arrived. In both Montreal and

Toronto, Bethune was a point of connection between the political left and artists.[11]

Like Pegi, Paraskeva found excitement in Bethune. "The Montreal contingent you sent from your gang has caused Toronto to wake up and think a little." Pegi wrote to Scott early in 1936. "The most effecting visit was Beth's. He took Bert Brooker and a few other pink artists for a fearful ride. The sound of the battle hasn't died yet ... We went to Paraskeva's and wrecked a very pretty party."[12]

Accounts vary about what happened, but apparently the Clarks were having a dinner party for the singer J. Campbell McInnes, Bertram Brooker, and Frances and Murray Adaskin when Pegi arrived along with Bethune and Fritz Brandtner. A scruffy-looking Bethune rudely barged in and asked, "Anybody got any beer? I want some beer." After stunned silence when no one responded, Bethune continued, "Philip, get me some beer." He made himself the centre of attention and broke up the party the Clarks were having with their friends.[13]

Murray Adaskin remembered another party the Clarks gave, this time especially for Bethune, when again many of the guests were musicians and artists, among them J. Campbell McInnes, Gordon Davies, Will Ogilvie, and Bertram Brooker. With Bethune as the special guest, the Spanish Civil War was the big topic of conversation. As Murray Adaskin remembered it, Brooker, very articulate, and Bethune "got into an argument about Communism, this, that, and the other thing, and why were they fighting, and what this was all about, and why we should help them, and so on ... I thought there was going to be a fist fight that night. It was a terrible experience. Fran and I were terribly upset about this because we weren't accustomed to this hot-headed political thing."[14]

Of course, Paraskeva would have enjoyed the argument between Brooker and Bethune. Like Bethune, she wanted to shake people loose from their set ways. In Bethune, she found a co-conspirator and wished he would stay in Toronto. In fact, Pegi reported, "Paraskeva was very annoyed that I did not somehow keep him here so we could get the whole town wakened up."[15]

Perhaps "Beth" was not in Toronto long enough to wake up the whole town, but he certainly was there long enough to jolt the Clark household awake. As Paraskeva put it, "... he started to go after me ... so there was a love affair." She claimed that even her husband loved Bethune.[16] Whether or not Philip loved him, Bethune did stay with the Clarks while he was in Toronto. "We looked after him," Paraskeva recalled many years later — he was completely broke."

Paraskeva told the story about how her affair with Bethune began. One evening they were going to Pegi Nicol's third-floor apartment on Jarvis Street. For some reason Paraskeva was riding with Bethune, and Philip was in another car. As they drove, Bethune put his hand on her leg. "You are like wine," he told her, and as Paraskeva recalled that moment years later, she rolled her eyes and jiggled on her stool as she sat in her studio at her drawing table. "*C'est commence*," she added. Then she sat for a moment, a pensive look on her face as though she was remembering and reliving her experiences with Bethune, who had called her "a great artist and a great human being."[17]

Speaking about sex, especially outside of marriage, was completely taboo in the 1930s despite the fact that infidelities and open marriages occurred. Pretending these behaviours did not exist seemed hypocritical to Paraskeva and she refused to participate in such duplicity, to the point of flaunting her infidelity.

Bethune had visited the Soviet Union the year before the two met. With the passing of thirteen years since Paraskeva had left, she must have been eager to talk with him about what he had observed there, especially since their political views were similar. Furthermore, Bethune was a poet and a painter, and his ideas about artists were similar to Paraskeva's. "The function of the artist is to disturb," he said. "His duty is to arouse the sleeper, to shake the complacent pillars of the world ... He is an agitator, a disturber of the peace — quick, impatient, positive, restless and disquieting. He is the creative spirit of life working in the soul of men."[18] Both Paraskeva and Bethune fitted his characterization of an artist as a person who "swims easily in the stream of his own temperament."[19] When Bethune first arrived in Montreal, he was described as a "breath of fresh air," which is exactly the comment Frances Adaskin made about Paraskeva's arrival in Toronto.[20]

Bethune went to Spain where he directed a mobile blood transfusion unit that travelled to the battlefield. He had difficulty working with other people, and after six months returned to Canada and went on tour to raise support for setting up homes for the many homeless children in Spain — he was distressed at the impact of the war on children. Upon his return in early summer of 1937, Paraskeva and Bethune met again and resumed their love affair. At some point they spent a weekend in New York together, and later Philip Clark would tell Murray and Frances Adaskin that he believed that Bethune and Paraskeva "lived together as wife and husband" that weekend, though he was never told that was true.[21]

After the New York episode, when Bethune was staying with the Clarks, he asked Philip for permission to have Paraskeva share his bed. Philip told Paraskeva that he would not prevent her from accepting Bethune's invitation. Philip took all this in stride, for, as he told his friends in the same letter, he viewed sex as an animal instinct and "a minor aspect of human life."[22] Then he added, "Paraskeva and I have always remained friends, affectionate friends, and I consider her to be a remarkable and beautiful woman ..." These sentiments were genuine. Gail Singer, who much later made the film about Paraskeva, *Portrait of the Artist as an Old Lady*, saw Philip and Paraskeva as "a man incredibly proud of his wife, and a wife who understood the sacrifices the husband had made to have a life with her. I mean, she says that in the film, in fact — what did his family think that he came back with a widow and a child?"[23] When Singer's crew was filming, at the end of the day's work Philip would say, "Drinks in the living room," and brought in a tray of cut-glass decanters with Scotch, Rye, and water, with nuts and cheesies to nibble on, and everyone sat down for conversation. "It was just extraordinarily civilized," Singer recalled. "It was just this is what you do, this is how you live."

It seems Philip, in the early years of their marriage, learned how to let his life flow around Paraskeva, her Russian persona dominating wherever she went, an anti-capitalist living her privileged existence provided by Philip's livelihood. With his Anglo-Torontonian conventionality, he was often embarrassed by her comments. For example, at one event someone approached her and said something like, "I understand that you knew Norman Bethune." Paraskeva, "wearing a black dress with sheer sleeves and black pumps and slouch hat," pulled herself up to her full height and said, " 'You are asking Clark if she knew Bethune, you are asking Paraskeva if she knew Bethune. Know him?

I fucked him.' And Philip was standing right there, and he said, 'Paraskeva, it's time to go home.'"[24]

Apparently, Paraskeva repeated this provocative explanation of her relationship with Bethune a number of times because several people remember this kind of scenario in completely different settings. Toronto in the 1930s was not the kind of city where a decent married woman would have an affair; and if she did, she certainly did not announce it in a loud voice in good company in front of her husband. One simply did not speak improper truths in public. However, Paraskeva's way of sustaining her own identity and surviving in Toronto's sedate culture was to speak from who she was without regard for mores and propriety. This is how her sense of self remained intact. Underneath Philip's embarrassment at her uninhibited behaviour and brazen comments — his patience with her wearing thin many times — he still admired Paraskeva, was proud of her achievements, and enjoyed the liveliness and spark she brought to his otherwise conventional life. With Philip, propriety was always something to take into account. With Bethune, Paraskeva could be completely free; bucking convention was the norm with him. In other words, she found in Bethune a friend she could count on not to censor her behaviour.

DURING THE EARLY part of the Spanish Civil War, Paraskeva continued with the same subject matter for her painting that she had used during the previous five years. Both *Caledon Farm House* (1936), a still life, and *Wheat Field* (1936) (Plate 16) were among her oils that year, and show the influence of Petrov-Vodkin: the former for the angles and the vantage point from above; the latter for her use of form and colour to capture the "essential inner forms" of the earth. "And we sense the solid bones of the earth beneath the soil ..."[25] The field is a rolling expanse beneath a high horizon with the farm buildings nestled between the slope of the field and the trees along the edge.

Another probable influence of *Wheat Field* was Paraskeva's friend Carl Schaefer's *Wheatfield, Hanover*, which he painted the same year.[26] It is not surprising that these two painters extended their frequent discussions on art and the role of artists onto the canvas in a visual dialogue about the activities of human beings in the landscape. However, on a deeper level, fields of grain were images riveted in Paraskeva's memory since her childhood visits to her grandparents in the Vitebsk region of Russia. The subject matter for her *Wheat Field* was a comfortable fusion of her two countries.

That year she also painted *Untitled (Trout)* (1936) (Plate 14), a still life picturing two slim fish on a plate, placed at an angle across the painting. The plate, asymmetrical and sitting on crumpled newspaper wrapping, has a plaid pattern with the stripes running into and across the fish as though they were part of the plate. The placement of the fish leads the viewer's eyes to the top of the painting where "$500.00" is printed in bold type on one of the pieces of paper.

At first, the image of the two fish seems completely incongruous with the large dollar figure above them. However, given the social conditions at the time, and Paraskeva's growing conviction that artists must paint about issues relevant to the people, the incongruity disappears and the watercolour reads as an effective statement about the Depression. Two small trout would not go very far for a meal, and the way the artist painted them with the overlapping stripes makes them seem less real; so, too, the $500.00 printed on the newspaper is fake, leaving the cook with nothing to feed her family. With this reading, the watercolour can be seen as a political statement, one of Paraskeva's Depression paintings.

In 1937, the year following the outbreak of the Spanish Civil War, Paraskeva painted an even more explicitly political work. The watercolour *Presents from Madrid* (1937) (Plate 15) is a still life depicting some of the objects Bethune had sent her from Spain: a magazine; an old, wrinkled parchment page from a Spanish missal, or prayer book; and a cap and red scarf of the International Brigade. When Bethune went to China in 1938, he and Paraskeva corresponded and she painted the watercolour *Portrait of Mao* (1938).[27] These works integrated several aspects of Paraskeva's painting life then: her firm belief that artists were responsible to depict real life, her awareness of political situations, and her personal relationship with Bethune.

Perhaps just as important, these political paintings tell us that Paraskeva understood the power that images and text hold, something she learned during the years following the Russian Revolution when artists' work depicted the upheaval in heroic terms. In those formative years, she had learned from

Petrov-Vodkin that still lifes could be dynamically political.[28] Now, the Spanish Civil War gave her an opportunity to experiment and build on what she had learned about the impact of art on society; this war was a pivotal phase in her development.

However, McInnes saw in *Portrait of Mao*, "the knotty question of art and propaganda," the only time in all his reviews that he took issue with Paraskeva's work. He felt the watercolour, created from a photograph and Chinese posters she received from Bethune, lost stature because she was speaking "in italics, which is not an artistic way to secure emphasis."[29] That this watercolour no longer exists leads to the question of whether Paraskeva might have destroyed it as a result of McInnes's comments, since his reviews had become extremely important to her — we know she destroyed other paintings.

In the background of the Mao watercolour, Paraskeva included the image of the face of a dead child, which likely alludes to Bethune's response to the hundreds of dead children he saw during the war in Spain. It was these dead children's faces that were the most distressing and haunting part of his experiences in Spain. In the hand of one dead child, he had found a tiny black leather-bound notebook and stooped to pick it up. Two dancing musicians, one playing a flute and the other a mandolin, were engraved in the leather of the front cover. The pages were blank except for a few childish scribbles.

After carrying the notebook with him, Bethune sent it to Paraskeva as a way of telling her about his emotions of that moment.[30] In a letter addressed "To my friends in Canada" in the spring of 1937, Bethune attempted to explain why he did not write letters more frequently.[31] "To share with you what I have seen, what I have experienced in the past six months, is impossible without art. Without art, experience becomes on the one hand, the denuded, bare bones of fact ..." and he went on to describe the inadequacy of words. "Only through art, can the truth of a non-shared experience be transmitted," he said. In that context, sending the small notebook to Paraskeva was an act of art that told volumes more than if he had used words. She, like Bethune, also needed art during a time of war.

In the middle of her work with the Committee to Aid Spanish Democracy, Paraskeva was offered her first solo exhibition in early 1937, the third one scheduled at the new Picture Loan Society (PLS). The Picture Loan

Society, which opened in the fall of 1936, was born out of artists' frustration at the dearth of galleries in which they could show their work. The organizing committee had put together a pamphlet announcing the new organization, outlining how it would function as a place for artists to show and sell their work and as a painting rental service to the public.

Douglas Duncan was in charge of day-to-day operations on the third floor at 3 Charles Street West, and eventually the PLS and Douglas Duncan became synonymous. Not only did Duncan show artists' work but, thanks to a family inheritance, he also bought their work, collecting hundreds of works of art that eventually would be placed in public galleries. Duncan was considered an "art angel" by many artists because he encouraged and supported them. However, many complained bitterly about his lack of business sense and his scattered nature. "I am fed up, bored and about through with you and the picture loan society," wrote one artist.[32] However, Paraskeva loved Duncan, for she was among those artists who considered him an "art angel" despite also becoming frustrated with him. She once told him, "If I didn't like you so much I'd hate you."[33] However, her irritation was surpassed by her support because he inspired artists. He was a friend with whom Paraskeva could converse intelligently about both Canadian art and European art — in French.

Not only did Paraskeva have her first solo exhibition that year, but she also participated in a conversation, or argument, in several magazines, making her debut in print. She read an article by Elizabeth Wyn Wood in *Canadian Forum*, a magazine with a socialist point of view, which covered arts and culture. Wood's article in the February issue argued that the strength of Canadian art lay in its freedom from the grubby day-to-day world. "Utter desperation such as is prevalent in Europe today is practically unknown to us by actual experience,"[34] wrote Wood. She continued by saying, "Politics and economics do not make the fundamental structure of life. They are the plumbing and heating systems of society, that is all." Then she went on with the question of what Canadian art should depict:

What should we [Canadian artists] do ...? Paint castles in Spain — crumbling? Paint the Russian proletariat standing on the fallen Cossack, a modern Saint George and the Dragon? Or shall we paint guns standing in rows, waiting? Such things are not authentic stimuli to the Canadian artist. Should we then turn to our own oppressors — make cynical statues of the academic capitalist with his paunch and silk hat? We have not the appetite ... Our millionaires are fine fellows who mush through the north as we do, eating hardtack and bully beef, and sometimes having their own doubts.[35]

She must not have realized what she revealed about herself: that she had distanced herself so much from what was happening around her that she was ignorant of — or perhaps was ignoring — the impact of the Depression in Canada.

Besides reading Wood's article, two months earlier Paraskeva had also read what prompted Wood to write in the first place, an article by the critic Frank Underhill who asked what effect the seven years of Depression had on Canadian artists. European artists, he observed, were "compelled to rethink the whole question of the relation to the artist in society," and "in our troubled generation the artist must be red or dead."[36] He suggested that the "rustic" Canadian temperament was too dominant among the country's artists because he could not find much evidence that "Canadian artists have been moved by the phenomenon of a civilization dissolving before their eyes."

Wood insisted that the Canadian artist was a trailblazer precisely because of "rustic rumination." She made the startling statement that "He [the Canadian artist] has always had some doubt about the importance of civilization ... He has walked off into the hinterland at every opportunity."[37] Clearly, she felt this is how it should be. Wood objected to Underhill's stance, saying he was "riding a presently fashionable wave" of art as propaganda. It seems she interpreted Underhill's "red or dead" statement literally, and for her it was complete heresy. Her proof was that art with political content, like that of the Soviet Union, was "essentially false, derivative and of little stature." She probably based her comments on an exhibition of Soviet art that had travelled to Montreal and Toronto in 1935.[38] This Slavic type art, she said, was "novel and colourful to us," but not aesthetically satisfying.

One can imagine Paraskeva pacing in her apartment, fuming and blustering after reading Wood's article. She disagreed, and vehemently. Given Paraskeva's total rejection of Wood's article, she was impelled to voice her opinion and write a reply. However, she felt the need for help to do it properly because she still had trouble using the English language, particularly when she wanted to articulate something fraught with intense feeling, and especially for an article that she wanted to have published. She went to her friend, the critic Graham McInnes.

Picking up on Wood's statement that artists would do well to stick to the Canadian approach to art and "camp for a while on our northern pre-Cambrian shield," Paraskeva titled her article "Come Out From Behind the Pre-Cambrian Shield."[39] "Who is the artist?" Paraskeva asked:

> Is he not a human being like ourselves, with added gifts of finer understanding and perception of the realities of life, and the ability to arouse emotions through the creation of forms and images? Surely. And this being so, those who give their lives, their knowledge and their time to social struggle have the right to expect great help from the artists. And I cannot imagine a more inspiring role than that which the artist is asked to play for the defence and advancement of civilisation.

The article is a true polemic on the artist in society, reflecting the influence of Picasso's words:

> What do you think an artist is? ... a political being, constantly aware of the heartbreaking, passionate, or delightful things that happen in the world, shaping himself completely in their image. How could it be possible to feel no interest in other people, and with a cool indifference to detach yourself from the very life which they bring to you so abundantly?[40]

In response to Wood's argument that Canadian artists have gone off to the "hinterland" to leave civilization behind, and that she herself has "lain on the rock between the sky and the water," Paraskeva suggested that such artists as Wood can lie on the rocks in peace and happiness because "... thousands suffered that they might do so. And you, artist of the Pre-Cambrian shield, have been born, unfortunately for your dreams, into an age when what one desires is not handed to one on a silver spoon, but has to be fought for, more grimly as each month goes by. It is to enable you to lie on a rock that castles are tumbling in Spain":

> Forget, if you wish, the troubles of Europe; there are plenty here. Paint the raw, sappy life that moves ceaselessly about you, paint portraits of your own Canadian leaders, depict happy dreams for your Canadian souls. But if you cannot do all this, for it is a new and difficult problem, at least have the grace to refrain from being scornful of those who do, those who are saying necessary things, and proving of immense value to their time. Think of yourself as a human being, and you cannot help feeling the reality of life around you, and becoming impregnated with it ... come out from behind your pre-Cambrian Shield and dirty your gown in the mud and sweat of conflict.[41]

Paraskeva knew the fallacy in Wood's portrayal of the capitalist in the same league as the artists who mushed through the North chewing on bits of dried beef. What they ate in the woods might look the same, but what they each found in their chequing accounts when they went to their various banks on Toronto's street corners looked very different.

Paraskeva's comments on the artist in society were rooted in Marxist philosophy and in the work of the "Father of Russian Marxism," Georgii Plekhanov. She read a copy of his *Art and Society*, which was still in her library at her death and is now among her papers in the National Archives of Canada in Ottawa.[42] Plekhanov's main argument is that in a society that spawns art for art's sake, a discord exists between the artists and their social environment; they are disconnected from society (both Paraskeva and Plekhanov would have described Elizabeth Wyn Wood this way). However, artists connected to their society create art reflecting that society and its class struggle, which Plekhanov calls "one of the most important springs in life's mechanism."[43]

During the 1930s in particular, it was images reflecting this class struggle that Paraskeva and some of her colleagues used in their paintings. In her copy of the book, she marked and underlined text having to do with the meaning of art for a person's life; for example, a reference to the "function of art as a judgment on the phenomena of life and a readiness to participate in social struggles ..."[44]

There is no question that reading Plekhanov strengthened what she already believed as she articulated her arguments for a Marxist philosophy of art. Furthermore, Plekhanov's book would have helped her put her early experience in St. Petersburg into context for her work as an artist. Although Paraskeva did not speak of being influenced by her observations of workers' strikes and her father's position as a factory worker, it seems almost inevitable that she would have absorbed the spirit of her milieu as a child. The thirties aroused that sense of class struggle.

Paraskeva sent a copy of Plekhanov's book, along with a copy of her article, to art critic Walter Abell, the editor of the magazine *Maritime Art*. In a letter of thanks, he commented on Paraskeva's place in Canadian art: "The combination of these ideas [in her article] as an impelling force with your technical equipment as a painter must certainly make you one of the creative centers in Canadian art at this time."[45] Being accepted as a Canadian artist was one thing; but being called "one of the creative centers of Canadian art" by someone like Abell would have made Paraskeva proud.

After her article was published, the next month she showed work in the "Exhibition of Paintings, Drawings and Sculpture by Artists of the British Empire Overseas" in London during the month of May, one of five exhibitions in which she participated that year.[46] Just after this exhibition ended, an article appeared in the *Toronto Star* about a steel workers' strike in Chicago, headlined "Five Steel Strikers Killed in a Clash with Chicago Police." An accompanying photograph depicted people trying to escape police; in another photograph, "a girl striker" argued with a constable holding a drawn revolver. Paraskeva read that two hundred striking workers had marched on the Republic Steel Corporation and broke through the wall of armed officers. At that point, the policemen charged into the crowd, killing five people and wounding seventy-five. Clipping this article, Paraskeva was galvanized into action and began a new painting.

She was frequently methodical in her approach, developing paintings in a series of steps: drawing sketches, sometimes on tracing paper on which she might pencil in a grid, which she overlaid on a subsequent rough drawing; then sometimes cutting out something from one study to collage onto another, or onto the grid. In this way, she developed perspective and proportion.[47] The roughs became her guide for the finished work. For her new painting that June, she made a watercolour and pencil sketch, laying out a scene of a puppet show. In a subsequent pen and pencil study, she drew in more details, such as the faces of the figures of the painting.

Dominating the centre of the painting called *Petroushka* (Plate 19) is a red puppet theatre. A policeman puppet holds a revolver in his right hand while wielding a stick in his left to beat a worker who slumps down over the theatre screen. A third figure is a capitalist, a man dressed in black tails and a top hat, clutching his money bags. To the right of the puppet theatre, a drummer beats his large drum and with his other hand gestures to the crowd gathered to watch the performance. However, the audience does not seem to like this show. Some are jeering, some scowling, others are raising a fist into the air. Even the baby in his mother's arms reaches out with a clenched fist.

The mother is Paraskeva herself, holding Clive, with her older son Ben at her side. These three are the only ones who have a vantage point from which they can see the puppeteer behind the screen as well as the audience.

Paraskeva's early childhood was the source of the images and setting of this painting, even though the catalyst was the article about the steel workers' strike. Paraskeva had a clear memory of travelling theatre troupes performing the story of Petrushka in the cobblestone courtyards between the worker apartment buildings where she and her family lived. People hung out the windows, watching, or gathered around the players in the courtyard.

For many Russians, the Petrushka stories are among the most powerful memories of childhood. Besides being performed by puppeteers, these stories were also the subject of a number of *lubok* (woodcut) editions published when Paraskeva was a child.

The glove-puppet Petrushka dominated the entertainment for the urban working class for a century between 1830 and 1930, a tale presented with many variations and combinations of characters, but the essential traits were consistent throughout the narratives of "a country boy's misadventures in town."[48] He was a hunchback, usually dressed in red, whose wooden, swinging legs were useless. Even though he was a wooden puppet he had human feelings, which evoked empathy and delight in the audience.

This working-class story was elevated to the theatre for the noble class when Stravinsky wrote the ballet, *Petrushka*, with Alexandre Benois designing the sets. In the ballet, Petrushka falls in love with Akulina and asks her to marry him. However, Akulina prefers his rival, a policeman. Petrushka strikes the policeman and, as punishment, is forced to become a soldier. A fight ensues with the two hitting each other with their sticks. When a lamb appears on stage, Petrushka strokes it and straddles the animal to ride it. Too late, Petrushka discovers the lamb is the devil in disguise as he tosses poor Petrushka into the air and gores him to death. The contradictory elements of tragedy and revelry are integral elements of the story, which was true to the experience of the oppressed and beleaguered, but unconquerable Russian people; Petrushka proved it by returning as a ghost.

Paraskeva's own *Petroushka* was partly completed by mid June when Bethune visited her. She showed him the painting and he had the audacity to take a brush and paint the brown building on the left a bright blue. After he left, Paraskeva "corrected it."[49]

In painting the capitalist, Paraskeva proved Elizabeth Wyn Wood wrong; one Canadian artist, at least, did have the "appetite" for depicting "the academic capitalist with his paunch and silk hat."[50] As with her words, Paraskeva was up for a good argument using her paints. And here she argued for the rights of workers exploited by the capitalist system.

This painting is among the most eloquent — and most visceral — of Paraskeva's works, the fusion of a variety of experiences and influences. "The brutalized features of the poor recall Käthe Kollwitz. The stylization of the drawing recalls Goncharova. The combination of savagery and elegance is pure Paraskeva Clark."[51] An early source for her capitalist came from the 1920 celebrations of the third anniversary of the October Revolution in Petrograd when she was twenty-two years old. Artists volunteered their time to orchestrate the re-enactment of the storming of the Winter Palace with thousands of Petrograd citizens. Puppet-like dancers were used to portray the capitalists "in tall hats, with enormous money bags."[52] We know that images of that era excited her, for when she was given a book on Leningrad depicting scenes from the Revolution, she exclaimed, "I was there, I remember that."[53]

In one of Paraskeva's working drawings, between the buildings in the background, stands a pine tree, shaped like the wind-weathered trees in Group of Seven paintings. In the final oil painting, the tree is stripped bare, appearing dead. In choosing this image, she reflected her friend Carl Schaefer's dead trees that he painted during the thirties. The black branches curve above the head of the capitalist, emphasizing his place in the painting.

During that period, some American artists such as Philip Evergood (1901–1973), for example, also used the plight of the worker as subject matter. The same year Paraskeva painted *Petroushka*, Evergood, considered a socialist realist artist — whose father was Polish but took on an anglicized name — painted *American Tragedy*, a scene of policemen beating up workers and their families. In the background stand the solidly closed factories.[54]

Simultaneously, as Paraskeva's new painting was evolving, her hero, Pablo Picasso, was completing his famous *Guernica* in Paris following the destruction of the town of Gernika by the German blitzkrieg.[55] The extent to which Paraskeva felt Picasso's painting expressed her own outrage at the violence of the Spanish Civil War is revealed in her efforts during the summer of 1937 to have this work shown in Toronto. As she told Harry McCurry, Director of the National Gallery of Canada, she was working as "an agent between Toronto Art Gallery and Toronto Committee to aid Spanish refugees" in an attempt to bring to Toronto Picasso's *Guernica*, along with sixty-five related drawings of the masterpiece.

In the midst of all her activities, her son Clive, who was only four years old, caught whooping cough. It was a very hot July, and Paraskeva made a special effort to amuse her son. Of course, she could take him nowhere for fear of contagion. He could go no further than the backyard and she was stuck at home with him.[56] While Clive was sick, Paraskeva painted a little and carried on her correspondence about *Guernica* with Evelyn Ahrend, an agent of the Spanish Relief Campaign.

In September 1938, Picasso sent the painting to be shown in London, England, designating that the proceeds be given to Spain through London's National Joint Committee for Spanish Relief. Two years to the day after Picasso began his sketches, *Guernica* arrived in New York. The Museum of Modern Art had requested the painting be featured at the opening of the museum's new space, but since their schedule would have interfered with a touring schedule for raising funds for Spain, Picasso turned down the request. The painting travelled to San Francisco, Los Angeles, and Chicago before it returned to New York in November where the MOMA staged a forty-year Picasso retrospective.[57] Paraskeva had hoped the painting would be brought to Toronto between the Chicago exhibition and the MOMA retrospective. However, Ahrend explained in a letter to Paraskeva the scheduling difficulties: time was required for the customs procedures and border crossings and for installing the large canvas and then packing it up again. For these reasons, despite Paraskeva's best efforts, the tour of *Guernica* did not include Toronto.[58]

Had Paraskeva lived in the United States during the early fifties, she would have been considered dangerous because of her efforts to show *Guernica*. The McCarthy hearings — when "cultural and political luminaries" were subjected to public, humiliating investigations — included those who made "efforts to bring before the American public a painted canvas called *Guernica*."[59] As the war in Spain continued, Guernica came to articulate the outrage many people felt about the horrors inflicted on that country's citizens. Now the painting, known around the world, has come to symbolize the outrage of war, from the bombing of Hiroshima to the attacks of the United States on Iraq.[60]

For two years running, Paraskeva was on the organizing committee that arranged art exhibitions to raise funds for the Toronto Committee to Aid Spanish Democracy. The other committee members were Paraskeva's colleagues, artists who, like her, had a social conscience, with whom she by then felt a sense of solidarity: Charles Comfort, Fred Haines, Yvonne McKague Housser, A. Y. Jackson, and Carl Schaefer. In 1938, a show was held at the Heliconian Club,[61] and in 1939 at the Lyceum Women's Art Association. As Paraskeva told the press, the exhibition included such artists as A.Y. Jackson, Fred Haines, and Carl Schaefer, and at the end of the week, there would be an art auction to raise money for Spain.[62]

Paraskeva also tried to recruit others. She wrote to J. S. McLean, asking him to be on the committee. He declined, saying that his company, Canada Packers, would have so many job applications he would not be able to cope;

Canada Packers had no jobs to offer. Instead, he gave her a cheque for five hundred dollars, but asked her to report it as proceeds from the Women's Art Exhibition since he wanted to remain anonymous.[63]

With the withdrawal of the International Brigade from the war in Spain in October 1938, a committee formed in Toronto to welcome home the Canadian volunteers. Paraskeva, along with Barker Fairley and Yvonne Housser, were among the thirty-seven names on the list of the Friends of the Mackenzie-Papineau Battalion, which raised money to finance the return of the volunteer soldiers, only half of whom had survived.[64] On a bitter February night in 1939, ten thousand people turned up at Toronto's Union Station to welcome home 272 men at an event organized by the Friends of the Mac-Paps. The two Toronto groups supporting the republican cause disbanded as their work dwindled, but being a part of them had given Paraskeva a sense of solidarity and belonging. Not only that, from her feelings about the war and the politics of the thirties, she had created her *Petroushka*, a painting that gave her great pride and is considered one of her masterpieces.

8

"Ambitious Aspirations" ✍

As the main and dominant feature in Canadian Art is Landscape
I became mainly a landscape painter too … I never exhibited before
and my painting developed and grew entirely on Canadian soil —
backed by memories of what I learned previously in Russia.[1]

One day as Paraskeva was leaving the Art Gallery of Toronto, she met a man she described as her "great fortune," the businessman J. Stanley McLean.[2] McLean, handsome and nearly six feet tall with a head of thick, dark hair, was an art collector and a staunch supporter of the Art Gallery of Toronto beginning as early as 1927, the year he became president of Canada Packers, a meat processing plant in Toronto. Certainly, by 1936 he was aware of Paraskeva's work, though it is likely he would have seen her paintings in exhibitions several years earlier.[3]

McLean sent her a letter at the beginning of 1938, addressing her as "Mrs. Clark," saying he was enclosing a one-hundred-dollar cheque for a painting. "As I have several times told you," he said, "I have been anxious for quite a while to have one of your pictures and I like this one. It is very bright and serene."[4] McLean suggested also that he could trade it for another since he sensed that Paraskeva liked one of her other paintings better. By the end of that year, McLean was sending her letters addressed to "My dear Paraskeva."

McLean frequented the Picture Loan Society, as did Paraskeva. The artists Duncan showed at the PLS "provided a general overview of the modern movement of painting then developing in Toronto. Clark and Schaefer received more attention than their colleagues in the Toronto community of painters ..."⁵ Duncan, with his broad knowledge of art, became McLean's advisor as he built his collection of Canadian art.

McLean developed friendships with most of the artists he collected; his closest relationship was with Paraskeva. That in itself is ironic, given McLean was a capitalist like Paraskeva's husband. Wentworth Walker, the grandson of one of the founders of the Art Gallery of Toronto and the Clarks' neighbour and friend, suggested that perhaps McLean as a capitalist helped Paraskeva, with her "communist feelings," to be more patient with Philip. Walker sensed that their differing philosophies created a barrier, which he thought McLean helped to ease.⁶

Paraskeva had no hesitation in speaking about her friendship with McLean, which became intimate. "He was my boyfriend for a while," she said, "and he bought about ten of my paintings over the years and he had quite a collection and his wife was very friendly with me in spite of everything."⁷

We do not know whether Philip was aware of the intimacies between McLean and Paraskeva. If so, he probably ignored the affair with the same attitude he had toward Bethune. An undated letter from McLean to Paraskeva seems to indicate that she must have been the one who terminated their affair. "I have your letter," he wrote, "and I am truly sorry. My first impulse was to go and see you. For I wanted to tell you how stimulating I've found our friendship, and how high a value I've set upon it. We've been pals — and we must still be so — please, Stanley."⁸ McLean had his wish. Their friendship continued until his death in 1954.

Their friendship benefitted both of them; he bought her paintings and she taught him about art, which helped him in his collecting. "I have visited many exhibitions with her," McLean said, "and I know of no one whose judgment of painting is more firm and more sure."⁹

Among the artists he purchased, he developed a particular fondness for David Milne's work; at his 1938 exhibition at the PLS, McLean bought twenty-two watercolours, and during the next three years he bought more than forty other Milne works.[10] McLean also bought the works of the Group of Seven artists, as well as a number by Carl Schaefer. Anne Savage, Yvonne McKague Housser, Isabel McLaughlin, and Jack Humphrey were also among the artists in his collection.

McLean had built a twenty-room fieldstone mansion on fifty acres in the north end of Toronto on Bayview Avenue near Lawrence Avenue, now a building incorporated into Sunnybrook and Women's College Health Science Centre. He turned his acreage into a beautiful park with plantings of trees and luxurious flower gardens. In this home for his family, he hung his Canadian art collection. McLean invited Paraskeva and Philip to his house to see his collection one spring when his gardens were in flower. And a month later, when he had rehung his collection, he invited them again.[11]

Most of McLean's collection was made up of landscapes; indeed, that was what most collectors wanted — Canadian landscapes. By the late thirties, even as she declared her staunch belief in the responsibility of an artist to paint about social issues, Paraskeva was feeling a pull toward landscape painting. She explained this attraction. "It's sort of from childhood, I have a kind of dreadish feeling about the woods, I adore that." And "all work is better perhaps because you have certain memories," she said.[12] Her memories related to landscape were rooted in the rural area, the forests and grain fields, south of St. Petersburg where her grandparents lived. The grip that the Russian landscape had on her — perhaps romanticizing her homeland — compelled her to paint the Canadian landscape, creating a set of contradictions in her work: landscape versus social issues.

However, there was a practical reason for the appeal of painting the landscape. Paraskeva had more time to paint when the Clarks took summer family holidays in Ontario's Muskoka areas and rural Quebec; it felt natural for her to paint this environment. In the summer of 1938, the Clarks took a holiday in eastern Quebec, about fifty kilometres north of Ottawa, around Val-des-Monts (Perkins) and Buckingham. They stayed in a cottage owned by a farmer on the edge of a small lake. Here Paraskeva spent her mornings and afternoons painting while Philip watched over Ben and Clive as they played in the water. Often Paraskeva produced her landscapes in summer and fall during holidays, whereas in winter and spring, she painted portraits and still lifes, or whatever interested her around her home.[13] McLean purchased two of her 1938 landscapes, *The Bush* (Plate 21) and *On Hahn's Island*.

In the late thirties, social issues were still on her mind, and it was likely during this period that she drew *Image of the Thirties* (Plate 17), an emaciated spectre of a man clutching his coat tightly around himself as he stands at the door. One's first impression is that this man is a beggar. His mittened hand, however, is open, holding a few pencils. This detail shows the artist's awareness of people's desire for respect in their desperation — the man did not want to be a beggar, but came to the door as a "salesman" instead. The image of the "beggar" is connected to her 1937 article in which Paraskeva argued with Wood about landscape painting. The art that Wood promoted, said Paraskeva, is "as useful today as a top hat to a tatterdemalion beggar in the midst of winter."[14]

Her *Evening Walk on Yonge Street* (1938) (Plate 18) depicts a woman, and a man on crutches, walking along the street, both thin and bent forward as though downcast and burdened. They pass a store without looking at the animated mannequins in fancy dresses positioned as though dancing in the window. They symbolize that many people continued their extravagance and turned away from the destitute during the Depression.

A coloured-pencil drawing that seems related, *It's 10 Below Outside* (1940) (Plate 27), depicts a large room, every inch of the floor taken with people lying covered with quilts and blankets. The artist's use of perspective gives the impression of a huge gymnasium-type space that must have been used as a shelter for the homeless.

A digression from both landscapes and Depression drawings came in her oil, *Bathing the Horse* (1938), a painting that refers specifically to Petrov-Vodkin's *The Bathing of the Red Horse* (1912). It is hard to know what prompted Paraskeva to choose the subject of this painting, so reminiscent of her young-adult years in St. Petersburg. It is possible that it was connected to the show of Soviet art at the Art Gallery of Toronto in the fall of 1936, in which three of Petrov-Vodkin's works were included, though *Red Horse* was not among them.[15]

It is more likely that letters in 1938 from her father prompted this painting with a Russian subject. He wrote to her saying he was sorry she was so far away living like a speck of dust among foreigners. He was not well, he told her.

He had enough to eat, but his clothes were worn out; he asked his daughter to send underclothes for him and for her brother, and something for Zakhar's three children. Apparently, Paraskeva sent her father a letter asking for a certain book from his library and a photo of her mother. Her father replied that his library was lost,[16] likely a casualty of the hard times during and after the Revolution. And he had no photos of Olga (her photo must have been missing from the old photo album for many years). Whatever memory fragments she retained of Olga, Paraskeva would never have a photo to help keep alive the image of her mother's face.

The next year, 1939, Paraskeva's father died. He was sixty-eight. In his life, he had given her a love of learning and reading. Now, with his death, she knew with finality that the strongest connection she had with her former life in Russia was severed. Coincidently, Kuzma Petrov-Vodkin also died in 1939.

This was a year of grief. Bethune, in China, had planned to return to Canada in November but contracted blood poisoning after he cut himself during battlefield surgery (there were no gloves) and died on 12 November. Although many Canadians do not know who Bethune is, a 2009 biography by the former Governor General Adrienne Clarkson will offer the current generation of readers a portrait of him.[17] In China, however, he is a major hero. During the SARS epidemic in China, when volunteers worked long hours, they were praised for "carrying forward the spirit of Bethune."[18]

"The Bethune story is still told in Chinese school textbooks, but his name has been fading from the media in recent years."[19] Over the years, however, he has appeared in artwork, posters, stamps, and statues; one of few Westerners so honoured. His last few months were documented in an essay by Chairman Mao Zedong — "In Memory of Norman Bethune" — which was required reading in China. The essay concludes with these words:

> We must all learn the spirit of absolute selflessness from him. With this spirit, everyone can be very useful to the people. A man's ability may be great or small, but if he has this spirit, he is already noble-minded and pure, a man of moral integrity and above vulgar interests, a man who is of value to the people.[20]

IN NOVEMBER 1939, Paraskeva visited New York for a second time — the first had been with Bethune. J. S. McLean paid for her trip so she could see the Picasso retrospective at the Museum of Modern Art. "She spent much of her time standing in front of the huge *Guernica*, absorbing and marvelling at the imagery, and studying the accompanying sketches, which documented its conception."[21]

In New York, she made a pencil sketch of what she saw outside her hotel window, and months later, wrote a short essay about the impact of seeing Picasso's work. She began it in English and switched to French to be able to express herself better, saying that the unexpected combinations of elements in his work show that, in a profound way, the artist grasped life's contradictions. At the same time, she said, he also had an understanding that the spiritual and sensual aspects of life fit together perfectly.[22]

The three days that Paraskeva spent in New York in front of Picasso's work made a deep impression on her. "I went to the show over and over again," she said. "I thought *Guernica* was so terrific." Then she went on to deplore that some of her best friends did not understand what Picasso was doing.[23] Not only was their lack of understanding upsetting to Paraskeva, but it also reinforced her perception of the ignorance and narrowness of Toronto's art world at the time.

Guernica fed Paraskeva's desire to paint about what was happening to people in the world. She was an artist of intense feeling with a humanist ideology of painting. But she was pulled back and forth between this belief and the enticement of landscape painting. Within her was growing a strong desire to be a truly Canadian painter, which, she thought, meant painting landscapes. She was represented in the late thirties in international exhibitions of Canadian art in Edinburgh, Scotland, in London at the Tate Gallery where she showed her *Wheat Field* (1936), and in several shows in the United States.

One of her paintings that had appeared in the "Exhibition of Paintings, Drawings and Sculpture by Artists of the British Empire Overseas" was purchased by the Napier Gallery in New Zealand. She was thrilled. Her "heart was swollen with pride of knowing that I belong to this group of Canadian Artists whose work is a contribution to the Common Stock of intellectual and artistic ideals, which is vital to the Spiritual Unity of the Empire, that is a grand feeling!" she wrote. She poured her "affection to the little spot on the Pacific Shore where my cold 'Snowfall' is going to be from now."[24] When she received the cheque for the painting, again she became effusive about her feelings, saying it was "a special kind of thrill to see this ... cheque. The first public institution having acquired my work. It makes a great moment in my life and brings such invigorating power to my whole being for the future work."[25]

Paraskeva participated in the exhibitions at the World's Fair in New York by submitting her work to three of the societies representing Canada: Canadian Group of Painters, Canadian Society of Painters in Water Colour, and the Canadian Society of Graphic Artists. *Petroushka* was one of her entries with the Canadian Group of Painters and her *Presents from Madrid* was in the show of the Canadian Society for Painters in Water Colour. She was particularly proud that *Petroushka* was reproduced in the *New York World Telegram* and mentioned in the review text among the names of such other Canadian artists as Charles Comfort, Emily Carr, and A.Y. Jackson. *Petroushka* represented Paraskeva again in the Great Lakes Exhibition that came to the Art Gallery of Toronto after touring American cities, including the Albright Art Gallery (now Albright Knox) in Buffalo, New York.

Paraskeva was also part of an exhibition at the Art Gallery of Toronto titled simply "Paraskeva Clark, Carl Schaefer, Caven Atkins, David Milne." In reviewing this show, Graham McInnes singled out two of her landscapes, *Wheat Field* (1936) and *In the Woods* (1939) (Plate 22). Both of these paintings are seen as among her most successful landscapes.

Paraskeva's main idea for *In the Woods* was to show the "charm of solitude, calm in the intimacy of walls made by trees ... the motion of soaring toward light above in everything growing ... The dynamism of so called inanimate forms and objects is one of the greatest attractions for me. Underlying this dynamism is making the hidden currents apparent to the eye."[26] A cubist rendering of the forest floor undergirds the verticals of the black tree trunks, giving the painting a feeling of energy. This somewhat abstract portrayal of the woods showed an awareness of contemporary European trends at the time, according to writer Roald Nasgaard. For this reason, he singled out *In the Woods* as a painting that broke through the "introspection that had characterized this nation's art with its fascination over the landscape ..."[27]

McInnes commented that in both *Wheat Field* and *In the Woods*, the artist "succeeds beyond all measure of doubt, and these works are fine art in any language." At the same time, he felt the viewer could detect the "immense struggle," which he also called a "grim and exciting tussle," as Paraskeva developed her painting.[28]

McInnes knew Paraskeva well. As she expanded in her painting, to most people she appeared sure of herself, with a sturdy sense that she was a good painter. In fact, these impressions of her were true, but they were also not true: underneath, her mind was often filled with misgivings as she worried over her work, frequently becoming discouraged. "I feel pretty doubtful about my work," she told her friends Carl and Lillian Schaefer. "I feel I am not bad enough to go on producing innocently mediocre paintings — feeling no great powers within to satisfy ambitious aspirations."[29] Beginning in the late thirties, she often spoke about her limitations in relation to the amount of time required to look after her family. She lamented the biological givens of women, which she said prevented them from being able to dedicate themselves to their art as men could do.

Paraskeva did not find many other people who spoke about these issues in public. However, she discovered that the critic Graham McInnes had some understanding of what women faced. In his article on Montreal artist Marian Scott, a friend of Paraskeva's, he discussed the quandary female artists experienced, saying their difficulties arose for reasons that were "biological, social and environmental," that women "cannot (except perhaps in literature) wrestle successfully with the greatest creative problems, and emerge — as men occasionally do — triumphant."[30] McInnes did not delve any deeper into the reasons women artists weren't considered what he called "triumphant" — the equivalent of "great" — saying he had neither the time nor the ability for that task.

McInnes pointed out the contradictions in society and the art world, the preoccupation with greatness and genius that puts men on top in a sphere where women encounter different "social and environmental" situations than men do. Apparently, he was more aware than most men that historically women were barred from the art-education opportunities male artists had; it was not common for men at that time even to see the barriers women faced, much less understand them. Likely, his friendship with Paraskeva sharpened his awareness, and led him to think beyond society's image of women.

Though not many specific details about their friendship exist, McInnes's son Simon McInnes remembers that his mother Joan "intimated that before she and my father got married … he and Paraskeva had a fling."[31] Certainly, the few letters that exist indicate they had a close friendship that included conversations on art along with their mutual respect and admiration for each other.[32]

However, despite her affairs, Paraskeva was devoted to Philip and her sons. They had been moving from one apartment to another for nine years when the sculptors Frances Loring and Florence Wyle told the Clarks of a house for sale at 256 Roxborough Street. This place would not have appealed to most people because it was perched on a steep hill, and it was impossible to drive to the front door. You had to climb up forty-three steps to reach the yard. However, Paraskeva liked the house; for one thing, in the basement was a finished room that would be suitable for a studio. With the way the house was situated, this room had ample windows to the south and west, overlooking a yard where she could develop a garden.

Philip would have been hard-pressed to come up with the seventy-five hundred dollars to buy this house. However, he was happy to benefit from Paraskeva's friendship with McLean and accepted the businessman's help. "For security he put 10,000 of Canada Packers stocks up and afterward we finally paid off the loan and he gave me all the stocks and he said, it's yours, don't say anything and don't you dare sell these, he told me right here in this house, or I'll kill you."[33]

The Clarks wanted Danish modern furniture, nothing like the heavy Victorian pieces that Philip's parents had. Paraskeva found a Danish carpenter and gave him photographs from the French *Vogue* magazine as his model to build the furniture they would use for the rest of their lives.[34] The living room was painted grey-blue, one of Paraskeva's favourite colours. In fact, the paint chip Paraskeva probably used for choosing the colour of Super Kem-Tone paint still survives, "Bluestone ck. 77."[35]

Paraskeva's friendship with her capitalist patron — McLean claimed he was the capitalist she painted in *Petroushka* — not only made possible this house for her and her family, but also her painting studio. No longer would she have to find whatever space she could to set up her easel in a small apartment. Now she had a space of her own where she could get away from the rest of the family, spread out her work, and hang on the walls whatever she chose. She hung up a hammer and sickle flag, and photos of Picasso and other artists she admired.

Philip could carry the mortgage; by then he was earning five thousand dollars a year in his position as Assistant Controller of the Province of Ontario.[36] With her husband's support, Paraskeva could feel financial security as she watched some of her colleagues, both men and women, scrambling to cope with financial difficulties after the Depression. Nevertheless, she had her complaints: more house meant more work, and in the 1940s something like laundry was not simply a matter of throwing clothes, towels, and bed linens into an automatic washer and dryer. Standing over an old wringer washer could consume most of a woman's day every week, and one can imagine her thoughts as she railed at the fates over the laundry because she wanted to be in her studio painting.

The Clarks took possession of the house early in 1940, and their first Christmas Eve on Roxborough Street was memorable, thanks to their friends Carl and Lillian Schaefer. Paraskeva was looking after the Schaefers' houseplants while they were away for a year in Vermont because Carl had been accepted for a Guggenheim Foundation Fellowship, which required spending a year painting somewhere in the United States.

Among the plants was a rare specimen, an exotic cactus native to southern Texas and northern Mexico, called the night blooming cereus, rather ugly and in its natural habitat resembling a dead bush. However, its beautiful trumpet-shaped blossoms have the most exquisite, fragrant scent. This cactus causes a great deal of excitement because it blooms for only one night of the year and then closes its blossom until another grows a year later. Unless you are awake most of the night, you never see the cactus in full bloom and you miss the exotic fragrance as well.

That Christmas Eve in 1940, the Clarks invited in some friends. Knowing the Schaefers' cereus blossom would open that night, they all stayed up until three o'clock in the morning. Douglas Duncan was among those who stayed. He and Philip spent part of the night photographing the spectacular white blossom. In a letter to the Schaefers several months later describing the Christmas Eve event, Philip told them that all their plants were thriving, and the cereus had already grown a whole new stalk.[37]

The Clarks enjoyed their spacious new home where they could entertain their friends and host dinner parties. With the front hall opening onto a sizable dining room on the right and an even larger living room on the left, the house could accommodate a large group of people. Guests could easily move back and forth and cluster in the different areas. Paraskeva produced memorable meals for guests in her domain, the kitchen at the back of the house, a room spanning the width of the dining room and the central hallway.

In the living room stood the baby grand piano Philip's stepmother had purchased years earlier. Oddly enough, Philip kept this piano out of tune. According to the Clarks' music-loving friend and neighbour Wentworth Walker, once when he visited the Clarks he asked Philip to play the piano. Philip refused, saying the piano was out of tune — deliberately so. "The idea of keeping a ... grand [piano] in your house, deliberately out of tune so nobody could use it, to me is quite crazy ... There's real frustration expressed by that."[38] Walker did not feel it was his place to talk further with Philip about it, but one does not need a degree in psychology to know that if a person goes to such an extent to squash his love of music there are bound to be personal repercussions. Life in the Clarks' new house would see the effects of that frustration as friction between Philip and Paraskeva developed over the years.

Outside the house, a few trees stood on the property, but Paraskeva knew that much more could be done with it and began visualizing her first garden. Trees, flowers, shrubs — before long she began the garden in earnest, a garden that offered her first intimate experience with flowers since she had hung over her mother's chair while Olga made flowers to sell.

Paraskeva was in a good mood at the end of the year because she had hired a woman to come in twice a week to clean the house. She took pleasure in her new home, especially when it was clean. However, as usual, her good mood also had its inverse side as a result of her perennial problem of not having enough time to paint. She considered resigning from the Canadian Society of Painters in Water Colour, because she was discontent with her work; everything she did in that medium was "so heavy and dry." Not only that, she worried over what she would send to the eleventh International Water Colour Exhibition at the Brooklyn Museum in New York in the spring. She seemed somewhat disgruntled about the idea of painting something for that show because of the politics. "It is not an honour in my case to be accepted [for the exhibition] just because politically U.S. wants to make a friendly gesture toward Canada."[39] Despite being malcontent, she did manage to finish new paintings that were shown in Brooklyn from the end of March until mid-May.

With ten years of working as an artist in Toronto behind her, she began to believe that she was indeed an artist — a Canadian artist. She had sold a painting for the first time just three years after she arrived in Canada, a still life called *Calla Lily Still Life* (1933), to her artist friend Bertram Brooker in 1934.[40] Since then, she had sold more than ten other works. However, after painting for ten years she felt she needed new stimulation and more training. Frequently, when she thought about her career, what she needed over-shadowed her accomplishments. Perhaps Paraskeva thought that if Schaefer applied and was successful at winning a Guggenheim Fellowship, she might also qualify.

For a Guggenheim application, she wrote out plans for work she wanted to do if she could live in New York for a year. She received great encourage-ment and "compliments" for her paintings and felt that she could "believe in my work only if I go in the direction of *composition* — of mainly figure composition. The political and sociological problems confront us nowdays [*sic*] with such insistence and vigour that we cannot help to taking some part in efforts to resolve to clarify these problems. The painter's job in it all still remains, the painting."[41]

She wanted to work from the model, sketching on the street and in parks as a way of developing her skills in what she called "figure composition." She also said she wanted to "study works of great masters, particularly modern which we lack entirely here in Toronto." The way of American modern artists was the direction she wanted to go with her own painting. If she were granted the Guggenheim Fellowship, she hoped, if possible, to work with an artist of the stature of Ozenfant.[42]

Paraskeva's notes convey the intensity of her desire to expand her skills and grow as an artist; we learn how knowledgeable she was when it came to what was happening in the art world outside Toronto. Few Toronto artists at that time would have known who Ozenfant was.

The most astonishing thing in these notes is that she felt her family could get along without her for a year by hiring a housekeeper. Unfortunately, her "ambitious aspirations" were unfulfilled, and she never received a Guggenheim Fellowship; she plodded on as best she could as she split herself between painting and her family.

The Artist as Comrade🙰

With my whole heart I am for a radical end to all this insanity.
Only from world-wide socialism do I expect anything.[1]

O n Monday 23 June 1941, *The Globe and Mail* in Toronto carried a huge
front-page headline — "Nazis Invade Russia" — that would have sent
a chill through Paraskeva. Her brother and sister and other relatives were still
in Russia and she feared for their safety.

Later that week, on Thursday 26 June, exactly ten years to the day since she,
Ben, and Philip boarded the *Empress of France* to sail for Canada, Paraskeva was
on her way to Kingston, Ontario, for the Conference of Canadian artists at
Queen's University. Within those ten years, she had given birth to her second
son Clive and established herself as a respected painter in Toronto.

Paraskeva seldom was away from her family. However, she decided she
could not miss this weekend in Kingston, a gathering of artists from across
the country. Not only would the conference give her a break from her daily
duties as wife and mother, but she would have a few days to feel herself
completely an artist among other artists — a *Canadian* artist among other

Canadian artists, who included her friends Pegi Nicol, Marian Scott from Montreal, and A.Y. Jackson.

The Conference of Canadian Artists was the idea of André Bieler, artist in residence at Queen's University, who, like Paraskeva, was a humanist painter. Because of his interest in the relationship of the artist to society, he was familiar with the American government initiatives benefiting artists: F. D. Roosevelt had earmarked one percent of the cost of public buildings for murals. This kind of support was the envy of Canadian artists, though money for this program disappeared once the United States entered World War II.[2] Even so, Canada had no such program and many of the artists at the conference hoped that they could unite with one voice and persuade Ottawa to offer one.

Bieler had attended two conferences in a series on international affairs between the United States and Canada held at Queen's, which the Carnegie Endowment for International Peace subsidized. That series was but one indication that the ties between the United States and Canada were tightening. Only two months before the artists met, Canada's Prime Minister Mackenzie King and American President F. D. Roosevelt signed a declaration of co-operation in producing defence equipment, giving Canada the prerogative of buying military supplies from the United States.

Furthermore, Queen's University had its own ties to the United States; it had bestowed upon F. D. Roosevelt an honorary degree in 1938. As historian Frank Underhill noted, Britain was being displaced by the United States in terms of importance to Canada.[3] In this context, it is not surprising that the artists' conference was funded by the Carnegie philanthropic empire.

As the 1941 conference on international affairs ended, the artists' conference was beginning. In that last weekend of June, from Thursday to Sunday, 150 artists, critics, museum directors, and others interested in the arts gathered at Queen's University. The conference marked a historic point in the history of art in Canada because it was the first time that artists from all regions of the country met to talk about art. In the opening session, Bieler, the chair, stated the purpose of the conference as two-fold: to provide an opportunity for artists from across the country to meet; and to study the function of art and artists in a democratic society. It was in the second area of discussion that

Paraskeva wielded some influence, though most people probably didn't know that.

She had given a copy of Plekhanov's *Art and Society* to Walter Abell, a professor at Acadia University and editor of the magazine *Maritime Art*.[4] Abell made a speech on "Art and Democracy" and drew on the ideas in Plekhanov as he developed that speech on the relation of art to society. In a letter thanking her for the book, Abell said, "It helped to crystallize in my mind a development of thought on the subject of the relation of art to society."[5]

In his speech, Abell spoke about art as permeating society in a broad sense that included not just painting, but "sculpture, architecture, town planning ... textiles and pottery, the industrial arts including everything from vanity cases to motor cars, and public utilities such as highways, dams, and bridges ... Art and democracy would take all these in." However, the picture he was portraying of art in society was not a reality in Canada, he said, because of the impact of the destructive aspects of the industrial revolution and because of "the concentration of wealth in our social system."[6]

Abell's speech must have been gratifying and exciting for Paraskeva, reminding her of her days in Leningrad at the Art Academy when these ideas were part of the air she breathed. She agreed with Abell, and she was known for these ideas. "She looks to a day when art will be recognized as an industry, with the people at large as consumers, not a little thing in a little circle," Pearl McCarthy said of Paraskeva.[7]

A theme closely related to Abell's talk on the artist in democracy emerged during the conference: the role of the artist during wartime. Paraskeva's alarm at the invasion of Russia was shared by other artists who felt that democratic freedom was being threatened by fascism; something that had became clear during the Spanish Civil War.

Even the workshops focusing on technique and media were presented in the context of artists working as responsible members of society, creating works of art of aesthetic merit with enduring value to society.[8] The regional painter, Thomas Hart Benton of Missouri and the members of "The Painters' Workshop" from Boston, Massachusetts, demonstrated the use of materials and methods in painting. Bieler and others hoped that interesting technical presentations and discussions would help Canadian artists loosen up and explore unfamiliar methods of working. Paraskeva, always interested in improving her painting, scrawled lists of ingredients for tempera emulsion and paint base all over her program.[9]

In the Friday afternoon session, when the all-male resolutions committee was announced, Paraskeva spoke up, pointing out there were no women on the committee — in a published list of nearly 150 conference participants, one-third were women. The chair that afternoon, Arthur Lismer, passed off her question about the exclusion of women by saying he could not change the committee and went on to other matters. According to the conference proceedings, none of the other women there backed up Paraskeva's objection. However, at the end of the conference the five-member continuation committee did include a woman, the sculptor Frances Loring.[10]

After the sessions at Queen's, the conference moved on to Ottawa, with Paraskeva travelling again with Loring and Wyle. The artists headed to the Chateau Laurier hotel for lunch, hosted by the National Gallery. Afterward, at the gallery they listened to speeches about painting, and then toured an exhibition of French paintings and the work of the Group of Seven.

This 1941 conference gave the artists a buoyant sense of community. In a letter to Bieler after the conference, Peggy Nicol MacLeod said she was still "threshing" conference ideas in her sleep and described the feeling from this democratic experience as "a mass emotion."[11]

At the official level, one outcome of the Kingston conference was the formation of the Federation of Canadian Artists (FCA), an association of professional and lay members to promote the arts and to lobby the government on behalf of artists.[12] Paraskeva was among the artists on the first Ontario region FCA committee.[13]

The FCA made recommendations for arts education across the country and the establishment of community centres. One effective action of the FCA was when it "gathered a thousand signatures and petitioned the federal government in February 1943 to establish a war artists' program and an arts council that would embrace not only artists 'but writers of all kinds, poets, playwrights [and] radio-dramatists.'"[14] As a result, the federal government authorized fifteen war artists who were assigned to a variety of locations to paint scenes from the war.

On a personal level, for Paraskeva the conference provided reassurance that she was an integral part of a community of artists and offered her a feeling of solidarity. The conference gave her a chance to talk with artists she did not often meet, for example Marian Dale Scott of Montreal. A photograph from the conference shows them in an intense conversation, Paraskeva talking with her fists clenched, and Marian listening.

THAT SUMMER, *New World Illustrated*, a magazine with a socialist point of view, commissioned Paraskeva to document life in Toronto. Graham McInnes wrote the text about "Toronto the Good" and Paraskeva made the drawings. The result was "Street Scenes: Toronto (Plate 24)." Paraskeva's drawings show the influence of the *lubok*, a type of nineteenth-century Russian peasant woodcut that resembled cartoon strips in which each frame captured a brief moment of action rather than a world complete in itself.[15]

"This is the first time that a national magazine has tried to anatomize a city in line," McInnes wrote. "However the drawing may strike the observer, he cannot fail to notice one thing: that the artist has uncovered a rich store of material in chronicling the life of a Canadian city." In a reference to Paraskeva's article in 1937, McInnes went on to say that Paraskeva's drawings show that painters have too long focused on the Pre-Cambrian Shield and have "plenty to paint in their very back yard."

These somewhat humorous, acerbic drawings poking fun at Toronto reveal some of Paraskeva's observations of the city during her first ten years there. A Toronto streetcar, with its "overwhelming dourness," has signs along the top: "Thou Shalt be dull"; "Thou Shalt not criticise Toronto"; "Thou Shalt not be Gay"; "Thou Shalt Not Ski on Sundays."

The other five smaller drawings do show Torontonians having fun in more diverse scenes: Baldwin Street markets, Hanlan's Point, Sunday afternoon in Queen's Park with a soldier lounging on the grass with his girlfriend, and strippers in a burlesque show. Timothy Eaton Memorial Church was also included, showing the fashionable churchgoers chatting after attending a service.[16]

These are the drawings of an outsider, a woman who dares to criticize the city in which she was both accepted and rejected. Her acceptance as an artist we already know about. Her rejection as a Russian immigrant, someone who

Plate 1. *Leningrad Memories — Public Bath* (1964), oil on board, 82 x 102.5 cm.
Private collection, Toronto. Photo credit: Dean Palmer.

Plate 2. *Memories of Leningrad* (1923), pencil and watercolour on paper, 16 x 16 cm. Private collection, Toronto. Photo credit: Dean Palmer.

Plate 3. *Landscape in Chatou* (1927), watercolour on paper, 29.7 x 39.8 cm. Private collection, Victoria, B.C. Photo credit: Anthony Sam.

Plate 4. *Self Portrait* (1925), oil on canvas, 28.3 x 22.2 cm. Art Gallery of Ontario, purchase with assistance from Wintario, 1979.

Plate 5. *Self Portrait* (1929–1930), watercolour on paper, 24 x 24 cm. Private collection, Toronto.

Plate 6. *Overlooking a Garden* (1930), tempera and watercolour on paper, mounted on paperboard, 40.1 x 51.4 cm. Art Gallery of Hamilton, gift from the Douglas M. Duncan Collection, 1970. Photo credit: Mike Lalich.

Plate 7. *Self Portrait* (1931–32),
oil on cardboard, 41 x 31 cm.
Collection of Museum London.
Photo credit: John Tamblyn.

Plate 8. *Portrait of Philip* (1933), oil on canvas, 126 x 126 cm. Art Gallery of Ontario, purchase, 1984.

Plate 9. *Fruit* (1931), oil on paper board, 45 x 58.3 cm. Private collection. Photo credit: Dean Palmer.

Plate 10. Waterfalls painting on the back side of *Fruit.* Photo credit: Dean Palmer.

Photo of waterfalls Paraskeva must have used for the painting that appears on the back of the 1931 still life *Fruit*, her first painting in Canada, which she gave as a birthday gift to her Philip's niece, Marguerite. The pencil lines show how she composed the painting. Note Ben sitting under the tree. Photo courtesy of Clive and Mary Clark.

Plate 11. *Myself* (1933), oil on canvas, 101.6 x 76.2 cm. National Gallery of Canada, 18311.

Plate 12. *Portrait of Naomi Yanova* (1934), 100 x 75.5 cm. Private collection, Vancouver, B.C. Photo credit: Cameron Heryet.

Plate 13. Working Drawing for Eaton's Windows (c. 1935), gouache, ink, graphite on paper. Ottawa Art Gallery.

Plate 14. *Untitled* (*Trout*) (1936), watercolour on paper, 61 x 50.8 cm. A.G. Rain Family Collection, Toronto. Photo credit: Dean Palmer.

Plate 15. *Presents from Madrid* (1937), watercolour over graphite on wove paper, 51.5 x 62 cm. National Gallery of Canada, 23666.

Plate 16. *Wheat Field* (1936), oil on canvas, 63.6 x 76.5 cm. National Gallery of Canada, 16452.

Plate 17. *Image of the Thirties* (nd), pencil on paper, 35 x 24 cm. Private collection. Photo credit: Richard Goldthorpe.

Plate 18. *Evening Walk on Yonge Street* (1938), watercolour on paper, 40 x 34.5 cm. Private collection, Toronto. Photo credit: Dean Palmer.

Plate 19. *Petroushka* (1937), oil on canvas, 122.4 x 81.9 cm. National Gallery of Canada, 18624.

Plate 20. *Pen Drawing for Petroushka*, pen and pencil on paper, 41 x 27 cm. Libby's of Toronto. Photo credit: Dean Palmer.

Plate 21. *The Bush* (1938), oil on canvas, 76.3 x 68.5 cm. Art Gallery of Ontario, gift from the J.S. McLean Collection, Ontario Heritage Foundation.

Plate 22. *In the Woods* (1939), oil on canvas, 77.5 x 69 cm. Hart House Permanent Collection, University of Toronto.

Plate 23. *Swamp* (1939), oil on canvas, 76.2 x 50.8 cm. Art Gallery of Ontario, gift from the Albert H. Robson Memorial Subscription Foundation, 1939.

Street Scenes: Toronto *drawings by Paraskeva Clark*

THE capital and largest town of the Province of Ontario speaks of itself as The Queen City. But throughout Canada its nickname is almost universally Toronto the Good. A good many conflicting emotions are summed up in the phrase: envy at Toronto's abounding prosperity, a sneer at its all too evident complacency, respect for its solidity, laughter at its blue laws, resentment at its financial domination.

The Torontonian, though he is aware of the phrase, is sublimely ignorant of its overtones. For he is, like all good citizens, immensely proud of his home town. "If ya don't like it, take the next train back" and "Go jump in the lake" are his some-

of material in chronicling the life of a Canadian city.

For too long our artists have had their eyes resolutely fixed in the Pre-Cambrian Shield with its rocks and lakes and spruce. These drawings show that Canadian painters have plenty to paint in their very back yard. In metropolitan Canada lies a fertile field for the artists of today.

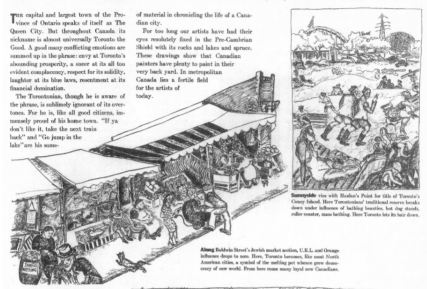

Sunnyside vies with Hanlan's Point for title of Toronto's Coney Island. Here Torontonians' traditional reserve breaks down under influence of bathing beauties, hot dog stands, roller coaster, mass bathing. Here Toronto lets its hair down.

Along Baldwin Street's Jewish market section, U.E.L. and Orange influence drops to zero. Here, Toronto becomes, like most North American cities, a symbol of the melting pot whence grew democracy of new world. From here come many loyal new Canadians.

what unsubtle rebukes to anyone who criticises Toronto. But it is a curious fact that Torontonians are made, not born. The old line families are dying out and the city recruits its ranks largely from rural Ontario, and in the immediate past, the industrial areas of the Old Country. Toronto is Canada's biggest stop-over town.

The Toronto spirit is something too subtle for words to analyze, and in the hope of probing into it by other means, and finding out what makes the city tick, NEW WORLD commissioned Canadian artist Paraskeva Clark to cast her eye around. The results are here; they will not please everyone, but no criticism or comment on Toronto ever did. The city has been Mrs. Clark's home for a decade; though deeply attached to the town, she can view it with the objectivity of a complete outsider. And if her pen dips occasionally in acid, it also dips in milk.

Here is Canada's second largest city (the "second" a source of secret shame to many of her citizens) with its foibles and virtues lightly indicated through an artist's hand and eye. This is the first time that a national magazine has tried to anatomize a city in line. However the drawing may strike the observer, he cannot fail to notice one thing: that the artist has uncovered a rich store

Crowd in typical Toronto street car combines qualities of Glasgow, Belfast and Buffalo. Overwhelming dourness is most noted feature.

Plate 24. Drawings for *New World Illustrated.*

was different, was more subtle. McInnes admitted that Torontonians tell those who criticize to "Go jump in the lake" or "If ya don't like it, take the next train back." In other words, "Thou shalt not criticise …" McInnes noted that the spirit of Toronto is too subtle for words, so the drawings are an effective way to probe the city. However, as Paraskeva had discovered when she arrived, often the spirit of Toronto had no subtlety when it came to the elitist nature of the old-line families, one of which she herself adopted. Class lines were clear and she had married up; even after ten years, she was still an outsider, now on Roxborough Street inside Toronto's upper-middle-class Rosedale. The artist side of her somewhat split identity did give her some feeling of acceptance; and some things about Paraskeva did give her respect in Philip's social bracket: she was a model housekeeper and mother and entertained in a grand style, particularly after they moved to Rosedale.

Alice Sutton, who was close to Paraskeva later on, thought that Paraskeva was insecure "about her social class in comparison to her husband's, and she lashed out against the practices of society by being overtly controversial in her political views."[17] From the time she first arrived in Toronto, she was outspoken to a degree that made many people uncomfortable. In some cases, she simply did not understand the parameters of what was and what was not acceptable. One example is an incident Paraskeva's friend, the sculptor Dora de Pédery-Hunt, recalled. One day de Pédery-Hunt and their friend Louise Comfort, who had recently had surgery, were on the Rosedale bus when Paraskeva got on. Immediately Paraskeva began asking Louise in a loud voice about her terrible operation. "Louise, how is it? Isn't this terrible? Who did it? blah, blah, blah. Louise, of course, stiffer and stiffer and stiffer and couldn't stop being very, very stiff." Paraskeva got off the bus first, and afterward Louise said to de Pédery-Hunt, "Dora, isn't this funny. She must be really a European. Nobody dared to ask me about the operation."[18]

Having emigrated from Hungary, de Pédery-Hunt had been taken under the wing of the sculptors who lived together in the old church, Florence Wyle and Frances Loring. They taught de Pédery-Hunt about Canadian taboos. Asking about someone's surgery — don't ever do that, they told her. You don't even go visit someone in the hospital unless you are invited. And if you do visit, do not talk about the surgery. Perhaps Paraskeva did not know about these taboos, but if she did, she would not have cared. There were many things like this that Paraskeva encountered, and to her these kinds of rules were silly. She couldn't be bothered worrying about whether or not saying certain things was acceptable when the mores seemed so arbitrary. Those who knew her well could piece together the kind of person she was and the way she depicted Toronto in her drawings.

THE DIRECTION THE war was taking must have always been on Paraskeva's mind. Toronto newspaper headlines during those months and into the fall of 1941 convinced people that the Nazis were out to obliterate Leningrad and the Russians. Germany simply ignored the Nazi-Soviet pact Stalin had reluctantly signed, and when all the evidence pointed to the Nazi invasion, Stalin declared no such attack would occur and did nothing. "If a dictator decrees that there will be no attack, an officer who prepares for one is liable to execution as a traitor."[19] When it became evident that Stalin was wrong, he withdrew in a state of collapse. One of the members of the Stavka, Admiral Alexei Kuznetsov, reported that Stalin was not in any meetings during the month of June, and not until almost the middle of July.

At the end of June, a Committee for State Defence was named, and this committee, which included Stalin's name, ran the affairs of the State until Stalin came out of his shell in the middle of July.[20] Given these circumstances, it is not surprising that by the beginning of September Leningrad was encircled by the Nazis, who expected to wipe out the city in no time. We know that is not what happened. The city was under siege almost nine hundred days until early 1944, during which time "a third of the population died, more than half of them from hunger ..."[21]

For Paraskeva, the war and the siege of Leningrad meant something different to her than it did to her friends and other artists in Toronto. It touched her in a personal way as she enjoyed comfort and safety in Canada while her native city suffered. Perhaps it was the war that prompted her to return to her earlier drawing *Memories of Leningrad* (Plate 25). She repeated it again, herself at a table reading as she cradled Ben in her lap.

Early in 1942, Paraskeva painted *Self Portrait* (a.k.a. *Self Portrait with Concert Programme*) (Plate 26). She presented herself seated in a chair in her living room;

in the background is her green Venini glass table lamp she brought with her from Paris. Dressed in a pink suit in a style typical of the 1940s, she holds a program she saved from a concert she attended at the end of the previous year called "Salute to Russia," a title that can easily be read in the painting.

To give the painting greater impact, she affixed the actual program rather than just drawing the concert program on the canvas. "I felt very terrifically about Leningrad being besieged, it's my native town, and just by pose and the expression of my face I wanted to point out the seriousness of that great moment with the whole world at war."[22]

Paraskeva's origin, the first twenty-five years of her life in Russia, entitled her to paint this image in a comment on this world event. The suit in a similar style to a uniform and her worried expression identify her as a comrade of her threatened people. This portrait stands in contrast to the way she presented herself in 1933 as a middle-class, confident woman. Her confidence had become overridden with anxiety and it is clear where her allegiance lay. It was an audacious act for a Rosedale woman in 1942.

It is significant that she placed herself in her living room, however, instead of her studio. She was making the point that even if she was a "society matron" sitting comfortably in her Rosedale living room she still had the prerogative to make a statement about the grave situation in Russia. But this painting was not just about the war; in her mind, she was helping the cause of socialism as well. And here again, we see the basic contradiction of her life: she championed socialism while "reaping the benefits of the capitalist system."[23]

Later that year, she would have an opportunity to not only meet some of her "comrades," but also to participate in events to honour them. The Soviet Union decided to send emissaries to both Canada and the United States to rally support for their beleaguered country, and Canada was receptive to the appeal. In the fall of 1942, when Leningrad had been under siege for a year, three Russian "heroes" arrived to solicit help: Lyudmila Pavlichenko, introduced as the "girl sniper;" Senior Lieutenant Vladamir Pchelintsev, organizer of snipers; and Nicolai Kravchenko, the organizer of Moscow's defences.

Paraskeva was on the welcoming committee for the three Russians, who arrived at Union Station on 21 September 1942. Toronto Mayor Fred J. Conboy, Ontario Premier Mitchell Hepburn, and other officials led a parade up Bay

Street, from Union Station to Toronto's city hall, with a military band playing and members of the Canadian Navy, Army, and Air Force marching. After a day filled with bands, receptions, and visits, an evening rally was held at Maple Leaf Gardens for the three heroes. Two hours before the rally was scheduled to start, long lines of people stood outside waiting for the doors to open. A half an hour before the start time, the Gardens was three-quarters full. Sixteen thousand people packed the arena, eager to hear the translated messages of the Russians. When they entered the arena, they drew "one of the most sustained ovations in Gardens history as flag-bearing veterans led the group in."[24] When the Soviet anthem was played, hundreds of communists, who until recently would not have dared to raise their arms in public, gave the clenched-fist salute with great cheers.

In an unusual show of common purpose, left-wing labour leaders, army personnel, and government officials shared the stage. Paraskeva was among them; she now had an opportunity to act the portrait she had painted. A. Y. Jackson wrote about the event in a letter to his niece. "Went to a big demonstration for a second front at Maple Leaf Gardens, to greet the young Russian lady sniper, who bagged 309 Nazis. She looked very charming," Jackson said. "Paraskeva was on the platform with Mitch Hepburn and a lot of C.I.O. boys."[25] What did Jackson think about his artist friend Paraskeva's position at this rally sitting with the "boys" and snipers? He does not say, but there on the stage she was as much Russian as Canadian — if not more so — and therefore still an outsider.

The Toronto newspapers played up "Girl Sniper" Pavlichenko and praised her for having killed her three hundredth German on 2 June, her twenty-sixth birthday. Newspaper articles also reflect the public near-hysteria of the time, with such shocking statements as "The only good German is a dead German," a declaration made by Attorney-General Gordon Conant when he introduced the Russian emissaries to the Canadian Club, saying he is sure the three Russians would agree with him.[26]

When Conant made this comment, barely two years had passed since communist groups had once again been declared illegal in Canada in June of 1940. And people seemed to have forgotten that during the 1930s the Communist Party was illegal. Now those antagonisms were subsumed by the common cause of fighting the Nazis when they invaded Russia, and the attitude of the Western democracies toward the Soviets took a dramatic U-turn. The signs of these changes were hard to believe: Eaton's flew the hammer and sickle; *Time* magazine in the United States carried Stalin on its cover; and the National Film Board of Canada produced a pro-Russian film called *Our Northern Neighbour.*[27]

Such is the fickle nature of friends and enemies in the political sphere, for it would take only a few years before mass hysteria would swing in the opposite direction once more; then people would make the same heinous declarations about Soviets during the Cold War, a situation that caused Paraskeva much grief. For the time being, the Russians were the "good guys." *The Globe and Mail* reported that "Premier Hepburn took the arm of both the girl [sic] and man snipers as he walked between them to his offices after welcoming them to Queen's Park ... 'We feel humble in the presence of you great warriors ... Your presence here will surely stir up a greater war effort in this country so as to assist you to drive the Nazis from your homeland.'"[28]

A groundswell of goodwill in Canada gave rise to a national organization to help the Russian people. On 25 November 1942, the Canadian Aid to Russia Fund was launched with Paraskeva's friend and patron J. S. McLean as one of eight organizers among a group of businesspeople and professionals who incorporated the organization as a non-profit corporation.[29] There is no question that McLean's considerable time and effort spent on organizing this group had to do with his friendship with Paraskeva. She not only taught him about modern art but also educated him on matters related to the Soviet Union.[30]

McLean, who became the national chair of the committee, made the opening address at the meeting that launched the fund. Its stated purpose was to send medical supplies and other life necessities — blankets, clothing, garden seeds, for example — to Russia. However, McLean also hoped that "the spirit in which these gifts will be sent to Russia ... may help in breaking down the suspicions and distrusts of the last twenty years — ours toward them and theirs toward us."[31] This organization was national in scope, with committees collecting clothing and donations in other parts of the country: Vancouver, Victoria, Calgary, Medicine Hat, Winnipeg and Minden, Manitoba, for example, and even small towns such as Armstrong, British Columbia, with a population of only 989. The Canadian Red Cross approved of the Canadian Aid to Russia Fund and offered to work with the group. The goal was to raise one million dollars.

To answer inquiries about the organization, the fourteen-page document outlining the range of work of the Canadian Aid to Russia Fund included a statement dissociating itself from the Communist Party. It declared that the Communist Party had no part in the group's management, and had nothing to do with it.[32] Given her support for Communism, Paraskeva had to swallow her own opinions if she was to continue working with the organization. One can imagine that she and McLean might have had arguments over these statements on the Communist Party.

From the beginning of the war, Paraskeva could not help but feel a great deal of distress for her people. Distress compounded by guilt as she lived in complete comfort, with the only "hardships" being a rationing of certain foods like butter and meat, while the rest of her family in Leningrad were struggling to find enough to eat. If, indeed, they were even still alive — something she had no way of knowing. She would have read whatever she could find about how the people of Leningrad were coping, including *Soviet Russia Today*, an English-language magazine published in New York, which detailed the progress of the war month by month.

There were heroic stories of packing up and shipping by train to the Urals thousands of the treasures of the Hermitage Museum; of thousands of girls and children chopping down trees and cutting firewood to help heat the city; of women and children planting seeds and harvesting gardens to help feed the city; of drawing water through a hole in the ice of the Neva and carrying it home.[33]

There are reasons why the people of Leningrad endured such intense hardship. In writing of Russians' characterization in their literature, Virginia Woolf notes that they have no inclination to rebel against sorrow. They are at home with suffering and sadness, and do not attempt to conceal them. The Russian people are strong and determined because they have what Woolf calls a "living core." This living core has no end, she says, as it suffers and toils.[34]

Paraskeva, too, had that core. The information she gleaned about what was happening in Leningrad stirred her deeply and filled her with sadness. "Sometimes I feel I should be working side by side with the women of my homeland," she told a newspaper reporter. "Since that is not possible, I must help them in any way I can."[35] She decided that the way she could help was by working hard in her studio. As she told Charles Hill of the National Gallery many years later, "During the war I saw a beautiful sunset and I thought should I paint that? I saw a poster, something like 'Russia needs coal' and I thought, 'Forget about sunsets. Help your country with your talent, with your works.'"[36] Art was essential for Paraskeva during the war, and as a way of reaching out and helping. (How similar her response to that of Bethune's during the Spanish Civil War.) [37]

In December of 1942, to raise money for Russia, Paraskeva showed twenty-seven of her oil paintings and watercolours in her second solo exhibition at the Picture Loan Society, donating the proceeds from sales to the Canadian Aid for Russia Fund. Instead of the usual charge for expense in addition to a ten percent commission, when Douglas Duncan wrote up her statement at the end of the show he stated, "In admiration of your own gesture, the P.L.S. is very glad to waive any profit, considering the destination of the proceeds." Because of her exhibition, Paraskeva was able to give more than four hundred dollars to the fund; this outcome gave her great satisfaction. "If I can transform even some of my paintings into food, clothing and medicine for Russia, I shall be content," she said.[38]

McLean sent her a letter in February 1943 to acknowledge her contribution, and included an interim report.

I had dictated a letter to you, acknowledging your contribution to the Fund, but when it came to my desk, I felt I would rather send you a written note.

The Fund has gone well. I enclose a copy of the Interim report issued this week.

One man came to the Fund office, during the severest weather. His shoes were cracked and he had no socks. He brought in $5.00. I felt his was the largest contribution to the Fund received.

Next to his I would rank yours. But you don't like me to say this.
So all I'm saying is thank you.[39]

McLean was right. The Fund had done well, exceeding everyone's expectations. In a speech he gave at a "Tribute to Russia" Meeting in the United States at the Chicago Stadium on 22 June 1943, he said "that instead of one million, more than four million dollars was contributed — $3,100,000.00 in cash and one million in clothing. The cost of the campaign was less than two per cent."[40]

It seems McLean and Paraskeva kept in frequent contact during all the activity in support of Russia. "I promised to send you a note while I was away," McLean wrote in an undated letter when he had been in the wilds of the West, hunting and fishing. "When I got out I was thrilled to learn the story of the Stalingrad defence — what a marvellous courage and staying power the Russians are showing."[41] McLean's appreciation of the Russians' mettle, and the work of her friends and other Canadians in the cause of the Russians, would have meant a great deal to Paraskeva.

The visit from the three emissaries, and speaking with them in Russian, would also have given her a tremendous boost. She must have spent the following months thinking about using the event in her work, for later that winter she painted *Pavlichenko and her Comrades at Toronto City Hall* (Plate 28), and in the lower left corner with her signature she scratched into the paint this inscription: "February 21st, 1942 /25th Anniversary of the Heroic Red Army."[42]

According to Michael Pantazzi of the National Gallery of Canada, this painting, which Paraskeva exhibited in the Ontario Society of Artists annual show at the Art Gallery of Toronto in the spring of 1943, was well thought out. The vantage point is the high steps of Toronto's Old City Hall and looking south on Bay Street, the heart of capitalism in Canada. In the foreground of the painting is Pavlichenko on the right and, on the left, her comrade Nicolai Kravchenko. The two heroes are in profile smiling at each other. In front of them is the speaker with his arms raised high above his head, facing the crowd, so one is left guessing who that person might be. By giving us the perspective of standing behind the three prominent figures,

Paraskeva draws us into the picture as participants as we look down Bay Street at the huge crowds.

She is there, too, in the bottom right-hand corner, the woman in profile wearing a hat, an image cut out of another piece of canvas and collaged onto the painting. As Pantazzi pointed out, "She places herself as a participant of the event."[43] With the heroes in the foreground, down the street the space is filled with people and the military parade. The crowds fade in the distance where, at the foot of Bay Street, a streetcar crosses, Toronto's old "Red Rocket."

This painting is a "combination of history and aesthetic concerns that characterized Paraskeva Clark's career in which she brings the elements together," said Anna Hudson, an art professor at York University. Though this painting is not as strong as *Petroushka*, Hudson sees it as an inversion, or reversal, of that painting. The formal elements are similar in the use of the buildings. However, in the Pavlichenko painting the centre of the canvas is empty by comparison to *Petroushka* with the puppet stage in the centre.[44]

The similarity in the composition of the Pavlichenko painting to that of a lithograph by American artist James Rosenberg portraying Wall Street is striking. Rosenberg was among the American artists of the 1920s for whom the skyscraper was a symbol of the modern era.[45] His *Dies Irae* is how he imagined Wall Street on 29 October 1929, the day of the stock market crash, which sparked the Great Depression. Rosenberg's painting is ominous with the skyscrapers as the home of the engine of capitalism toppling and the people, looking like death itself, in the streets. In contrast, Paraskeva's Bay Street skyscrapers have a solidity about them and are standing so tall their tops shoot off the edge of the canvas; and the people are not delineated enough to show any features. However, both images are politically charged: Rosenberg's shows the fall of capitalism and Paraskeva's depicts two contradictory philosophies embodied in the Russians and Canadians under the towers of Bay Street.

The same month that Paraskeva painted *Pavlichenko*, her "Thoughts on Canadian Painting" appeared in *World Affairs*. The article could just as well have been called "My first eleven years in Canada" because she wrote about her progress as an artist since arriving in Toronto, along with her evaluation of Canadian art at the time. She admitted to still feeling somewhat embarrassed at being called an artist or painter, partly because she felt the enormous responsibility of those titles. And she talked of painting as "very hard work, a slow painful struggle with my awkward hands, my inner eyes lifted to the great heights while the eyes of my face were shedding tears of defeat." This comment may be melodramatic, but the intensity of the feeling was genuine. Some of her difficulty arose from having her heart pulled in two directions: to her past with her country now under threat, and yet living her present life.

Paraskeva made a case for artists' working to record the war and for co-operation of people around the world for peace. She believed that art could be a great force during wartime. "But it has to be, of course, an art depicting the human being, human action, in order to produce in people's minds and hearts the desired effect. And here is where Canadian Art in War-time should take its lesson." And she repeated the theme of her 1937 article: "In our overgrown 'pioneering' delight in our wilderness, we neglected the study of the 'pioneer', of the man [*sic*]. And we must not continue this sad mistake."[46] Perhaps as she looked at the painting around her, she felt the artists had not yet heard her message. And now in wartime, she felt what she had to say was even more urgent.

"400 Blows"

> *To give birth to a child, to raise him, and after eighteen*
> *precious years to see his talents developing, to see what*
> *rich fruit the tree will bear — and then to have it cut short ... !*[1]

Paraskeva had no way of knowing what was happening to her brother and sister in Leningrad during the war, whether they might be starving, barely surviving amid a pile of rubble, or even still alive. Nor did she know the fate of her other relatives, that her cousin Anastasia, a dear childhood friend, was shot by the Germans in 1942. Another cousin, Elena, who worked in Russia's secret service also died the same year as a result of her war work. Another cousin died of typhoid; still another died of starvation just six months before the war ended. Paraskeva would have wanted to know about all this but she could find out nothing; "bitter truth is better than a sweet lie" says a Russian proverb.[2] Her anxiety arose not only about the fate of her family, but also about the survival of the whole city of Leningrad. She tried to keep her anxiety at bay by working to generate support for Russia, mobilizing her friends to make donations.

Her family in Russia was not her only worry; as soon as the war began, she became anxious about Ben. In a 1939 letter to Douglas Duncan, she had expressed her fear that she could be harmed, but was even more frightened about what could happen to Ben. She had heard on the radio that the Russian army had

> passed the Polish border ... possible unpleasant suppositions rushed through my mind. Anything can happen and I really don't give a damm [*sic*] except for my kids — especially Ben. I think that Clarks will look after Clive, but I am not so sure how they'll act toward Ben. Douglas dear — please keep an eye on Ben if anything happens to me — help him if necessary in any way you would be able to. You probably think I am crazy but I think of Germany and how it all can turn out.[3]

In other words, the way different nationalities can turn on each other, depending on who would become the enemy, made her anxious. She told Duncan that she lay awake at night with her worries. This letter makes clear that Paraskeva's apprehension had to do with Ben as a "foreigner" — Italian and Russian.

In 1943, something did happen to Ben, though not what she had anticipated. He became seriously ill. Ben had been attending Central Technical School and was doing very good work in the art program there. People such as the Toronto artist Harold Town recognized that Ben had potential as an artist, and Paraskeva spoke of him with great pride. Yes, she herself was known as an artist, but would she someday also be known as the mother of the artist Ben Clark, just as the French artist Suzanne Valadon, whose work Paraskeva admired, had become known as the mother of the painter Maurice Utrillo? She wrote to Carl and Lillian Schaefer that Ben got a scholarship, and was fourth in his class, but only "because the whole class is very good," implying that he would have been first had there not been so much competition. He also received an honourable mention for a poster.[4]

Like other Canadians, the students and teachers at Central Tech were focused on doing what they could to contribute to the cause of the Allies. Students were assigned to design and paint posters for recruitment. Knowing how talented Ben was, his teachers kept pushing him to improve his poster designs. However, Ben was not a typical young Canadian student dispassionately doing his drawing and observing Europe from a distance. He was half-Italian and half-Russian; his two countries were enemies. That aspect of the war gave rise to inner conflict, and is likely one reason he had trouble creating posters that measured up to his record of producing exceptionally good work.

Besides making posters at school, Ben was also drafted into the Reserves and became part of the Signal Corps. Any young man who did not want to join up was made to feel like a "wimp" as the pressure to join the military was enormous.[5] "By mid-war 1943, the drive to get volunteers became very aggressive. Volunteering was like hitting the donkey with a crowbar over his head until he agreed. There was tremendous pressure from the army, from the public, from everybody to make these men volunteer for overseas service and the guys that wouldn't volunteer were called 'zombies.'"[6]

Clive, who was nine or ten years old at the time, remembers his older brother wearing a uniform, going to the armoury and marching in drills. Being in the Reserves meant the possibility of being sent overseas, an unpleasant thought for Ben, and an unbearable one for Paraskeva.[7] She had endured enough pain in her life; the prospect of losing Ben in this war that was devastating her country was unthinkable.

As for many Canadian families, the world conflict was a constant presence for the Clarks, especially for Paraskeva. According to Clive, when the war artists were home on leave, they would drop in at the Clarks' house to visit. They came in "roaring drunk, Schaefer and Miller Brittain, Will Ogilvie, Charles Comfort ..."[8] And the Clarks listened to the radio almost every evening. Clive remembers coming home from school, doing his homework, and when his dad came home for supper, he would turn on the radio and they sat listening to the reports on the war while Paraskeva was in the kitchen cooking. One radio serial called *L for Lanky*, Clive remembers, was a particularly vivid dramatization of the air war, in which a flight crew went out on raids in a Lancaster bomber, or "Lanky," which was the show "narrator."[9]

Life was focused on this war in which Italians were considered enemy aliens in Canada. With all the pressure about posters and joining the Reserves churning around inside Ben, given that he was both Italian and Russian, and had lived in France, he was torn apart: how could he possibly fight for either side?[10] This quandary was too much. Ben suffered a nervous breakdown in early April of 1943, experiencing delusions and hearing voices.

When he was taken to see a doctor, the diagnosis was schizophrenia. Paraskeva was crushed and extremely distressed as she saw the change in Ben's personality. He was given an honourable discharge from the Reserves, and his mother told him to wear his pin so people would not question him about not being in the military.[11] For all her nonchalance about people's opinions of her own behaviour, when it came to her son she did care what people thought of Ben and how they treated him.

As any parent would do, Paraskeva searched for possible reasons for Ben's illness, trying to find a shred of understanding. According to Clive, she questioned herself, likely thinking it was her fault, something in her background, possibly the medication she took when she was young. She also thought about how Ben had lost his father; she believed that episode could have affected her son so profoundly that it precipitated his illness. This is what she told her friends: as she stood on the shore of the Neva River holding three-month-old Ben, such despair at her husband's drowning changed her body chemistry and Ben must have sensed it all. Whether or not her perception was true, the horror of Oreste's drowning was still in her voice, even in her seventies.[12]

Paraskeva also wondered whether heredity was a factor. The Allegris, she thought, had "a strain of abnormality in the family." Her evidence was that one of Oreste's sisters was mentally ill.[13] In the midst of all her probing, Paraskeva knew that the immediate question was what she could do for Ben, and what treatment he should have.

In 1943, there was much less understanding of mental illness, and it carried a profound stigma. Many people thought it was a sign of moral weakness or poor character. Because of the behaviour of the mentally ill, people regarded them as troublemakers and offenders. A study of Canadian psychiatric services describes these most extreme attitudes in society: "Mental illness ... is all too often considered a crime to be punished, a sin to be expiated, a possessing demon to be exorcised, a disgrace to be hushed up, a personality weakness to be deplored or a welfare problem to be handled as cheaply as possible."[14] Paraskeva, besides coping with her own agony, had to deal with other people's attitudes.

If the attitudes were extreme, so were the treatments. In the first place, the environment of a mental hospital was "abominable." For schizophrenia, "insulin coma therapy" and electroshock were the two most popular methods of treatment by the early 1940s. A study conducted in 1944 showed that electroshock was not effective for schizophrenia; nevertheless, it continued to be used "indiscriminately," even though the study reported that it "might be 'harmful in cases diagnosed schizophrenia.'"[15] The Clarks searched for the best institution and chose Surrey Place, the Toronto Psychiatric Hospital just north of College Street. Surrey Place as a teaching hospital was better than most. Even so, the treatments there were not very different from other hospitals.

Seeing the change in Ben and thinking about him in hospital being given electroshock was distressing for the whole family. Clive remembers that the summer of 1943 he was sent off to summer camp, and speculates that his parents were trying to shield him from the distress of his older brother's illness. "I suspect they had a concern about how I would deal with all this so they in subtle ways would try to minimize my involvement." Clive does not recall feeling any shame about Ben, but knew his illness simply as a tragic reality that became part of their family that year.[16]

Clive has a clear understanding of how Ben's illness affected Paraskeva. "It's amazing she survived to do anything," he said. "It sucks all the life out of you as a mother to have your son fall apart who was so brilliant and bright and good looking and everything else and [becoming] virtually one hundred percent dependent."[17] Though Clive's description of the effect of Ben's illness seems accurate, and Paraskeva had stopped painting when Ben became ill, about two months after his diagnosis she had completed a new painting, *In a Toronto Street Car*. That she was able to paint at all indicates how forceful was her desire to do something about the plight of Leningrad. Her painting is a scene of streetcar passengers smiling and talking to one another about the Toronto newspaper headlines, "Reds Break Siege of Leningrad."

It didn't really matter that Paraskeva's painted headlines were not accurate. The siege did not actually end until January 1944, but Russian troops had scored a major victory in which 13,000 Germans were killed and 1,250 taken prisoner.[18] Every sign, no matter how small, that the city would endure gave the citizens of Leningrad hope. They celebrated this victory without knowing that the worst was yet to come.

During the following dark days in the winter of 1943–1944, Leningrad City Council was redesigning the city and planning for the future even though it was still besieged. In Canada — a world away from Leningrad — Torontonians joined in every sign of hope. Keeping that hope alive was the intent of a group that formed in 1942 and incorporated in 1943, the Writers', Broadcasters' and Artists' War Council. A four-page document outlined the group's purposes and ideas for ways artists, writers, and broadcasters could join together to educate the public on issues related to the war, and through the universal language of art, offer solidarity and understanding. The group organized a number of projects, among them, painting a mural in Toronto's Union Station and holding an exhibition of sketches and paintings created in war plants, as well as a show of war posters at the Art Gallery of Toronto. They also sent a collection of Canadian paintings to Leningrad as a gesture of friendship and goodwill.[19]

Paraskeva's *In a Toronto Street Car* was among the selections of Canadian books, music, and paintings that were sent. Paintings by other artists depicted a variety of subjects related to the war; some were by children from the Saturday morning art classes at the Art Gallery of Toronto, as well as classes for Winnipeg children whose families had come from Ukraine. Several of the children painted a scene of caravans of vehicles carrying supplies to Leningrad across the ice on Lake Ladoga. Artist Isabelle Chestnut Reid submitted a stylized painting of women carrying on with their daily life during the war, washing clothes at holes in the river ice because the city's water system was not functioning.

The paintings that would be going to Russia were shown in an exhibition in Toronto at the Fine Arts Gallery at Eaton's College Street that June. At the opening of the exhibition, the paintings were presented to the Soviet minister to Canada, the Honourable Feodor Gousev.[20] More than a year later, the *Toronto Star* reported that the forty paintings were exhibited in Moscow and drew large crowds. Accepting the paintings for the city of Leningrad, V. Serov said, "One proof of the persistent friendship of Canada is this gift of paintings, books and music. We Leningrad artists are particularly touched by this attention. We had to work despite hunger and cold. We worked in the feeble light of tiny kerosene wicks. We worked at night while enemy bombs were raining on our city."[21] This was an article that Paraskeva clipped and kept all her life. That one of her paintings of a scene in Toronto would hang in Moscow and Leningrad must have given her enormous satisfaction.[22]

Another group was formed in early summer of 1943, the National Council for Canadian-Soviet Friendship, with the purpose of fostering friendly relations between the people of the two countries. The public launch of the organization, announced days in advance in Toronto newspapers, was held at Maple Leaf Gardens in Toronto on 22 June. The group did not charge for tickets, but announced that donations would be accepted for the work of the organization. Between fifteen thousand and seventeen thousand people attended; more came, but even with extra seats being added, many could not get in.[23]

Prime Minister Mackenzie King chaired the meeting, and spoke of how Russia and Canada — neighbours — are similar in their diverse populations. The rally, which had the support of dozens of political and religious leaders, featured a four-hundred-voice United Nations choir singing national anthems and marching songs. When the anthem of the USSR, "The International," was sung, many people rose to their feet, something they would not have dreamed of doing a few years earlier. The next day, the newspaper reported the Russian salute as "thrilling," with tributes that left many teary-eyed.

Paraskeva's name was missing from the articles mentioning those who participated. This could only have been because she was preoccupied with Ben and could not help with the event. However, by the fall when Ben was home from the hospital and seemed to be recovering, she again took on more outside responsibilities. She was on the Council's National Arts Committee, chaired by Group of Seven artist A.Y. Jackson.[24]

When the Second Congress of the National Council for Canadian-Soviet Friendship met in Toronto's Royal York Hotel in mid-November, Paraskeva was on an arts panel. She also organized a display of photographs on Russia, and Russian crafts and art. Judging by her handwritten list of 221 items, she spent a great deal of time and energy on this project. For the documents in the exhibit, she wrote out captions in English. Her photo appeared in the Toronto newspapers, along with the other participants, among them John

Grierson, then head of the National Film Board of Canada, who led a discussion on the art of cinema.[25]

While Paraskeva was preoccupied with the war, she painted one of her most perplexing still lifes, an oil she called *Deck of Cards* (1943)[26]. On a small round table, she placed a pineapple, two lemons, a blue and white teapot, and a deck of cards. The ace of hearts is about to slide off the table directly above a pair of red sling pumps; the ace of clubs has already fallen to the royal blue rug. Why these particular objects? She would have argued that each thing is interesting in itself for its form, and that is true, but what is the relationship between, for example, lemons, a deck of cards, and shoes?

The band around the edge of the round table holds the elements of the painting together in the centre, even though the objects themselves are incongruous, even bizarre. The cards sliding off the table lead one's attention to the red shoes and then the eye follows left to the ace of clubs on the floor. It's the two high-scoring cards that Paraskeva is losing, symbolizing her feeling of loss — loss of her son, loss of her country, loss of her brother and sister.

AFTER RETURNING HOME from Surrey Place on probation in September, Ben was discharged the following February; it seemed, for the time being at least, he had made a recovery. However, Paraskeva must have sensed that his difficulties were not over and became reluctant to be separated from Ben for long periods; vacations were planned according to whether Ben could participate. "It's complicated — woman's life ... and there's so much involved and once you have a child, you're just forever with him. It's just there, and particularly when you have a child who at twenty becomes schizophrenic. I'm a mother ... it has nothing to do with any decision."[27]

Ben also complicated her life by keeping her linked to the Allegris, despite being separated by the Atlantic Ocean. During the war, the number of letters from Oreste Allegri increased, particularly throughout 1944 and 1945.[28] By then Ben's grandfather was nearly eighty years old, and was thinking back over his long life. He wrote of the misfortunes he experienced in both wars and his grief over his family disasters. Certainly, he had in mind his daughter's mental illness and his son's death and the death of his wife in 1937. Now, sliding deeper into his old age, he had little hope of ever seeing an end to his troubles because food was scarce and new clothing nearly impossible to find, except through the black market with prices so exorbitant he could not possibly buy anything. To make his point about his difficulties, he listed the cost of clothing: a pair of socks more than a hundred francs; a shirt twelve hundred to three thousand francs; a man's suit was twenty to twenty-five thousand francs. Allegri, when he could find work with the ballet or the opera, was being paid ten thousand francs a month.

Besides all this, his son Paul, who had been Paraskeva's lover in Chatou, was in the French army in Bavaria and Allegri never knew when he would see him again. Telling Paraskeva all this would have been like placing a heavy stone on her shoulders. Apparently, Paraskeva did not write to Allegri about Ben's illness until two years after his diagnosis. Most likely, she hoped he would make a complete recovery, in which case there would be no need to tell his grandfather about it. However, it was not to be. Allegri wrote that he was deeply saddened by the news, and after his first response he frequently inquired about how Ben was doing. In response to a letter in which Paraskeva wrote about her despair and anxiety over Ben, he tried to make her feel better by telling her there was a great defect in all the Allegris: laziness. Then he quoted the French saying that "Laziness is the mother of all defects." However, he himself escaped from that defect, he said, because the difficult situation of his family meant that he had to work hard to support everyone. He assured Paraskeva, however, that this defect in Ben would disappear.

He suggested that Ben come for a visit because Paris was a good place for young men to put their lives onto a better footing. As a way of trying to persuade the Clarks to send Ben to him, Allegri told the story of two young men — one a Canadian — who had not been doing well at all but came to Paris and began thriving and making dramatic changes in their lives. Allegri was positive the city would have the same effect on Ben. Although Allegri had good intentions in his "diagnosis" of Ben's problems and what to do about them, his comments would have done nothing to alleviate Paraskeva's distress over Ben's health. As for "laziness," she would have thought that ridiculous because Ben had certainly not been lazy. Paraskeva would not have even considered allowing Ben to travel to Paris.

It is unfortunate that her letters to Allegri have not survived. However, his correspondence suggests that she wrote to him frequently during the war, which would have taken time away from her painting. As she "listened" to his difficulties, she also wrote of her frustrations of not having enough time to paint and about not being able to express on canvas all she saw with her internal eyes. In an effort to console her, Allegri responded that all artists feel the same. But he seems to have had little sympathy for her complaint about housework eroding her time for painting; he asked that in between, in a small moment of leisure, she write to him.

Given that she had a comfortable life, and that he had helped her out when she was desperate twenty years earlier, she could not refuse his requests for letters and parcels, even though his need for her attention robbed her of precious time to paint. It was all part of what she considered to be a "complicated family life."[28] She and Philip were extremely generous to Allegri. In one of his letters, he thanked them profusely for sending him a thousand francs, the equivalent of about forty Canadian dollars at that time. The Clarks also sent packages of food: butter, cheese, conserves, meat, bacon, tea, coffee, sugar, and chocolate. Allegri requested that they continue to send tea, coffee, and sugar regularly.

By fall of 1945, Allegri was desperate. Paraskeva must have asked her friend Will Ogilvie, in London working as a war artist, to help him, because Allegri wrote to Paraskeva that Ogilvie sent him underwear, a vest, and a scarf. Around the same time, the Clarks sent Allegri a suit, shirts, a sweater, gloves, and socks, among other things. Allegri responded that there were no words to convey his profound feeling of thanks to them. He continued making requests, even as late as 1950 when he asked Paraskeva to encourage his contacts in New York to pay him money he felt they owed. This was one request that Paraskeva did not take up.

BEN'S ILLNESS DEEPENED his mother's feeling of having primary responsibility for him even though Philip loved Ben and was a father to him. Paraskeva invested a great deal of energy in her sense of claim on Ben, became protective and worried over him, diverting her energy away from painting as she tried to find ways he could use his time. He had graduated from the art program at Central Technical School and then took courses at the Ontario College of Art. Paraskeva tried to help him find jobs where he could use his talents. She still saw him as a gifted artist who could do productive work if he had the right environment. However, she could not deny that Ben's illness shattered his abilities, for she counted his illness as yet another in her long list of hardships. She saw herself as having so many troubles it reminded her of the François Truffaut movie, *400 Blows*. At the end of this film, the main character is caught between land and sea, between the past and the future. This must have been how Paraskeva felt as she looked back trying to understand what happened to Ben, and forward to ... she did not know what.

In an attempt to keep her sanity, she poured her frustrations and sorrows into developing and expanding her garden, ferociously digging and carefully planting. Gardening would become her lifesaver in a way that painting could not because her studio work demanded a presence of mind, a psychic space of interior calm that was lacking in times of distress. Gardening became for her an alternative source of what artists need: "time alone with oneself when reflection, the generation of ideas, and the production of the work are carried forward."[29] The garden also gave her and Philip a lovely place for summertime parties that their friends still remembered fifty years later.

Like many women with similar responsibilities, Paraskeva paid a high price for her domestic situation, and the demands Ben placed on her. Her life — and of even greater consequence, her energy — was divided into "two unequal parts."[30] The mother and wife aspect always took precedence; she fitted painting into her days as best she could.

During her summer holidays with the family, when she had many opportunities to paint scenes with no sign of human habitation, Paraskeva frequently painted landscapes that included buildings and figures, an indication of her interest in human elements. One such painting is *Evening After Rain* (1946) (Plate 29), which might have been a scene from one of the trips to Quebec. The strength of this work lies in the contrast of the small figures with the dominant blue form, the house in the upper half of the painting and reflected in the water. The figures, which appear to be women, close together in conversation on the veranda in the middle ground, along with the man straining in his efforts to pull the horse up the hill, animate the composition anchored by the large weathered tree remnants in the foreground in the water. The choice of subdued colours helps to set the mood of quiet in the evening after a day of rain, a picture with a feeling of an era long past — it was painted more than sixty years ago.

Her 1945 landscape of Ben painted from the back as he sits on a rock along a stream uses a different approach to figures in the landscape (Plate 30). Ben's figure looms in the immediate foreground with the rather chaotic rendering of the rocks, stream, and bushes extending out away from him in the distance. This watercolour gives the impression of the large figure as master of all that is visible beyond him as he sits with his massive torso, large, angular legs and spindly right arm all reflecting Cubist and Cézanne influences.

Ben stands as a symbol for what her son became for her, the pivotal point around which her life would revolve for the rest of her days, long after he was no more a child, nor an adolescent, according to his years.

The Artist as War Worker

The grave mood that comes over one when one knows: there is a war,
and one cannot hold on to any illusions anymore. Nothing is real
but the frightfulness of this state, which we almost grow used to.
In such times it seems so stupid that boys must go to war. The
whole thing is so ghastly and insane.[1]

The New Year finally brought some better news for Paraskeva as she scanned newspaper headlines. The siege of Leningrad ended on 17 January 1944 with red, white, and blue rockets streaming over the city. This salute marked the end of the longest siege of a city in modern history, 880 days, and the news that it was over spread quickly around the world.[2]

Paraskeva returned to one of her most cherished childhood memories as the subject of a painting she called *Public Bath — Leningrad* (1944) (Plate 32). Her working drawing for the bathhouse painting shows how methodical she was: she drew a grid and then worked up the sketch in watercolour, ink, and graphite.[3] She painted her bathhouse memories several times, and in this watercolour, the mother in the painting holds her young girl by the hand, a child being rude as she passes a stooping woman. Twenty years later using the same subject in oil, the little girl is behaving properly.

The subject Paraskeva chose, female nudes at their bath, has been a part of art history for hundreds of years; similarly, in Russia, the public bathhouse has

been part of the cultural history for centuries. As a child, Paraskeva regularly
went to the bathhouse with her mother and sister. These pleasant excursions
with only women and children, away from daily routine, provided a break from
the pressures of the hard life in Russia.

In the large bathhouses, "One proceeded from a steam room, where birch
switches were provided for people to use on their backs and legs, to a shower
room, a scrubbing room (in the more expensive variety there were scrubbers
to do the work for you), a pool, and finally a dressing room."[4]

Paraskeva's painting of the bathhouse is reminiscent of a painting by Kuzma
Petrov-Vodkin. His *Morning Bathers* (1917) depicts a female nude holding the
hand of a child in much the same manner as that of the dominant figure in
Paraskeva's painting. However, as Mary MacLachlan pointed out:

> Paraskeva's statuesque and graceful mother figure ... is psychologically
> set apart from the other women in the composition. Goddess-like, she
> hovers between the space of the picture, which is all bustle and chatter,
> and the space of the spectator; she is poised on the threshold, a symbol
> of womanhood and motherhood. In this respect, more than in actual
> form, do Paraskeva's figures resemble the mother/child group in Petrov-
> Vodkin's painting. Paraskeva, however, has more sense of humour than
> her teacher, and while his mother figure holds the hand of a shy, gentle
> boy-child, Paraskeva's mother hangs onto a rather rude little girl straining
> to get away.[5]

The dominance of this mother figure symbolizes Paraskeva's preoccupation
with maternity and the central responsibility of women in the family. She never
let go of speaking about the hold of that reality on women.

Paraskeva's sense of responsibility to Russia continued to dominate her life,
but she managed to enter her paintings in a number of shows during the war.
Her *Trout* (1940) was selected by Yale University for an exhibition, *Canadian
Art 1760–1943*, that spring.[6] When she received a letter from Harry Orr
McCurry of the National Gallery in May saying he was sending a cheque
for the self-portrait on which she had affixed the "Salute to Russia" concert
program, Paraskeva was ecstatic. She replied:

It brought me from the deepest of depressions brought on by the sight of my painting in the currant [*sic*] shows where it seemed to me so dull and boring beside all the daring bright northern painting of my colleagues.

The fact that National Gallery acquired some of my portrait work is particularly significant to me and gives me all the courage to attack again and again that subject.[7]

In fact, it set a fire under Paraskeva, so much so that less than a month after she sent McCurry her letter she began work on a portrait of her friend Murray Adaskin (Plate 31), who had played in an orchestra during the war that provided music for radio dramas on the Canadian Broadcasting Corporation (CBC). The painting of Adaskin is a particularly fine portrait of a musician. Adaskin himself said he had seen many portraits of musicians, and it would be impossible for a violinist to play in the way that many artists positioned the hands. This was not the case in Paraskeva's portrait of him. "Those are marvellous hands," he said, "the way she's got that bow: it could be swung into position instantly, and the hand, the way it's around the violin is absolute perfection. If I didn't know this portrait, I'd say, 'Well, this person was a professional violinist, no question about it.'"[8] That Paraskeva could paint the position of the violinist's hands so accurately demonstrated her acute powers of observation.

Though the National Gallery purchase gave her a burst of energy to begin Murray's portrait, Paraskeva was still focused on work related to the war; she did not complete his portrait until the following year.

McCurry's letter about the purchase of the concert-program portrait included an invitation to work on two war-related projects. One was the Silk Screen Project, initiated to boost the morale of troops. The idea was that if soldiers overseas had images of the Canadian landscape hanging in their barracks and mess halls, they would be inspired and feel good about the cause for which they were fighting. Military personnel in camps in Canada also needed something to relieve their bleak environment.

In consultation with A.Y. Jackson, H. O. McCurry invited artists to create images that would work well for the process of silkscreen printing. The prints could be reproduced in quantities that were needed and could easily be shipped, which made this particular medium the most suitable. The printing was done by Sampson-Matthews under the supervision of the artist A. J. Casson, who was the company's artistic director. McCurry told Paraskeva, "Several sets have been asked for to be sent to Russia."⁹ McCurry knew what he was doing in telling Paraskeva that prints would be going to Russia; he knew she would not be able to pass up the opportunity, as is clear from her reply to McCurry.

> I am very grateful too for suggesting to get busy on a silk screen, — truly — I would be feeling unhappy to have missed opportunity (without trying) to have my work in the collection going to Russia ...
>
> I had difficulty to start working on it having very little time, and mainly no subject matter as I didn't go out of Toronto for the last three summers.
>
> However — after your letter — I feel ready to start anything. I phoned A.Y. for advice. He told me to go for a week to country and thus get some fresh material for some sketches for s. screen. Well — here I am — on a farm in Caledon country ...¹⁰

It seems to have been the assumption that the silk-screens would be landscapes. This is not surprising. In the 1930s, the National Gallery of Canada had initiated an educational project, reproducing works from the gallery collection for use in schools. These were primarily landscapes from central Canada painted before 1930 by male artists: the idea held that Canadian nationalism was bound up in portraying nature.¹¹

As art historian Joyce Zemans has pointed out, these reproductions became part of nation building and played a dominant role in establishing "a Canadian art canon whose iconography would dominate the Canadian psyche for more than half a century."¹² The Silk Screen Project of the 1940s became an extension of what had begun in the thirties. In fact, in the early forties the National Gallery and the CBC joined in an educational venture called *Young Canada Listens*, which was aired from 1945 to 1947. Were the National Gallery and the CBC surprised at the astuteness of their knowledgeable listeners? The writer of one letter of response thought the discussion of J. W. Morrice's painting *The Ferry* was simple-minded because there was no mention of Impressionism or

Post-Impressionism. And a response from an art instructor from Neepawa Public School in Manitoba said her students "would like to hear some stories about Canada's Women artists."[13] That kind of comment would have pleased Paraskeva.

For the Silk Screen Project, artists from different parts of the country were solicited, including women. Landscapes still dominated the nine thousand prints that were sent to many service headquarters in Britain — J. S. McLean, Paraskeva's patron, subsidized two thousand prints for the British army[14] — North Africa, the Middle East, and Gibraltar. Some artists' submissions were rejected if there was the slightest chance of offending someone. For example, Ann Savage's *Sunflowers* was turned down because an official thought there was an outhouse in the painting. And Fritz Brandtner's *Potato Pickers* was also rejected because it did not depict a "true" Canadian,[15] whatever that was.

In the end, "The project was so popular that it was extended after the war, and the prints distributed in schools, and community centres."[16] Thus, the National Gallery continued to promote a nationalism based on the Canadian landscape, the iconography of the Group of Seven.

Paraskeva Clark, the proponent of painting the human situation, contributed to this nation-building exercise. Her *Caledon Farm* (1945) is an overview of a farm with its buildings, a few cows, some sheep, a tractor, and several farm workers, with southern Ontario's Caledon hills in the distance, in her typical colour palette of muted greens and umber along with some soft reds. This was the last print in the series created for the benefit of military personnel.

The second invitation from McCurry for Paraskeva to consider was even more important than the Silk Screen Project. In a handwritten note, McCurry said he put Paraskeva on the "R.C.A.F. artists list but do not know if the minister will agree to appoint a woman artist!!"[17] She responded:

The adventure would be great and would've done lot of good to my painting — but — on the other hand — I was worried about my family.

Forgive me please of taking so much of your time and please believe me that I feel a great honour Canada gave to a Russian that came here 13 years ago — so utterly unsuspecting it might be waiting for her.

Thank you for everything — dear Mr. McCurry — and please accept my kindest regards.[18]

Hardly even thinking about the idea, Paraskeva knew immediately that she could not leave her family — especially Ben and her big house in Rosedale — for months to join the air force to paint. She told McCurry she had only two or three hours a day away from housework for painting.

Canada had led the way in appointing artists to record the fighting during World War I, but this was not the case in World War II because the Department of National Defence was reluctant to spend public money on art. In contrast, artists' organizations and the National Gallery were enthusiastic about the idea. Certainly, the artists at the conference in Kingston in June of 1941 were in favour. It was not until the fall of 1942 that an Order-in-Council authorized the program, and Cabinet approval came at the beginning of 1943. A number of the Clarks' friends — Charles Comfort, A. Y. Jackson, Will Ogilvie — joined up and were assigned to work as war artists. At the point when the art program was in full swing, thirty artists participated.[19]

It is not surprising, then, that Paraskeva wanted to be included even if she could not go overseas. Thanks to McCurry, she had an opportunity. The National Gallery commissioned her to paint the activities of the Women's Division (WDs) of the Royal Canadian Air Force (RCAF). Paraskeva's friend Pegi Nicol MacLeod had a similar assignment in Ottawa, and since she was working full time, she was being paid the same rate as other war artists.

McCurry understood that Paraskeva's situation was different from Pegi's. "We will pay for your work on whatever basis you wish, either time or by individual canvas ... You may wish to give only part time," he told her, "but let us know and we will make some satisfactory arrangement. When you have finished with the W.D.'s you can go on to the Wrens [Women's Royal Naval Service] or the CWAC's [Canadian Women's Army Corp] if you wish." He gave her a broad choice of what to paint, but he did say he wanted something of "an inspirational nature," rather than more sketches of girls working in kitchens and offices.[20]

McCurry might have wanted Paraskeva to paint something other than women working in these traditional jobs, but that is where the majority of them were assigned in both the armed forces and the naval services. Most of the women, if they were not doing clerical work, were cooks, telephone operators, canteen helpers, or mess waiters. Many of those who enlisted had envisioned exciting assignments overseas, but only one in nine served outside their country, and even then, they usually did the type of work thought suitable for women — similar to the work they did at home.

The traditional stereotypes of men's and women's roles held fast during the war, which is not surprising since even the women's branches were under the command of a male-dominated bureaucracy.[21] Women's war activities were just a temporary break in their work environment; once the war was over, they were expected to slide into place again and be content to stay at home in traditional roles. During the war, the media depicted women active in helping the war effort, but after 1945, it was back to vacuum cleaners and kitchens.

Given what women actually did during the war, Paraskeva realized that this commission would offer her a big challenge. She corresponded with McCurry about the job throughout the summer and until the end of the year. They were both putting some effort into finding ideas for paintings to compensate for the lack of drama in the work of women in the RCAF. McCurry was reaching: "What I should like to see is something that will signalize the great human advance which has been made in the English speaking world at all events by the admission of women to the fighting forces."[22] Paraskeva likely scoffed when she read this comment. How could a woman working in a mess hall or in an office equal anything as grand as a "great human advance"? It was especially ludicrous beside the memory of "girl sniper" Lyudmila Pavlichenko.

In early January 1945, Paraskeva arranged to have someone take care of her Rosedale household for a week. McCurry had contacted the army and navy to secure the necessary letters of introduction for her, stating clearly that she was working for the National Gallery of Canada. She spent the week in Trenton at an RCAF training base about 175 kilometres east of Toronto. There she stayed in a house with the senior officer of the Women's Division and ate in the officers' mess. She felt out of place, but it took her into a world outside her own and gave her a complete break from her regular family routine.

Paraskeva was pleased to have the assignment, and was determined to scrape up something dramatic to paint. She told McCurry she had found five or six subject areas she wanted to consider: "girls folding parashutes [*sic*]"; "Quaickers — girls at wireless"; "girls in the 'dope' shop ... jobs with repair of parts and applying paint with air-gun"; "girls working on the motor in the hanger"; "girls painting on the plain [*sic*] and putting patches on the plane in the hanger [*sic*]."[23] These were the activities she sketched in Trenton to be worked up for paintings when she returned home.

Right after she returned from Trenton, she had to prepare a lecture on Russian art scheduled at the Women's Canadian Club in Parry Sound. "Imagine them being interested in Russian Art," she told McCurry. "I realized they don't know much about their own Canadian art but they are so keen about everything Russian that it was inspiring to go there."[24]

Later in the winter, Paraskeva arranged to go to Ottawa for a few days for a reception in celebration of the twenty-seventh anniversary of the Red Army. She stayed with her old friends, Graham and Joan McInnes. While she was in Ottawa, she met with McCurry to talk about the problems she was encountering with her war paintings. She wanted to visit the gallery as well, and see "many other highly attractive points and people in Ottawa."[25]

By the end of March, Paraskeva had finished her first canvas for her commission, *Bedtime Story*, which she described as somewhat humorous in nature, "6 women in house coats — brushing hair — buttons — shoes (RCAF uniforms) in the evening hour."[26] As it turned out, she felt ambivalent about this new painting, and even though she sent it to McCurry by the end of March because he wanted to take the payment from his current budget, she said she might want to take back *Bedtime Story* later when she had time to paint a better one. McCurry agreed.

That same month Paraskeva also went to Galt, Ontario, for two days on the training ship, *HMCS Conestoga*, an experience she felt was exciting. There she found women who were not doing domestic work, and she would have sensed their exhilaration with living on the ship. She came home with more ideas for paintings.

Paraskeva wrote to McCurry to tell him about her progress, and at the end of her letter said how exciting it had been to have lunch with him and

Mrs McCurry when she was in Ottawa. It is obvious from her letters that Paraskeva liked McCurry; and why wouldn't she? He appreciated her work and gave her opportunities that helped her career. She loved the recognition. However, she couldn't resist toying with him and told him, "I would like to paint a portrait of you — I am intrigued with the strange eyes you have — tell that to your wife — I am sure she agrees — about the eyes."[27] In a subsequent letter, McCurry seemed nonplussed at the idea and suggested postponing doing the portrait. Paraskeva replied that the "talk about your portrait — it was really a joke — although at heart I had this wistful desire all that time — but I know it is impossible."[28]

Paraskeva's "wistful desire" was not just of that time and place. It was a quality Murray Adaskin sensed from the moment he first met her. "I just feel I'd like to take her into my arms and hug her ... I always felt that way about her right from the early days. You just feel that you almost want to mother her into cheering her up, somehow."[29] It's the kind of inner longing originating from personal loss; her loss of her great love in 1923 had not left her, the kind of experience that pushed its way up through whatever was happening in her life.

She continued in her discontent with *Bedtime Story* and became flustered about getting something to McCurry by the end of March, the closing of the gallery's fiscal year. She packed it up and sent it, along with another unfinished painting, so he would have something in hand for which to pay her, with the understanding that he would return the paintings so she could finish them or replace them with something better. As it turned out, not only did she take back *Bedtime Story*, but later on she thought it was so bad that possibly she destroyed it, because it no longer exists.

Paraskeva was extremely conscientious about trying to do things the way McCurry asked, to the point of being overly scrupulous. She even sent him a tally of the number of hours she had worked on the paintings. He replied that he had not meant that she should give an hourly record because he did not intend to pay her "like a carpenter!"[30]

When $550 arrived from McCurry, she said it was the biggest cheque she ever received. She told him that being paid for the paintings put a "big responsibility on my shoulders — too. And my poor old shoulders begin to creek [*sic*]. But I'll be coragious [*sic*] ..." By then Paraskeva had her own personal bank account where she deposited her income when she sold a painting. It made her a little less dependent on Philip because with her own money she bought art supplies or perhaps a dress.[31]

By mid-May, Paraskeva sent McCurry *Maintenance Jobs in the Hangar* (Plate 35), which she completed on the first day of the month. She worried over how long these paintings were taking, that she wouldn't be finished before the war was over. In fact, the Germans had surrendered just a few days before she wrote her letter on 11 May 1945. For her the war was over. "Victory is here," she wrote. "Isn't it too late with war paintings — I guess it's a stupid question but my slowness is very depressing — but under the conditions of my life — I have very little hope for improvement."[32]

To add to her frustration, McCurry was holding out for something dramatic, an outdoor scene perhaps. She reminded him that he had said he wanted something that would mark the great development of the inclusion of women in the armed forces. And then she followed with a long explanation of her thoughts on the subject of painting women in the war, saying she wanted him to think of her letter as written to him personally and not to the Director of the National Gallery. What she told him is worth quoting at length because it shows that she saw the contradictions of the situation: fitting together her idea of where the drama could be found with the commission of recording women's war work. The incongruities of the situation made her task difficult.

I argued the point of dramatic subject before, but after having some personal experience with life and activities of the Women's Divisions in the R.C.A.F. or Wrens, I lost all hope to see "any drama" there. But I found exciting enough the fact that in some activities — women performed the jobs, previously done by men and thus-released (perhaps) some men for fighting duties or for war industries. I thought that portraying some of such activities in their authentic setting might present a worthy subject for war record ...

You see I feel that dramatic subject in Canadian Womens life is not among C.W.A.C. but among millions [of] women, who stayed in their homes, carrying on some jobs, some responsibilities plus their usual home duties, — with their hearts full of constant pain and longing and sorrow for their men going fighting. Being C.W.A.C. was the easiest thing to do, the most pleasant. Throwing off the eternal chores and drudgery of woman's life — women entered a regulated orderly life, with one duty set upon each, for so many hours each day, with the glory and glamour of uniform to top it! The jobs — mostly clerical, or as servants, cooks. All that is important but where is the drama? We had ... no women in fighting planes, or in command of ships ... If I see a dramatic subject here in Toronto, it is like this: group of 3 or 4 legless young soldiers, laughing and joking, pushing along in their wheel chairs with few others hop[p]ing beside on crutches. "A promenade" — a narrow crooked window in the second storey of a slum house, elaborately decorated with flags and inscription:"Welcome Home Son" such a home! — I see a drama in a scene when Toronto mair [mayor] proudly and happily presents a mesely [*sic*] \$200 Victory Bond to the only Toronto V.C. winner — But National Gallery wouldn't want such War Records and I am not sure that I would be able to put on canvas the drama and pathos of such subjects.[33]

This letter to McCurry tells us how clearly Paraskeva was able to see through situations that most people took at face value. She used her acute powers of observation not only when she painted but also when she looked at real-life situations to see beneath the obvious, as though she could see through the surface of the ground to the roots. She understood the interior drama in people who experienced pain and loss during the war.

She did succeed in finding pictorial drama for *Maintenance Jobs in the Hangar* (1945) (Plate 35), painting women doing work usually assigned to men. Perhaps Paraskeva had seen Edwin Holgate's painting with a similar subject matter (*Grooming a Spitfire*, c. 1943). In Holgate's painting, the Spitfire is the dominant form; the workers, who are men, seem mere accessories. In *Maintenance Jobs in the Hangar*, the women making repairs are the most important elements in the picture.

The composition of Paraskeva's painting succeeds in depicting an energetic seriousness about the tasks of the three women dressed in chartreuse-coloured coveralls in three different postures at work on bright yellow planes or plane parts. The woman in the foreground leans into her scrubbing or sanding, the lines of her body leading the eye of the viewer to her right arm, the focus of her energy. Behind her, the sweep of a plane's wing catches the viewer's eye, intercepted by the propeller close to where another woman is working as she leans in close to the base of the propeller. A third woman in the right-hand side of the painting works on the end of a wing, the plane itself off the canvas.

The woman working by the propeller is the figure featured on a one-hundred dollar fourteen-karat gold Canadian coin minted in 1994, eight years after Paraskeva's death, and circulated worldwide. How proud Paraskeva would have been, had she known, especially since these war paintings were so difficult for her. It would have been another indication to her that Canada claimed this Russian artist as one of its own.

During the summer of 1945, Paraskeva and her family went for a holiday in Tadoussac, Quebec, on the North Shore of the St. Lawrence River, and to the nearby Gaspé Peninsula. From that summer vacation she worked up at least a dozen paintings, among them *View on the St. Lawrence Shore* (1945) (Plate 37), an oil conveying the feeling of that region, *Percée* (1945) (Plate 33), *Noon in Tadoussac* (1946) (Plate 52), and the watercolour of Ben from the back.[34]

After her holiday, she still had to tackle completing the other war paintings for McCurry. In November, she told him that seeing her *Bedtime Story* was painful — she was on the jury of a Canadian Group of Painters show and despite the insistence of the other jury members that the painting be kept in the show, she persuaded the president to withdraw it. "There in the gallery — standing on the floor this canvas looked to me terrible with its incompetent drawing — bad proportions etc. I never meant it for your definite possession ..."[35] She promised McCurry another canvas of the same size as a replacement.

Two years after her week in Trenton, Paraskeva sent McCurry two paintings, *Parachute Riggers* (Plate 36) and *Quaicker Girls* (1946) (Plate 34). With the first painting, Paraskeva again succeeded in creating the pictorial drama for which she was searching. She used a sense of perspective she learned from her teacher Petrov-Vodkin as though she were observing the women at work from above, along "two great diagonal lines of workbenches thrusting from the lower right to the upper left corner of the canvas ..."[36] As in *Maintenance Jobs*, the arms and hands of the women and the movement of the figure in the centre background of the painting convey the energy and concentration as the women focused on their work. From the women in the foreground, one's eyes are drawn upward to a parachute, a splash of bright orange-red colour near the top of the canvas.

Quaicker Girls (named for the sound made by the keys of the telegraph) is a more placid painting, with more subdued colours, though within the picture it seems Paraskeva is telling a story. In placing the man — presumably the boss — as a dominant figure in the painting she is giving us a picture of the power structure in which men are in charge. The woman to the left is bent to her work, speaking into a microphone, and the man stands with his sheaf of papers in his hand, a bemused, condescending expression on his face. Through the large window that forms the background of the painting, a bright yellow airplane is visible, and one woman, shielding her eyes from the light is trying to see the plane.

Paraskeva sent *Parachute Riggers* to McCurry as her replacement for *Bedtime Story; Quaicker Girls* (1946) was thrown "'into the bargain,' because I took such a long time to give you the second canvas, paid for already in 1945. I had very difficult time with these works and realize now that it was beyond my abilities. Besides, my complicated family life does not present a very suitable atmosphere for a job that is so difficult for me." She apologized for causing McCurry trouble with these war paintings. "Now I do hope that you will allow them to join the hundreds of other war canvases, which are being stored somewhere in the sports building."[37] Paraskeva's sense of the absurd comes through — all her hard work and the paintings in storage somewhere in a sports building!

With this typed letter to McCurry several years after the war was over — most of Paraskeva's letters were in her scrawling handwriting — the three-year correspondence about war painting came to a close. She was unhappy that her paintings took so long that the war had ended before she finished them, but she did the best she could given the time her family required.

PARASKEVA CONTINUED TO receive letters from Oreste Allegri, and he begged for news, especially about "little Benois." It seems he still thought of Ben as a young boy although he was in his early twenties. Thinking a visit from Allegri might help Ben, Philip wrote a letter in the spring of 1945 inviting Ben's grandfather to come for a visit to Toronto. Making travel arrangements at that time was extremely complicated and expensive. Despite the problems, the Clarks persisted. With the war over in the fall of 1945, they bought tickets for Allegri, and finally in June of the following year when he received his tickets the airline informed him there would be no planes available until October.

By then Allegri was hesitant to make the trip because of the cost — 100,000 francs. He was unhappy about the sacrifice that would mean for the Clarks. He wanted to reimburse them by selling some of his work from his portfolio. He discovered, however, that there was no interest in Paris in his set paintings and maquettes, so he packaged some of them and mailed them to the Clarks, hoping they could sell them. Of course, there was no interest in his work in Toronto, either, as no one would have ever heard of him.

Allegri did visit the Clarks, but it did nothing to help Ben. By then, they hardly knew each other anymore. It could not have been easy living in the Clark household, even for a week, especially since he could not speak English. Ben was not his cute little grandson anymore, nor was Paraskeva the same young woman he remembered. And Allegri would have had difficulty relating to Philip. Allegri stayed only a week before going on to New York in an unsuccessful attempt to renew his contacts there in the world of opera and ballet.

With the end of the war, great celebrations took place all over the city at the end of the summer of 1945. Clive remembered it as "a fantastic time," that everyone was coming home; they were meeting people at the armoury; people were looking for new jobs. There was a feeling of life starting over. But with the end of this war came the beginning of another one: the Cold War, accompanied by a hostility that would push Paraskeva and her family into a period of great apprehension.

The Rosedale Russian in the Cold War

I am deeply concerned about the lack of peaceful and friendly
feelings between Canada and the Soviet Union — and I also
have a profound faith in the paramount enlightening powers of art.[1]

The name of Toronto's affluent area of Rosedale came from the abundance of wild roses sprawling across a wooded hillside of the ravine that cut through the city to the Don River. In early Toronto, the Jarvis family — William B. Jarvis was Toronto's sheriff in the 1820s — called their home on Yonge Street near Roxborough Street, "Rosedale." When the one-hundred-acre Jarvis estate was sold off into lots in the 1850s, the whole area was called Rosedale; then it was the suburbs, considered to be far from downtown Toronto.

In the 1940s, nearly one hundred years later, Paraskeva Clark could look out her south windows to see the same wooded ravine where the Jarvis family had walked. Wooden sidewalks for pedestrians ran along Roxborough, all the way from South Drive near Bloor and Sherbourne. On these sidewalks, which were very slippery after rain, Paraskeva faithfully carried bags full of groceries on her way home from downtown.

That Paraskeva did her shopping on foot, and did it daily, as was the custom in Europe, seemed odd to the other housewives on her street who drove to the Summerhill Market, not far to the north, in their wood-panelled station wagons. Paraskeva had her own unique routine: she walked downtown, had lunch at Simpson's lunch counter, stopped in at a gallery or two, did her shopping, and then continued her walk home and began dinner preparations for her family. What heavy bags Paraskeva couldn't manage to carry home, she had delivered by the downtown Loblaws store where she shopped.

Paraskeva never did learn to drive a car. Walking was her statement of rejection of the capitalist system, her way of expressing her identity as a peasant and a socialist. She was not one of the bourgeoisie; she made friends with sales people, the wait staff at the restaurant at Simpson's, and any other "workers" she encountered. "All this was part of her ethic," explained Clive. "It was carry your own stuff, you do your own shopping."[2] For Clive, this was only one of the many contradictions in his mother's life and philosophy: she lived in a nice house in Rosedale but wouldn't drive a car.

Of course, not driving a car seemed absurd to the Clarks' neighbours and it was not something they understood in their lives of "ordered mediocrity."[3] They were accustomed to a culture of uniformity, and began thinking of Paraskeva, who was sometimes seen at the bottom of the steps in her bathrobe doing a task at street level, as "quite a character."[4] She did not hesitate telling neighbours what she thought of the paintings they hung on their walls. "Goddamn decoration," she declared about a painting the O'Brians hung above their fireplace. No wonder another neighbour described Paraskeva as someone who "called a spade 'a damn shovel.'"[5]

Even the way Paraskeva walked was something her neighbours noticed: she "moved aggressively through space."[6] Her intensity and feisty nature were not characteristic of other mothers on the street, and the neighbourhood children knew she was different, not just because of how she walked, but also because of how she talked. "Oh, Geoffrey, you're so, you're so — oh my beautiful boy," she said to young Geoffrey O'Brian. He knew that no other mother on the street would say such a thing directly to a child, and not "in those extravagant tones that stick in one's mind."[7] Not only that; when Geoffrey turned twenty-one Paraskeva gave him a bottle of wine and said,

"Take a woman to bed."[8] She defied the taboo of sex as a suitable topic of conversation.

Bay Cardy, who then was a young girl in the Cochrane family and lived across the street from the Clarks, remembered that in the forties Paraskeva kept to herself and did not talk much to neighbours.[9] Cardy's mother felt sorry for Paraskeva, who did not have domestic help and not only lugged heavy bags of groceries along the streets, but up the forty-three steps to her house on the hill. Had Paraskeva known of her neighbour's pity, she would have pooh-poohed it — she had no regard for that kind of sentimentality.

Throughout the forties, these neighbours would have seen Paraskeva's photo in the newspapers from time to time in relation to exhibitions of paintings and her activities in support of Russia. They knew where she came from. But at the same time, "most of the people on the street simply had a traditional Anglo reaction to meeting the Clarks, letting them be, because that's what you did, you didn't pry."[10]

During the 1950s, a more diverse group of people, less concerned with conformity, began buying houses on the street, among them, the late Donald Coxeter, famous mathematician and University of Toronto professor who lectured all over the world, as well as set designer Murray Laufer and artist Marie Day. However, when the Clarks arrived in Rosedale in 1941, the lines of conformity were fairly rigid and many of the old traditional families remained there for years.

Paraskeva, who by then had developed her own defence system when she did not fit in, figured she had better things to do than taking tea with the neighbour ladies. She valued her time, and furthermore, when she was not preoccupied with the war or thinking about Canadian-Soviet relations, she was worrying over Ben. She would have thought her neighbours unable to comprehend her situation, and she was probably right.

Her work as an artist during the war led Paraskeva into finding yet another avenue for helping her country: educating people about Russian art. Through the visit of Lyudmila Pavlichenko and the other Russian emissaries in 1942, Paraskeva had become known to Russian officials. Several years later, the Russian Embassy in Ottawa asked her to take on the task of educating Canadians about Russian cultural life. Even though she said that she was an artist and not a speaker, she could not turn down their request. She was born and raised in Russia and, as a Russian, she learned to do the tasks assigned to her for the good of the country.[11]

Did Paraskeva know that as a cultural ambassador for the Soviet Union she became part of a massive propaganda network presenting a facade of what life was like there? She certainly would have read articles and seen photos in the Soviet magazines to which she subscribed, but she would have taken these at face value because she had given up so much in leaving her homeland that she would do almost anything to defend it as a way of hanging on.[12]

As an active member of the Federation of Russian Canadians, Paraskeva also served on the central committee and wrote articles on art for *Vestnik* (Herald), the group's Russian newspaper. She was respected in the organization because she didn't put on airs even though she spoke intelligently and was better educated and better dressed than most members who had come from different parts of the Soviet Union and were struggling just to keep their families alive.[13] In 1944, she was elected vice-president of this four-thousand-member group, and held the position for two years.[14] Of course, all the time she spent in this work meant she had less time for painting, but given who she was, she couldn't *not* do it.

In February 1944, she spoke to two groups about Russia's art and artists: the Women's Art Society and the Art Association of Montreal at the Museum of Fine Arts. The Art Association, in celebration of February as the anniversary month of the Red Army, mounted an exhibition of Russian posters and held a "Russian Night" featuring Russian music and dance. Paraskeva was the guest speaker; her speech, "Art in the Soviet Union," provided an overview, beginning with the October Revolution.

Several small notebooks still exist with Paraskeva's handwritten notes, presumably jottings of her thoughts as she developed her speeches. The one set of undated notes is titled, "What are current opinions about Soviet Art?" This notebook contains excerpts from articles and books about what Canadian and American writers said about Soviet art.

The other set of notes could well have been her first draft of the speech for Montreal because she refers to "the pictures hung on these walls. They are so simple, so unpretentious, so comprehensible to anybody — But all these last weeks I cherished the idea — a very ambitious one — to tell you about Soviet Art, something that would strike the sparkle of enthusiasm, of lively interest in the art of my native land — the irresistible desire to follow its growth, its progress."

A comparison of this small brown notebook and the typed speech she gave is striking. Her handwritten draft, spontaneous, spirited, and defending Soviet art, is filled with references to the revolutionary struggle, "living actual art," art as the "property of the great working masses."

The typed speech, the one she likely read at the Russian Night at the Montreal Museum of Fine Arts, is more restrained, carefully developed, and not as laudatory of the Soviet system. She explained that immediately after the Revolution, groups of artists sprung up, each claiming to be the most faithful to the new ideology of Soviet life. The conflict was resolved with the Committee of the Communist Party establishing one united organization on 23 April 1932. "From then on, the fundamental principle of creative work for Soviet artists became Socialist Realism, that is, the concrete historical representation of reality in its revolutionary development."[15]

Paraskeva pointed out that in the West there was much misunderstanding of Soviet art. There was no Russian school of painting in the sense that art history regards the Flemish, French, or Italian schools. However, she suggested that the Soviet Union was taking its first steps, and she ended her speech by asking that her fellow Canadians not condemn these first steps, but, rather, admire the courage of her people and respect their difficulties.

A year later, when Paraskeva spoke in Parry Sound at the Women's Canadian Club, she took a different approach by delving into early Russian art history. Her speech was illustrated with art reproductions projected on screen through the use of lantern slides (glass-covered images used until the 1950s when slide transparencies became available). It is likely that this was the same lecture she had given in November 1944 at the Art Gallery of Toronto when the Toronto Council for Canadian Soviet Friendship met, a speech of nearly thirty typewritten pages, which she presented along with the lantern slides on a number of occasions.[16]

This talk was a panoramic view of the history of Russian painting, beginning with the religious iconography in the ninth century.[17] Paraskeva highlighted the artists whose work stood out from the twelfth to the sixteenth century, and used the slides to show how techniques changed and how Western influences began when Ivan the Terrible invited foreign artists into the country. By the mid-eighteenth century, the influence of the post-Renaissance Western culture secularized Russian painting while some artists attempted to keep the old traditions. In 1757, Catherine the Great opened the Academy of Fine Arts in St. Petersburg, a school that imitated French institutions rather than being rooted in the life of the Russian people. By the end of that century, Russian artists had begun landscape painting, and portrait painting was flourishing.

The nineteenth century was characterized by a return to interest in old Russian art; artists returned to the great churches in the old cities to study. Ilya Repin (1844–1930), and his student, Valentin Serov (1865–1911) were two of the "giants" of the beginning of the modern period in Russian art.

At the beginning of the twentieth century, the artists who formed the "World of Art" movement were among the most creative and innovative of the time. Of course, with the 1917 Revolution, the focus shifted to art that would inspire the masses. Various artist groups formed and dissolved during the early years after the war and the Revolution.

This is the period when Paraskeva herself experienced what was happening in the art world in Petrograd when she was studying at the Academy of Art. However, in her speech she held strictly to her "textbookish" approach. She talked about the influence of Petrov-Vodkin on his students, but did not talk about her own experience with him at the Academy.

She did explain what happened after she left Russia. In 1932, the Central Committee of the Communist Party decreed that the artist organizations that had evolved were useless and did not reflect the reality of Soviet life. By then Social Realism was the only "true" art for the Soviet Union, excluding Expressionism and Constructivism.

Paraskeva concluded her lecture by emphasizing that art was a part of everyday life in the Soviet Union and quoted the artist Ilya Ehrenburg: "Now, when our people are fighting in the vanguard with other peoples, friends of liberty, against barbarism, against inhuman Hitler Germany, the muses are blessing the Front line; they comfort and inspire soldiers. A Death Battle is raging for freedom, for human dignity, for beauty, for Art."

It is clear from this lecture that Paraskeva had educated herself on Russian art, and was intent on helping her fellow Canadians understand her native country. This had become her own mission, and the Soviet embassy could not have found a person more committed to educating Canadians about the Soviet Union. However, after the war Canada's attitude toward the Soviet Union changed dramatically, which caused Paraskeva much grief.

The about-face occurred when a Soviet spy ring was discovered immediately after the war, in September 1945. Since 1943, when the Soviets and Canada were allies, Lieutenant-Colonel Nikolai Zabotin, a Soviet attaché, was in charge of intelligence, collecting military and scientific information. He and his staff were located at, but worked separately from, the Soviet embassy in Ottawa.

Working under Zabotin in Ottawa was the cipher clerk, Igor Gouzenko, who handled the transmission of information between Ottawa and Moscow. When Gouzenko was ordered back to his own country, he was not sure he wanted to return because he and his wife had come to appreciate the freedom Canadians enjoyed; he left the embassy one day, carrying more than a hundred secret documents, and never returned. When Canadian authorities examined the documents, they discovered evidence of a comprehensive spy ring operating not only in Canada, but also in Britain and the United States. Meanwhile, the Gouzenko family was offered police protection until they were able to relocate and take on a new identity.

Under pressure from both England and the United States, Prime Minister Mackenzie King established a Royal Commission into espionage. On 15 February 1946, King announced to the nation that there was evidence of a spy ring and invoked special measures to investigate and detain suspects. That same day, the RCMP began conducting pre-dawn raids to detain people suspected of being communist sympathizers, who might have fed classified information to the Soviets.

A month later, when Parliament opened in Ottawa, Fred Rose, a Labour Progressive MP for Montreal, went to work as usual and appeared in his seat in the Commons. That night after he returned home, the RCMP arrived at his door and arrested him. Rose had helped a man named Sam Carr with operations in the Communist Party since the twenties, and in 1943 Rose did feed classified information to the Soviets, but at that point, it was not illegal. However, Rose was now a prime suspect.

During the time of the Rose trial, the Soviet Union "issued a statement: its ambassador wasn't involved; the secrets supplied were of little interest to the U.S.S.R. given its more advanced technical achievements; Colonel Zabotin had been recalled because of the actions of members of his staff." Only four days after Zabotin had returned to Moscow, news reports stated that he had died of a heart attack.[18]

This series of events would have sent a chill through Paraskeva. She knew Colonel Zabotin. When the 1945 Congress of the Federation of Russian Canadians met in Toronto, Colonel Zabotin stayed with the Clarks. Paraskeva was totally enthralled with this tall, handsome Russian. A photograph of the two of them standing on the street shows her, a blissful expression on her face, nestling against him as he smiles down at her, putting his arm around her. She told her friends several accounts that reveal the intensity of her feelings for him — when he left the house in the mornings to go about his business, she'd "jump into his bed to feel the warmth of this big strong man." And after he left Toronto, she did not make up the bed for two weeks because she liked to spend time lying where he had slept.[19] She had no hesitation telling her friends about this.

Besides the account of Zabotin, the articles in the magazine *Soviet Russia Today*, to which Paraskeva subscribed, were distressing for the stories of increasing suspicion of the Soviets, not only in Canada, but also in the United States. By 1946, the House Committee on Un-American Activities in the United States was investigating "subversives," and attacking the National Council of American-Soviet Friendship.

Given Philip's position with the Ontario Government as Assistant Controller of Revenue, he and Paraskeva must have spent hours talking about the situation and would have experienced tension and anxiety over the climate of fear and suspicion they encountered. Philip and Paraskeva could not have missed knowing of the RCMP raids and investigations of people with links to the Soviet Union. Even the Aid to Russia Fund had become suspect, an organization that had been perfectly acceptable during the war.[20] Through the investigations, twenty-one people in Canada were eventually charged and eleven convicted. Member of Parliament Rose was among them. News of the arrests and convictions was carried in major newspapers around the world. The Cold War had enveloped Canada, and a climate of paranoia escalated in Britain and the United States.[21] All this continued to have an impact on the Clarks. The anti-Russian attitude as Clive was growing up led him to "just not be curious" about his mother's native country.[22] Nor did Paraskeva ever encourage him to learn the Russian language though he often heard her speaking Russian on the telephone to other Russian-Canadians.

As a child and a teenager, Clive had to sort out what to say and what not to say to his friends about Russia. When he was in elementary school, he did not invite his friends to his house very often. For one thing, his mother had a hammer and sickle flag in her studio, as well as Lenin's portrait. These were an anathema to the families of his friends.

Accordingly, Clive spent a lot of time at the house of his best friend, whose dad was a stockbroker. This family had little sympathy for the plight of the Russians. Paraskeva advised Clive not to talk to people about his Russian side. It was for his safety that she told her son to keep to himself his connections to Russia — likely, she had heard about the harassment Fred Rose's daughter experienced. Ten-year-old Laura Rose was taunted in the playground, her playmates calling her father a spy while he was on trial.[23] Paraskeva wanted to save her son from that kind of abuse.

Clive kept his pride about being part Russian secret even though he *was* proud of his heritage, having come from these heroic Russians who "were superior, struggling and winning out over incredible odds over the Germans and all of that. I just had that feeling, but I never went around talking about it because people would say, 'You're a Communist,' and that was that."[24] For someone so proudly and completely Russian, asking her son to deny his — and her — Russian heritage was painful, like the amputation of a limb to save a life.

The paranoia and the surveillance in Canada had a profound impact on the lives of many other immigrants from the Soviet Union. For example, Adam Rayco, who knew Paraskeva, was also a member of the Federation of Russian Canadians and a strong trade unionist. He was a skilled tool and die maker who worked the night shift at Massey Ferguson in Toronto. After he left the company in the late forties because he no longer wanted to work nights, he applied again two years later to learn that the same foreman he had before was still there. Though the foreman said he would like to hire Rayco back because he was good at his job, he could not do it because Rayco was on the RCMP black list.

The extent of the distress of RCMP activities for such people as Rayco is obvious: fifty years later in an interview he asked me whether I work for the RCMP, and quickly said, "I'm being sarcastic." And yet, when I replied that I definitely did not work for the RCMP, but that I could understand the reason for the question, his eyes filled with tears.[25] For sure, Paraskeva was aware of what was happening to people like Rayco, and that must have caused tremendous anxiety.

The harassment of Rayco and others led me to wonder whether the RCMP investigated Paraskeva. Her Russian connections were known all over, so it seems she would have been a likely suspect. However, Clive Clark has no memory that she ever talked about it. A search under the *Access to Information Act* did not yield any evidence that the RCMP had files on her, but many of the records not considered "historically significant" were destroyed, so we may never know whether, in fact, she was investigated.[26]

However, we do know that her apprehension about the Cold War sapped her time and energy as she tried to think of ways to bridge the antagonism between Canada and the Soviet Union. She expressed her anxiety in letters to H. O. McCurry, suggesting ways art could be used as a bridge between Canada and the Soviet Union. She proposed in her letter that the National Gallery bring to Canada an exhibition of the work of four Soviet artists, which had travelled to Vienna, Prague, and Belgrade. Paraskeva had read a review of this show of portraits, landscape, and genre painting of Soviet life in the local Russian newspaper. "Such an exhibit might reassure masses to some extent — that there is still a shred of friendly relations between Canada and the Soviet Union — and might mean *more* confidence in *our* government among certain sections of Canadian masses [emphasis in original]." Paraskeva not only wanted this Russian exhibit to come to Ottawa; she wanted to send a show of Canadian art to the Soviet Union. However, H. O. McCurry sent on a copy of Paraskeva's letter to the Department of External Affairs because the National Gallery did not organize international exchange exhibitions.

In the meantime, while waiting for a reply from External Affairs, Paraskeva worked at other ways to help relations between the two countries. She corresponded with VOKS, an arts group in the Soviet Union, who also had an arts magazine by the same name. At one of their meetings, they read parts of Paraskeva's letter about the work and lives of Canadian artists. She had also sent a letter A.Y. Jackson had written about the history of the Group of Seven, and his letter received a "very enthusiastic reply."[27] VOKS sent greetings to Canadian artists, and asked for more information about Canadian art — monographs and photos.

Paraskeva began collecting material on Canadian art to send to the VOKS office in Moscow. She spoke of her idea to Carl Schaefer and he, too, wrote to McCurry. Once more, she apologized for taking McCurry's time, but said she had gathered up whatever she herself could find to send, and hoped he would do what he could to help her.

During 1947 when Paraskeva was exchanging letters with McCurry, the National Conference on Canadian-Soviet Relations sent a memorandum of suggestions for improving the situation, followed by correspondence between the Congress and Lester B. Pearson, Under-Secretary of State for External Affairs. These were valiant efforts on the part of the Congress, whose national committee included such respected persons as A. Y. Jackson, poet and professor E. J. Pratt, and Rabbi A. L. Feinberg. The Goethe scholar and writer Barker Fairley was the Chairman of the Executive.[28] However, by the late forties it became obvious that the break in relations with the Soviet Union was too solid to penetrate.

Fear of an all-out war with the Soviet Union was increasing and the anti-communism sentiment was at a feverish pitch. Paraskeva's notes for her lectures reflected her own fear, but she also articulated her faith in the effectiveness of art to bring about peace:

> We are living in a difficult dramatic epoch of great struggle to win the peace and to the masses of people of the world the danger of a new war seems almost unavoidable — the hope to win the peace seems dying

— the chances of success for victory of Peace — so slim; and if we really know and believe that arts are inspired by most peaceful instincts of [the] human race — then all artists and all scholars of Arts and Culture like you should turn to the problems of Arts and Culture with greater devotion and study than ever before. Then Peace will be won.[29]

The Cold War affected not only Paraskeva's family life, but also her professional life. She stopped writing for *Vestnik*; and she gave no more lectures — no one wanted to hear her talk about Russian art. Nor did she do overtly political paintings. There were new still lifes, but landscape became her predominant subject matter, scenes from her own neighbourhood or from family holidays in Ontario or Quebec. It was as though both the Cold War and the conventions of painting Canada's landscapes wore her down and silenced her earlier passion for pouring her social conscience into her work.

Essentials of Life (1947) (Plate 54) is one of her still lifes painted during the Cold War, an oil remarkable for the artist's careful consideration of the arrangement of objects and the impact of the angle of the table's edge. Standing in front of the painting, one feels off balance and is inclined to tilt one's head, something she must have intended, as though she wanted to jolt viewers into seeing something new and keep us shifting and moving.[30] "To me all things are moving,"[31] she once said; a statement very close to Petrov-Vodkin's idea that movement is a sign of existence.

At that time, Paraskeva's thoughts about the artist's need to make a living and the need for patronage consolidated. These ideas were part of the thought process of this painting. For her, life's essentials included not only food, but also books and other things that nourish the mind, the spirit, and one's aesthetic sense. The loaf of bread is there, with a candle for light, but so are gifts of nature: butterflies and flowers.

Her teacher's painting called *Herring* (1918), painted not long after the Revolution during World War I, could also be called "The Essentials of Life," with its fish, two potatoes, and a hunk of bread. But the feeling in this Petrov-Vodkin work is one of scarcity, whereas Paraskeva's painting conveys abundance.

The dominant object in the still life is a book, open to Canto XXVI, a volume of the American poet Ezra Pound's epic poem. One theme of Cantos

Plate 25. *Memories of Leningrad* (1941), watercolour on paper, 41.1 x 50.4 cm. Winchester Galleries, Victoria, B.C. Photo credit: Anthony Sam.

Plate 26. *Self Portrait* (a.k.a. *Self Portrait with Concert Program*) (1942), oil on canvas, 76.6 x 69.8 cm. National Gallery of Canada, 4592.

Paraskeva wearing the suit she wore when she painted the 1942 self portrait holding the Russian concert program. Library and Archives Canada, e006078597.

Plate 27. *It's 10 Below Outside* (1940), wax crayon, ink, graphite on paper, 28.5 x 30.2 cm. Ottawa Art Gallery.

Plate 28. *Pavlichenko and Her Comrades at the Toronto City Hall* (1943), oil on canvas, 127.7 x 128.3 cm. Art Gallery of Ontario.

Plate 29. *Evening After Rain* (1946), oil on canvas, 45.8 x 40.6 cm. Private collection, Victoria, B.C. Photo credit: Anthony Sam.

Plate 30. *Ben* (1945), pencil and watercolour on paper, 43 x 48 cm. Libby's of Toronto. Photo credit: Dean Palmer.

Plate 31. *Portrait of Murray Adaskin* (1944–45), oil on canvas, 98.7 x 75.0 cm. Library and Archives Canada, C51465K.

Plate 32. *Public Bath — Leningrad* (1944), watercolour, pastel on paper, 29 x 59 cm. Private collection, Toronto. Photo credit: Dean Palmer.

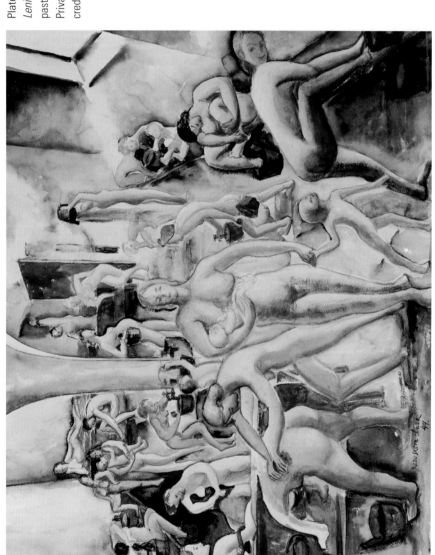

Plate 33. *Percée* (1945), oil on canvas, 51 x 61 cm. Art Gallery of Ontario, gift of Dorothea Larsen Adaskin, 2004.

Plate 34. *Quaicker Girls* (1946), oil on canvas, 73.8 x 89 cm. Accession Number 19710261-5680, Beaverbrook Collection of War Art, Canadian War Museum.

Plate 35. *Maintenance Jobs in the Hangar* (1945), oil on canvas, 81.6 x 101.6 cm. Accession Number 19710261, Beaverbrook Collection of War Art, Canadian War Museum.

Plate 36. *Parachute Riggers* (1946–1947), oil on canvas, 101.7 x 81.4 cm. Accession Number 19710261-5679, Beaverbrook Collection of War Art, Canadian War Museum.

Plate 37. *View on the St. Lawrence Shore* (1945), oil on canvas, 80 x 100 cm. Private collection. Courtesy of Masters Gallery, Calgary. Photo credit: John Dean.

Plate 38. *Road Builders* (1948) oil, 50 x 60 cm. Private collection, Toronto. Photo credit: Dean Palmer.

Plate 39. *Diana Hunting in Caledon* (1948–1951), watercolour on paper, 52.1 x 83.8 cm. Private collection. Photo credit: Dean Palmer.

Frances James Adaskin. This is the photo Paraskeva used as reference for her portrait. Library and Archives Canada, a215154.

Plate 40. *Boathouse, Still Life* (1954), oil on canvas, 76.2 x 68.6 cm. Private collection, Toronto. Photo credit: Dean Palmer.

Plate 41. *Portrait of Frances James* (1950–1952), oil on canvas, 121 x 85.4 cm. Library and Archives Canada, C151469K.

Plate 42. *Melancholy of a Winter Day* (1951), oil on board, 60 cm x 50 cm. Private collection, Markham, Ontario. Photo credit: Dean Palmer.

XXIV–XXVII is Venice sinking into the sea as a metaphor for degeneration: "the degeneration of the painter's relation to his patron, the degeneration of painting itself."[32] And, specifically for Paraskeva, the degeneration of her hopes for friendly relations between her two countries.

Another theme of Canto XXVI is the artists' need for money and patronage, and it opens with Pound's writing about himself in Venice, a young poet without a patron, almost broke. Then he leaps back into history, to the 1400s, when a number of personalities who have figured prominently so far in his epic tale all gather in Venice. It's a long story, but these characters came to Venice to obtain patronage for their enterprises. The Canto closes with Pound's version of Mozart's dealings with the archbishop of Salzburg in 1777 — Mozart wanted to leave Salzburg because he wasn't being paid enough.

If we look beneath the surface, we can ferret out other reasons why Paraskeva might have chosen to include Ezra Pound in this painting, and in the process, we learn more about her. For one thing, her choice of Pound shows her knowledge of literature and illustrates the aspects of her as a person full of contradictions: she included in her painting about life's essentials a poet whose politics she abhorred because he was against socialism and supported Mussolini and Hitler. He was an American but had been living in Italy since the 1920s. During the war, he made more than one hundred broadcasts on Rome Radio supporting fascism, praising Benito Mussolini and attacking the United States President, Franklin D. Roosevelt. These broadcasts were carried by shortwave radio to the United States. An American grand jury charged Pound with treason.

In May 1945, when Germany surrendered to the Allies, Pound was arrested and kept for two weeks in solitary confinement, exposed to the elements in a steel pen. The inhumane treatment — surely a form of torture — resulted in a breakdown of his mental and physical health. When he was moved to better accommodations, which included a typewriter, he went back to his writing. He was held at the U.S. Army training camp for six months and then flown to the United States, examined, declared mentally ill, and imprisoned in Washington D.C. in a hospital for the criminally insane where he continued writing his poetry. After he was finally discharged in 1958 as a result of a petition signed by other writers, he returned to Italy to live out his life.[33]

Whether or not Paraskeva was conscious of it, there are some correlations between Pound and Ben. It was during the time that Ben's illness occurred that Pound was making his broadcasts. Some literary critics have theorized that Pound had become psychotic, citing that as the reason for his rants on radio. We know that Paraskeva thought of Ben as a great, talented artist, whose divided loyalties — one being Italian — struck him down and made him mentally ill, wasting his life, with the war as a contributing factor. Similarly, Pound suffered because of his choice of where he placed his loyalty, also because of the war. Paraskeva would likely think these connections ludicrous; she denied any symbolism in her work, calling herself a realist with the images being exactly what they are. However, one cannot take her idea about symbolism in her paintings at face value because she was a complicated person whose reasons for doing things were layered with meaning, and she would not arbitrarily place a poet such as Pound in such a prominent place in her painting.

Paraskeva was preoccupied with artists' need for support, so choosing Pound's Canto xxvi in her painting makes sense. She engaged in a conversation in print, as she did in 1937, but this time about travelling exhibitions of artists' work and their need to be paid for what they do so they can make a living. It started at a meeting of "museum people," which was attended by "several leading Canadian artists and we became involved with Paraskeva Clark in a highly stimulating (though unresolved) discussion on the value — or lack of value — of travelling exhibitions to the Canadian artist."[34] Subsequently, *Canadian Art* magazine asked Paraskeva to elaborate on what she said at the meeting. Her article, "Are Painters Being Imposed Upon?" appeared that fall. "Any nationally recognized artist is really working in the service of the national culture," she began. She argued that artists should be paid for their work just as other professionals are paid, so artists should be paid because they work in "the service of the nation." Society was not completely to blame, she said, because artists often were "too humble" or "too romantic" about their art to expect remuneration. She pointed to the bind artists feel when it comes to travelling exhibitions. If they don't participate, their work does not get shown; if they do participate, their painting might be travelling for two years and when it returns it is often damaged and/or soiled; this, after all the hours of hard work and the cost of materials. And yet, they were not paid, not even rent for the paintings hanging in museums and galleries. The paintings "come back, in their shabby frames, but they keep to themselves the bitter secrets of their long sojourns in dark cellars in which they were stored between the holding of little advertised exhibitions. They return somewhat dated, with a sense of failure."

In her typed, unedited copy of her article, Paraskeva concluded by saying that if society wants the services of the artist, it "should set him free from the constant torment of wanting to give his services, and of feeling such a sucker by giving them free." The unvarnished language of her draft was smoothed over in the published version: "Our society, if it wants the services of the artist, should set him free from this constant torment of desiring, on the one hand, to give his services, and of feeling on the other hand, that he is constantly being imposed upon by giving them free."[35] Paraskeva had something at stake in this. Earning a living from her painting would have freed her from her dependence on Philip.

Her personal interests aside, she linked the artist with the nation, an ideology which she maintained even after nearly twenty-five years in Canada. One senses a disillusionment — bitterness, even — with the capitalist society that adopted her. When she spoke of the life of artists in the Soviet Union, she pointed out that they were employed by the State and did not have to worry about earning a living. This was yet another area of her life in which she experienced the push and pull of contradictions, the advantages and disadvantages of where she came from and where she landed.

Although Paraskeva was dissatisfied with the system in which artists operated, she continued to receive the praise of critics. Andrew Bell wrote an article about her that appeared in *Canadian Art* in the last issue of 1949.[36] "There is no Canadian painter quite like her," he stated; "... her pictures reveal truths about the Canadian scene just as sure, in their own way, as, say, those of A.Y. Jackson or Emily Carr." This was high praise, sweet meat for a Russian-turned-Canadian artist, particularly for one who had originally so condemned Group of Seven landscapes. She succeeded in showing that one could paint landscapes — Canadian landscapes — without copying the Group of Seven.

When she said painting was very hard for her, what she left unsaid was that as a young woman she discovered the importance of painting and learned that getting it right was hard work; now, she refused to take the easy way of falling into work like the other artists around her.[37] It was hard to paint her own way, and to do it better than the others, which she thought she did, surrounded as she was by the Canadian idiom.

Most of the time she worked at home slowly and laboriously in a manner that required intense concentration to produce portraits of friends and herself, as well as still lifes and landscapes of scenes within a stone's throw of her house. "It may in fact be this very concentration within a limited orbit which has enabled her to absorb and express, within relatively so short a time, such basic truths about the Canada she knows."[38]

The critic Andrew Bell saw in her work two influences: Cézanne and Picasso. Cézanne because Paraskeva used colour to define form; Picasso, for the way she organized her portraits and still lifes. The tilt of the surfaces and the placement of the objects show she understood Picasso as she put him together with Petrov-Vodkin to turn out her own Paraskeva Clark still lifes.

By the late forties, Toronto's art world, which had become so familiar to Paraskeva, was changing. The cluster of artists in the city was considerably different than it had been in the thirties when a cohesiveness among them and their societies had offered Paraskeva a sense of community. During the thirties, the formation of the Canadian Group of Painters, the Depression, and the Spanish Civil War all stimulated artists' thinking, and gave rise to many conversations about their place in society, conversations that had brought artists together. The Kingston conference in 1941 and the formation of the Federation of Canadian Artists (FCA) built on that desire for focus.

Although the FCA was instrumental in artists' contributions during the war, afterward it did not provide the cohesiveness that Paraskeva and others had hoped for. In 1948, Andrew Bell wrote that in Toronto "the local painters are hard to ferret out." He described them as "largely lone wolves, spread all around and about the sprawling metropolitan area, most of them working on their own, and in their own way."[39] Nevertheless, Bell said, Toronto's serious artists continued to work, among them the former war artists and the sculptors.

"Paraskeva Clark, meticulous craftsman and sensitive observer, has carved out her own special niche."

Her February 1947 solo exhibition at the Picture Loan Society included a number of landscapes, among them *Boats in Tadoussac* (1946) and *Evening After Rain* (1946). She was called "A Painter of Sylvan Canada" for capturing the cool, blue light of Ontario skies. This description of her as an artist gave her great pleasure, for she spoke of it years later.[40]

She won a one hundred dollar award for her painting *Road Builders* (1948) (Plate 38), which she showed in the first Annual Winter Exhibition at the Art Gallery of Hamilton in 1948. This painting is a scene from her street when Mount Pleasant Road was being constructed from Bloor Street northward, passing a short distance from the Clarks' house.[41]

Paraskeva continued showing with the artist societies and contributed to six international exhibitions of Canadian art. She was also elected president of the Canadian Society of Painters in Water Colour in 1948.[42] That same year she began a curious watercolour, *Diana Hunting in Caledon* (1948–1951) (Plate 39), a playful rendition of the Roman goddess who has been an artistic subject for centuries, usually portrayed in the landscape.

The setting for Paraskeva's *Diana* is the rural, hilly Caledon area north of Toronto where she visited Alice and Stewart Sutton's farm near Mono Mills. She had met the Suttons through Douglas Duncan, became fast friends with Alice, and was a frequent visitor to "Balmagillie," named as a whimsical take-off on "Balm of Gilead."

With her origins going back at least as far as the sixth century BCE, Diana was both a wood nymph and goddess of the woodlands, hunting, and the moon, as well as ruling over fertility and childbirth (the equivalent of Artemis in Greek mythology). She appears in literature throughout history and has also been portrayed by such sixteenth- and seventeenth-century artists as Titian and Peter Paul Rubens, who painted at least three different scenes of Diana with her nymphs.

Paraskeva's Diana is a deftly light and fanciful painting, so unlike her other work over the years that it is very hard to imagine what prompted her to not only choose this subject matter, but to give it such a capricious interpretation.

Diana, particularly her head with its strange halo above the forehead, is surrounded with a background of brown billowing hills, which become the focus of the painting. Her face and slim body communicate a youthful energy and joy that is reminiscent of the young Paraskeva.

If we pay close attention to the details of the painting, we discover that Diana has brown hair and brown eyes, but all her nymphs have blond hair and blue eyes. Seven nymphs (don't miss the one in the upper left corner, whose head could be misinterpreted as a piece of fruit tossed into the air) pick fruit and cavort in the grass where native plants are growing — goldenrod, dandelion, violets. The fruit tree, which began growing off to the left, has been chopped off; the new growth curves to the right, which works better for the structure of the painting. Most significant is the date: "48" written in green and "51" in blue. A case can be made that the parts of the watercolour in the same blue of the "51" were painted in 1951, when she finished it. With the movement of the bow and the tree to the right, as well as the hilly vortex swirling to the right, she could see that the blue tree trunks on the left edge were needed to anchor the painting.

A strong representation of the Caledon countryside is a part of the water-colour, with fences and tiny farm buildings in the distance at the top edge among the hills, including the landscape as a vortex, catching in its sweep a fox running toward the forest in the upper right corner. The foregrounding of figures with the high horizon and buildings in the background is pure Petrov-Vodkin.[43]

That Paraskeva began this major watercolour the same year she became president of the watercolour society has significance because she claimed it was a difficult medium for her. In tackling a subject used by artists throughout history, she established her ability to use watercolour at the same time as she claimed a place in art history. In her position as president of this society, Paraskeva was the judge for the Canadian National Exhibition hobby show in the summer of 1949. She looked at more than two hundred paintings entered by amateur artists from across Canada, and some from the United States, and chose the winners of the prizes.[44]

The backdrop to the success of her professional life was that she received more sad news about her own family in the Soviet Union. Apparently, Paraskeva had sent a letter to Zhabina, the village where she had visited her grandparents as a child, asking about certain relatives. In the spring of 1949, Paraskeva received a letter from Vasilly Nossenkov, a cousin in Zhabina.[45] This heartrending letter told Paraskeva what happened to some of her family during the war. He said the village was destroyed and the people killed or driven away. The Nazis shot his mother (Paraskeva's childhood friend Anastasia) and sister in 1942; he did not say how he had escaped.

Nossenkov's account corresponds to the records of the sequence of events in the war. Zhabina, which was in the Nevel area on the rail line running north to Leningrad, was regained by the Soviets in January 1943, after the Nazis had held that part of the country for almost a year and a half,[46] during which time Paraskeva's extended family would have been killed. However, according to Nossenkov, the younger generations returned to Zhabina and rebuilt, working for the good of the motherland.

When his mother Anastasia was alive, she had told her son about Paraskeva and expressed regret that she lived so far away in another country. Nossenkov thought that Paraskeva's brother Zakhar had survived the war, but did not know what had eventually happened to him. However, he was wrong. What Paraskeva never found out was that Zakhar died on 26 February 1942 during the siege of Leningrad. He was helping take people out of the city to escape the Nazis; one night when he returned, he died in his sleep.[47] He was only forty years old. Given the situation at the time, it is not surprising that Nossenkov did not know what happened to Zakhar. Paraskeva's sister Palenka also died during the war.

Nossenkov asked that Paraskeva reply, and promised to try to find out what happened to her brother and sister when he went to Leningrad. Sadly, no letters arrived again from this cousin until the early nineties after Paraskeva's death.

The chances are slim that Paraskeva's correspondence would have reached Leningrad in the late forties, even though her letter to her relatives in Zhabina apparently slipped through the censors undetected. However, corresponding with people in the Soviet Union, a relative or not, was suspect then. Philip, who was working for the Ontario government, probably would not have wanted letters going back and forth between his house and the Soviet Union.

The Cold War and new trends in the art world affected both Paraskeva's personal and professional lives. She did continue working, but the intensity of the fiery spirit characteristic of her during the thirties and forties diminished when, simultaneously, antagonism toward the Soviet Union grew in Canada and Abstract Expressionism began dominating the art world.

God and Gremlin
at Mid-Life

A society without art would seem unimaginably impoverished.[1]

Paraskeva was fifty years old at the end of October in 1948. This was the time of her life when she would have wanted to be in full flight, in contributing to Canada — and the world — the images that were hers to give.

At mid-life, Paraskeva was an artist who had been altered and influenced by major political developments, first in Russia when she was young, and then during the Spanish Civil War and World War II, as well as through changes in Canadian society. Her personal history during the first fifty years of her life fuelled her firm beliefs about art in society and the need to work for change, something she had done with passion during the war. In 1943, as she looked forward, she had written something that sounded like a manifesto, stating that post-war art would have to be "strong, great inspiring" and "depicting the human being, human action ..."[2] However, these were words she wrote when she was in the swing of working to build a friendship between Russia and Canada and before her son was struck down with schizophrenia. Now, at age fifty, her world was much different from what she had hoped for; it seemed that larger circumstances over which she had no control were pressing in on her and casting huge doubts over the two important parts of her life: art and Soviet–Canadian relations.

The new trend of Abstract Expression unsettled Paraskeva. In November and December of 1949, a show of contemporary art from the United States, Great Britain, and France was held at the Art Gallery of Toronto.[3] Paraskeva would have made a point of seeing the paintings in the show, which included such American artists as Willem de Kooning, Jackson Pollock, and Robert Motherwell. Then in 1952, *Abstracts at Home*, an exhibition organized by Alexandra Luke, took place. For Paraskeva, all this abstract work triggered a worry that she was being left behind.

During the Cold War, Paraskeva knew that artists who tackled social issues were seen as suspect — even communist. It meant that her opinions on Soviet–Canadian relations could hardly even be spoken outside her own house without recriminations, for she saw what happened to artists who dared to speak out as tentacles of McCarthyism invaded Canada. Six members of the Toronto Symphony were denied entry into the United States because the authorities claimed the musicians were communists. And members of the executive of the Canadian Society of Graphic Arts were attacked for making art that was considered communist propaganda.

Working with many Canadians in aid of the Soviet Union during the war and seeing the support for her native land during that time had energized Paraskeva. Within herself, she held stubbornly to her vision of a healthy tie between Canada and the Soviet Union. Alongside her hope for Canadian–Soviet friendship was her belief in the power of artists to effect change in society. As it became clear to Paraskeva that her two countries had once more become highly suspicious of each other, she experienced not only disappointment but also a correlated disillusionment about the role of the artist in Canada, especially her own role, in responding to social issues. The convergence of these two facets of her life — the fundamental shift in the art world and the Cold War — each one of major consequence for her, surely was a principal reason for her retreat, beginning in the late forties, from social issues in her paintings.[4] She conceded that she fell in with "landscapes, landscapes, landscapes" as a national form of art, that she "lost the system of that kind of

thinking" for painting human beings.[5] Feeling frustrated, she continued painting landscapes, and she often escaped into her garden as a way of keeping her
sanity. When suspicion and paranoia in Canada mounted in the mid-twentieth
century, the climate of fear contributed to a loss of faith within Paraskeva,
which would continue into old age and give rise to bitterness.

In the early fifties, probably the summer of 1952, a visit from her old friend
from Paris, Sonia Liber, provided a refreshing break. The reason for the trip
was that her daughter was going to the United States to attend university;
Liber would be accompanying her there and also wanted to visit Paraskeva.
It was a time of catching up on what had happened during the twenty years
they had not seen each other. Paraskeva introduced her old friend to Toronto,
and also took her to see Niagara Falls.

After Liber's visit, Paraskeva returned to her routines. At the beginning of
the decade, even though she no longer lectured on the art of the Soviet Union,
she was still participating in exhibitions and speaking about issues related to
Canadian art. As before, she held the belief that art was a serious matter, an
attitude that was born during her art-student days in St. Petersburg. For her,
art was the soul of a nation, and she wanted people to recognize its meaning,
to respect and cherish it.

Her lectures on art were based on her broad reading and showed her ability
to synthesize her reading to formulate cogent ideas about art. In a lecture at
the Art Gallery of Hamilton, she articulated clearly the intensity of her beliefs.[6]
She first summarized the 1950 spring season exhibits in Toronto and the
activities of women's volunteer committees in Vancouver and Winnipeg; then
she launched into a passionate discourse about art and what it contributes
to a nation. The context for this part of her lecture was a recent "action of
Public Representatives in the Ontario Legislature": the purchase of works by
amateur artists. That the provincial government's art committee would not
purchase "serious" work meant that the government officials did not have an
understanding of the meaning of art as an expression of the soul of the people
and a repository for the spirit of a society.

Since early human history, Paraskeva said, art as "manifestations of <u>souls
yearning</u> toward beauty were somewhat <u>like a prayer</u> and gradually most of
those early forms of art became the Attributes of religious rytes [*sic*] and

ceremonies" [emphasis in original]. She spoke of the meaning of art for oppressed people, their yearning to express beauty and their inner world of "absolute freedom" from which art was born, "forms of rhythmic motions, of plastic forms," music, song and dance, and objects beautiful in proportion and colour. The prayer-like yearning of masses of people giving birth to all forms of art became a process of growth of people's souls, Paraskeva declared.

Her comments were reminiscent of the language and sentiment of a letter printed in the *Ottawa Citizen* ten years before she set foot in Canada: "The art of all ages has concerned itself with things considered supremely beautiful and therefore good, that is capable of inspiring good."[7] Eric Brown, the director of the National Gallery in Ottawa from 1910 to 1939 and an adherent to the Christian Science religion, was the author of the letter. He, along with his successor, H. O. McCurry of whom Paraskeva was extremely fond, were both Christian Scientists and their religious beliefs are evident in their discourse on art.

Paraskeva professed no religion, but in truth, her religion was art mixed with socialism, both of which were rooted in her Russian heritage — the Russian culture held an esteem for art to a much greater extent than did the cultures in the West.[8] While Christian Science flavoured Brown's writing, it was Marxism mixed with Christian influences that gave Paraskeva's ideas their expression, for in her Hamilton lecture she used such words as "enslaved," "masses," and "the people" for whom art was a ray of light in the face of "enslavement" by "power-loving leaders." She told her audience that "one of the main virtues of the good artist is an utter humility of a Disciple in front of that great thing — Art" [emphasis in the original]. This was why the action of the Ontario legislature art committee upset her: they disregarded these deep meanings of art in their frivolous purchases of amateur work.

Her view of the artist as "disciple," is similar to how the Group of Seven leader Lawren Harris, who espoused Theosophy, described artists: "The genuine, creative artist," he said, "pioneers for the soul of a people."[9] He believed that artists were the spiritual leaders of the nation, an idea close to Paraskeva's belief that art was the soul of the nation.

These ideas that Brown and Harris articulated had infiltrated Canadian art, and because they were close to Paraskeva's own beliefs about art, she, in spite of herself, was drawn into the stream of Canadian painting and it made her feel she could contribute to it. We know she also had contradictory feelings about Canada's art and artists; that she thought they "didn't think," read, and learn about art, or pay attention to the development of form in painting.[10] The contradiction she felt about Canadian art was like a gremlin on her shoulder that couldn't be shaken off.

All this fed into Paraskeva's lecture, which she concluded by addressing the people of Hamilton directly with an almost religious fervour:

> The consciousness to Art Matters is growing in your city of Hamilton
> in the last few years. I hear that the new art gallery at last is going to be
> built because in a city like yours with [a] population of many Nations
> the well organized art gallery is like a Church of All Nations — the
> place of teaching and inspiration to all that is beautiful inspiring uplifting
> and broadening the moral values in any and all Nations.[11]

In the spring of 1950, she participated in the art associations' exhibition at the Art Gallery of Toronto. She showed *Mid-Winter in Rosedale* (1948), a scene from her neighbourhood, and her watercolour, *Still Life: Plants and Fruit* (1950). She also was represented in "Canadian Painting: An Exhibition Arranged by the National Gallery of Canada" at the National Gallery of Art, Smithsonian Institute, in Washington DC. She exhibited her oil painting *In the Woods* (1939), and the same still life she had shown that spring at the Art Gallery of Toronto. She enjoyed showing in Toronto because she received personal responses to her work from people she knew.

By the 1950s, she had lived in the city long enough that she knew it well and observed its changes. Sidewalk cafés began cropping up. The city's art scene was expanding, particularly with the increasing popularity of the Isaacs Gallery, which Paraskeva visited from time to time. And Toronto's artists had their favourite spots for socializing — Malloney's on Grenville Street, the Pilot Tavern, and Angelo's. But Paraskeva's sense of responsibility to her family would have kept her at home instead of spending her nights drinking with other artists.

The city was expanding at a rapid pace, and the changes reached into the

Clarks' neighbourhood. In 1947 Clifton Road was extended, and in 1948 work began on building Mount Pleasant Road, which cut Roxborough Street into two segments. Because of this, a city bylaw was passed renaming the two segments, which changed the Clarks' address from 256 Roxborough Street East to 56 Roxborough Drive. Paraskeva documented this roadwork in *Building Clifton Road* (1947) and *Road Builders* (1948) (Plate 38).

At that time, Toronto was one of the fastest growing cities in the Western world. "About 2.7 million immigrants arrived in Canada between 1945 and the mid 1960s and at least a quarter came to Toronto."[12] Many Toronto families moved from the central part of the city to the suburbs and their old houses were happily filled by new Canadians. To the north, Don Mills, begun in 1952 when the wealthy E. P. Taylor developed two thousand acres of farmland into a mix of residential and commercial areas, evolved as a unique example of urban design — "a Canadian compromise — between an American plan for a dormitory town replete with industry and all services ..."[13] With the expansion, Metropolitan Toronto was formed in 1953, a new political entity joining a dozen municipalities into one city under Metro Chair Frederick G. Gardiner.[14]

With all this growth, Toronto's streetcar system was no longer adequate; the city had begun the "big dig" for Canada's first subway in 1947, laying track from the foot of Yonge Street just north of Lake Ontario to Eglinton Avenue, about seven and a half kilometres north. After the novelty of inspecting the digging process wore off, Toronto's citizens — including Paraskeva since she walked downtown nearly every day — became annoyed and frustrated with the mess of the big hole on Yonge Street. But when the subway began operating on the next to last day of March 1954, like a mother who forgets her birthing pains, Toronto's frayed nerves were soothed.

Paraskeva could not have guessed that nearly fifty years later her granddaughter and namesake, the artist Panya Clark Espinal, would win a commission for artwork in the Bayview Avenue subway station, part of the new Sheppard Avenue line opened on 24 November 2003. What would Paraskeva think of her granddaughter's two dozen large, sprawling, hand-drawn black images integrated into the white tiles of the walls and floors? From some angles, the objects appear abstract but as one walks along, they come into focus as recognizable, familiar things: a child's tricycle, a watch, a coffee cup. On one of the landings between two tiers of steps, a drawing of a ladder on the tiles begins flat on the floor and climbs the wall, a particularly clever placement. Paraskeva, with her curiosity, would have enjoyed the playfulness and sense of humour of her granddaughter's work in the subway.

Since Paraskeva never learned to drive a car in her one-woman protest of bourgeois life, she used the new subway from time to time but usually went about the city on foot. Of course, if she and Philip were going somewhere together, she rode with him in his car. One of the places she might have walked was to visit her friend Alice Sutton, who lived north of Roxborough Drive in the Yonge and Lawrence area. Paraskeva had met Alice in the late forties through Toronto's music circle and the Adaskins — Alice played a violin, though she never became a professional musician. Sometimes Paraskeva spent ten days at a time with Alice at a cottage near Honey Harbour on Georgian Bay.[15] By the 1950s, Paraskeva preferred vacationing at the Adaskins' cottage, or with the Suttons — she rarely wanted to go to the Clarks' cottage. She complained there was too much work, more than there was at home.

Perhaps it was during her 1950 summer visit at the Sutton cottage that she decided she wanted to paint Alice's portrait (Plate 43). When she asked Alice, Paraskeva knew exactly what she wanted her to wear, which dress and which hat; and Alice's opal ring, which had belonged to her grandmother. Back in Toronto, Alice posed in the Clarks' living room over a period of several weeks, sometimes in the morning, sometimes in the afternoon. After they finished working, they had drinks and talked, while Ben dropped in and out of the room.[16]

Alice's daughter, Anna Sutton Anderson, feels Paraskeva captured a particular characteristic of her mother. Anderson remembers that at age eight she thought her mother had a "severe, pulled-together look — [the] tight face was one I remember well ... My mother was a very disapproving person and that's what [Paraskeva] picked up there."[17] When other family members first saw the portrait, they complained that it did not look like Alice, it was too fierce, to which Paraskeva replied, "She'll grow into it." Alice herself also did not think the portrait a good representation, even though it was "handsome." However, she also said she had no idea how she looked, but she could not connect with that image on the canvas.[18] This portrait attests not only to Paraskeva's competence as a painter, but also to her honesty, even if she was painting a friend, as she took the risk of showing Alice's more brittle, flinty side. The severity in the Alice Sutton portrait is reminiscent of Fred Varley's *Janet P. Gordon* (1925–1926). However, Varley's portrait is stark for its empty background, whereas Paraskeva included her living room in the background of the Sutton portrait.

Alice's feeling about the portrait did not interfere in the two women's friendship. They confided in each other, having frequent long telephone conversations and visits. They had a great deal in common, each having lived in Europe. But what gave them a special bond was that each had lost the great love of her life in youth. Alice's first husband died in Paris, after a short marriage, when she was only twenty-three. Like Paraskeva who grieved all her life for her Oreste, Alice grieved all her life for Fred McCulloch; at age ninety-one in an interview about Paraskeva, Alice would happily have spent most of the time talking about what a wonderful artist her Freddy was.[19] Nevertheless, four years after his death, she was married again to Stewart Sutton, a social worker.

The Suttons hosted many parties, including New Year's Eve celebrations, with artists and musicians as guests, among them Jack Nichols, Will Ogilvie, and the Clarks. From these parties, Paraskeva is the one who stands out in the childhood memories of the Suttons' daughter Anna. She still remembers her eight-year-old self, roaring into the room with noisemakers in celebration of the New Year. Paraskeva would say, "Children are meant to be seen and not heard." Anna was frightened of Paraskeva because she never knew "when she was going to turn and say something in an angry voice."[20] To Anna, Paraskeva seemed angry and unpredictable. How uncharacteristic of Paraskeva that, in that instance, she took upon herself the persona of the proper Torontonian, a stance she so despised.

The year she painted Alice Sutton, Paraskeva began a portrait of another friend, Frances James Adaskin, but she did not finish it until 1952 (Plate 41). It is interesting that Murray called this portrait of his wife "exaggerated, almost a caricature."[21] He would have experienced Frances's warmer, softer side instead of the independent and self-contained aspects Paraskeva conveyed.

Like the Alice Sutton portrait, it reveals the rigid aspects of Frances Adaskin, albeit also her elegance. Perhaps it was her public, performing persona that Paraskeva chose to portray. It was the last portrait Paraskeva painted.

Both of these women, her most intimate friends at the time, would leave Toronto. The Adaskins moved to Saskatoon, Saskatchewan, in 1952 when Murray accepted the position of head of the music department at the University of Saskatchewan. The Suttons left the country in 1954, not returning until 1966 to live in Ottawa. Paraskeva had many acquaintances and casual friends, but very few close friends. It was these more intimate friends she missed when they left Toronto.

She needed her friends and she needed her time in the Ontario forests as it strengthened her feeling of belonging to Canada. She loved the feeling of "dynamism of so-called inanimate forms and objects," which she experienced when she was among trees."[22] At least she spent time with the Adaskins most summers in the forest. With Murray's teaching job came summers off, and he and Frances continued to spend the warm months of the year at their cottage on Canoe Lake. This cottage became a refuge for Paraskeva. Whenever she stayed with the Adaskins, in the mornings Murray would take her in the boat to a spot where she wanted to paint for the day and would pick her up in time for dinner.[23] Being alone with her paints in the forest by the lake would have restored her inner calm, and provided images she could work on in her studio after she returned to Toronto.

An important event of one of her visits to the Adaskins' was her trip by boat to the Tom Thomson memorial at Hayhurst Point. On top of the Thomson cairn, more than twenty metres above the water line of Canoe Lake, a totem points toward the sky. Alice Sutton's son David was the oarsman who took Paraskeva there to paint the memorial, which she painted twice; the first and smaller one she gave to her dear friend Murray Adaskin. When Paraskeva visited the Adaskins at their cabin, they likely had many a conversation about Tom Thomson. Adaskin, in his memoirs, recorded a conversation he had with the proprietor of the local grocery store explaining why he believed that Thomson was murdered. However, "Though intriguing, it wasn't this story that I wanted to capture," Murray said of his 1958 composition, *Algonquin Symphony*, "but Algonquin Park that Tom Thompson [*sic*] and all of us so dearly loved and that gave so generously of its quiet and beauty."[24] Murray knew what he was talking about, for he spent many summers there, playing and composing music.

He had a deep appreciation for Paraskeva's painting of the Thomson memorial. Perhaps that is why she gave it to him, inscribing the small oil, "Paraskeva to Murray, 28 March 50." The larger memorial painting was signed 1951. Ten years later, the Taylor Statten Camp in Algonquin Park reproduced the painting in colour on its Christmas card and Paraskeva was delighted. She sent one of these cards with a note to June and Bill McLean (her friend's son), which is important for what it tells us of her feeling for Canadian art by that time. She wrote on the card to the McLeans:

> I wonder if you received this card from Taylor Statten Camp in Algonquin? If not, I hope you will be interested to see it — for me it was an event — seeing this painting ... reproduced in colour and sent to thousands of people. Just what I hoped for — when I painted it in 1950 — moved by the feeling of the place and subject and sorry that nobody sees it it is so remote — high up above Canoe Lake. Now my dream that through this painting more people will know about it is realized and I am very happy about it.[25]

With this statement, Paraskeva revealed that she had adopted the myth of Tom Thomson, and accepted him as a Canadian icon, which made visiting the memorial a profound experience. Wanting people to know about the memorial means she took on the mantle of responsibility for passing on the significance of Thomson, a symbol of the North, and the memorial's celebration of what Canada is.

"If he had lived," writes Sherrill Grace in *Inventing Tom Thomson*, "or so the story goes, he would have been a founding member of the Group of Seven, which formed in 1920, but dying as he did, during the war but not in the war, his loss seemed to represent the losses so many suffered."[26] Thomson became the hero Canada needed after the Great War ended. For Paraskeva, his tragic end by drowning in Canoe Lake resonated with the death of her Oreste Allegri in the Neva.

It is ironic that just as Paraskeva seemed to have grown into a feeling of kinship with the Group of Seven, their grip on English Canada's art no longer held; the shifts in the art world made her feel as though the ground was being washed out from under her feet. And during the Cold War, she stood out as though "RUSSIAN IMMIGRANT" were etched on her face. Her identity was a constant point of inner conflict — she slipped in and out of the garb of Toronto's culture of the 1950s while inside she still maintained her strong Russian identity. Even after nearly twenty years in Canada, it seemed impossible for her to resolve her personal dilemma: assimilating into a Canadian culture struggling for a clear identity, or retaining her own "strong cultural identity" she had never given up.[27]

What kept her going was praise from the critics for her work. In 1950, she had just concluded her two-year term as president of the Canadian Society of Painters in Water Colour. Andrew Bell, in his critique of a show of the Society, described Paraskeva's work as both sensitive and powerful. "Her paintings are always sensitive, sometimes poignantly so, yet not in the delicate way. They are powerful in exactly the manner of a telling oil." Later in the article, he says, "Powerful art may be a consequence of slow, laboured thought or a sudden, incandescent concept."[28] "Slow" and "laboured" is exactly how Paraskeva described the way she worked.

Her friend Graham McInnes had published a history of Canadian art in 1939; in 1950, he published a revised, updated edition. After seeing the new edition, Paraskeva wrote to McInnes:

> I am profoundly grateful — to the Fate — I suppose — that in your criticism I can find one of the few sources of encouragement of that necessary impetus to go on working — to pull myself up from the constant falls into despair and frustration ... If it would be for Toronto Newspaper Critics I would've stopped painting long ago. So please accept my compliments for the excellent qualities of your book — and my great thankfullness [sic] ...[29]

Packaged with the praise from critics were uncomfortable contradictions — the old stereotypes of the female artist, which were obvious in many articles about Paraskeva: of course, since she is a wife and mother she paints domestic still lifes, the wonders of her own back yard, and landscapes within a stone's throw of her house because she cannot leave her husband and sons. And only *after* she has completed her household duties.[30] She herself said that is the way she arranged her life, but the assumption that this state of affairs was "natural," is problematic for its stereotyping and contributed to yet another of the contradictions that made up her life.

One critic, who visited Paraskeva in her garden and called her "A Painter of Sylvan Canada," concluded, "Perhaps she feels her artistry is best used tending the flowers, and that a woman's glory is to be had not winning laurels for herself, but in spreading joy and gaiety about her."[31] Paraskeva enjoyed being described as a "Painter of Sylvan Canada," but the stereotypically sentimental view of her "spreading joy and gaiety" diminished her strengths as a painter in the minds of readers and compartmentalized her in a way that reinforced her growing opinion that women's place in society was completely unfair. The cheery way in which reviewers wrote about this aspect of her life must have been especially irksome when she was already angry about it.

Despite her domestic duties consuming much of her time, she showed thirty-nine paintings in a one-woman exhibition at The New Laing Gallery in the spring of 1951, a few still lifes but mostly landscapes, among them *Melancholy of a Winter Day* (Plate 42), a scene she might have seen from her second-floor balcony.[32]

Paraskeva lived on the side of a ravine, so in this painting we look down on a hunched dark figure trudging alone up the street that angles up the hill. In the distance, when the leaves were off the trees, she could see houses on the far side of the ravine. We know the artist's house is even higher than her neighbour's because the corner of the brick house next door, with its electrical feed fastened to the edge of the roof, is lower than the position from which she painted the scene. It was completely natural to her, given where her house stood, that her outlook would emulate the high, overall perspective of her teacher twenty years earlier in St. Petersburg.

The soft greys of the painting establish the mood of melancholy. Big snowflakes fill the air; the roofs are covered, and as the snow becomes deeper on the ground, one can imagine the muffled sounds of a snowy day. The artist captured that feeling of the totality of winter that can envelope Toronto in mid-January or early February when the city endures one grey day after another.

IN JANUARY 1952, Paraskeva had another solo exhibition of twenty-six paintings at Victoria College, University of Toronto, a third of which were owned and loaned by J. S. McLean. This exhibition included her 1933 *Myself*, as well as *Petroushka*, which she listed at three hundred and three hundred and fifty dollars, respectively.[33]

Two of her friends wrote her notes of appreciation. Yvonne Housser said, "Your clear colour held its own — it is a fine show, not a bit of shoddy painting in it and sincerity plus intellectual handling of the subject — exciting show." And Carl Schaefer responded that "It did me a power of good" to see her paintings, and they reminded him of the good momentum that their group of artists had in the thirties and forties that was smashed by the war. He, like Paraskeva, was discouraged by the shift to abstraction that led the art world increasingly to overlook the artists of their circle.[34]

Schaefer and Paraskeva exhibited together in a two-person show at the Art Gallery of Toronto two years later. She wanted to show her 1942 *Self Portrait* (a.k.a. *Self Portrait with Concert Programme*), which she also called "Salute to Russia." In a letter to H. O. McCurry at the National Gallery, she said she wanted to show the painting because "I would like the variety for this show — which helas! will be predominately landscape. However, she was worried about vandalism. "... there are so many crazy Russian hating Uranians [*sic*] [Ukrainians] etc. that someone might damage it." In her anxiety, she appealed to McCurry, "Please help me with your opinion." Paraskeva did show the portrait with the concert program, and it was not damaged.

Paraskeva was smart enough that she caught the irony about her show being "predominately landscape" since she had complained from the beginning about Canadian art as "nothing but landscape, landscape, landscape." No wonder she exclaimed, "helas!" — clear evidence that she had mixed feelings about the direction she took in her work away from human subjects. One paragraph is worth quoting simply because it conveys how insecure she felt by the mid-fifties:

> My words of doubts about the quality of my works already belonging to National Gallery — must sound crazy to you. But in the last years I grew so scared of critics and of my own feeling about my painting which I feel is so void of excitement originality adventure — in comparison to what is going on. I am always scared to face my works which I didn't see for [a] long time.[35]

Many artists fret over looking at paintings they have not seen for many years, so in that regard Paraskeva was not unusual. At the same time, she wrote so frequently of her insecurity and anxiety about her work over the years that there must have been basic reasons we have not yet explored. According to cultural critic Carol Becker, "women have internalized centuries of oppression" and have been trained to put first the needs of others — their families — hence they experience anxiety when they pursue their own personal goals and creative enterprises.

As women develop creative careers, they "push against external limitations that attempt to contain and control them," which gives rise to internal anxiety. If this is true of some women's experience in our time, it was even more intense for women in Paraskeva's time when conventions dictated that their primary responsibility was to be a wife and mother. "Anxiety itself embodies a creative component," Becker explained. "Since anxiety is an anticipation of the unknown, a person must imagine that which has not as yet occurred ..." which generates anxiety. "The creative act, focused as it is on the unknown, dependent as it is on the confidence to allow that which does not yet exist to manifest itself, generates anxiety."[36] This kind of anxiety must have underlain Paraskeva's entire career.

And yet, despite her fears she drove onward with her work and continued to show at every opportunity. Once again, she wrote to McCurry in 1954, asking to borrow a painting for a Montreal show with Henri Masson. "I am happy and scared of Montreal critics and public but it is not in my character to refuse meeting the challenge — and I'll try to work as hard as possible for an old girl."[37] She allowed herself to vent her feelings to McCurry, and was grateful that he put up with her and encouraged her so that she could conquer her "chronic state of frustration." She was disappointed when McCurry retired in 1955 and wrote to thank him for his help. During his sixteen years as director of the National Gallery, Paraskeva had come to count on him.

The new director of the National Gallery, Alan Jarvis, would not have been as receptive to her work — and her difficulties — as he was much more interested in changing the thrust of the National Gallery. He set about his mission of showing abstract art and collecting works by international artists, particularly American. Furthermore, he had no time for "'liberated house-wives' who aspired to paint," telling them to "relax and play bridge."[38] These comments resulted in angry editorials in newspapers, as well they should have, and Paraskeva would not only have been highly offended by this attitude; she would have been enraged.

Ironically, around the same time that Jarvis had made these grossly sexist comments about housewives, an article called "Families in the Arts" appeared in *Saturday Night* magazine.[39] "Canadians have a familial approach to the lively arts," it began, featuring artist couples and families. Paraskeva was featured in a photograph with Clive, who was then a third-year architecture student at the University of Toronto. She would have been proud to be featured in the same article with theatre doyenne, Dora Mavor Moore and her son Mavor Moore. People who came to look at her work, Paraskeva said, also were excited by Clive's mobiles. At the same time, the fact that Ben's illness prevented him from developing his talent enough to be included would have been painful for Paraskeva.

In 1954, Paraskeva suffered another loss; her dear friend and patron J. S. McLean died. For a number of years he had been ill, and was too weak to climb the forty-three steps to visit Paraskeva. On a Sunday afternoon, McLean's day for visiting artists, she would go down to street level when he came to 56 Roxborough Drive, and the two would sit in his car and talk.[40] As his letters show, McLean was supportive in a way that reassured and encouraged Paraskeva, especially when she had difficulty with her work. However, when things were going well, she said, "it's as if god was on your shoulder."[41] Conversations with McLean put her into a frame of mind for "god" to appear.

She was then in a stream of landscape painting, but curiously, in the middle of the decade, she returned to her past to paint her fourth rendition of *Memories of Leningrad* (Plate 55). She added more details to the picture of the artist-mother in her loneliness: Ben's cradle made by Oreste is still there and now a guitar-like instrument, probably a Russian balalaika, hangs on the wall. In this new oil, Paraskeva again sits reading with Ben in her lap, but her artist's tools sit idle on the table: books, a pot of artist brushes, a T-square, a triangle, and paper. This is the closest Paraskeva ever came to portraying herself as an artist, but the mother has again taken precedence. A large, heavy shadow behind Paraskeva looms darker in this painting. It is a work that gives visual expression to her life-long complaint that God unfairly targeted women when he distributed responsibility for the young, preventing the time and focus needed to be good artists.

Her mind was drawn away from her sadness and her troubles when she was invited to show her work in Montreal, this time a solo exhibition at MacDonald College, McGill University, in January 1956. She was back in Montreal again in March, taking a short break from her household routines to serve on the jury of the Montreal Museum of Fine Arts annual spring show, travelling at the museum's expense. The organizers had decided to include one out-of-towner on the jury and Paraskeva was that person. She liked the artists in Montreal, and this bit of business gave her an opportunity to visit with friends.

To Paraskeva's delight, Lilias Torrance Newton threw a party for her in her studio. The Montreal artists made sure they had plenty of Paraskeva's favourite beverage — beer. Often, if Paraskeva had any doubts about whether good beer would be available at a party, she brought her own, as when she visited Will Ogilvie.[42]

In the fall, she had another one-woman show, this time in her hometown at Hart House, University of Toronto. Apparently, Premier Leslie Frost, Philip's boss, sent her a letter of praise about her show. She replied, "I was deeply moved that the Premier of our great Province took some of his precious time to write such a kind and friendly message to a woman painter about her exhibit." She said she would always keep his letter as a "precious memento of my painting career."[43] The tone of this letter shows yet another side of Paraskeva, that she could fall in with the hierarchy of society and present herself as a lowly "woman painter" hardly worthy of the premier's time — she was putting herself down.

Paraskeva's show, predominately landscapes, also included eight still lifes, along with her portraits of A. Y. Jackson and Alice Sutton. She also showed an abstract experiment, a dark painting of her kitchen cupboard doors called *Kitchen Cupboard Aspect* (1956) (Plate 56), which was described by her daughter-in-law as "an abstract that she lived in."[44]

To take that idea further, her kitchen was not only where she lived. The painting also "indicates her feeling of enclosure in the home. She has taken the forms of kitchen cupboards and has attempted to break them down into flattened spaces, sustaining a manageable subject matter while attempting an incomprehensible stylistic change. The familiarity of her home now thwarts her ..."[45] Showing this painting would have taken some courage; it was completely different from the other works in the exhibition, but she probably wanted at least to be seen as attempting to explore abstraction for this Hart House show.

At the time, Hart House was still a bastion of men, with university women allowed into the gallery for two hours on Wednesday afternoons. "The public is never invited to come into the gallery unescorted," Hart House's undergraduate secretary told Paraskeva.[46] Nevertheless, the opening was not restricted, for Paraskeva reported that she had a

nice opening attended by my oldest and youngest friends — and I am bragging about the fact that 4 members of the "Painters 11" honoured me by visiting me that evening — and made me happy by their encouraging comments and compliments. For [an] old timer like myself — I think there is no greater satisfaction than to get a word of recognition from young avant garde! One feels then not quite useless — although one should never be discouraged by being in arrière-garde as it has not as glamourous [*sic*] and heroic role in the army but most essential in protecting the life lines of the army.[47]

Paraskeva did not name the artists in Painters Eleven who attended her opening, but it is likely one of the guests was Harold Town with whom she had formed a friendship. This show at Hart House seemed to be a high point in 1956, which had been a good year for Paraskeva.

Feeling rewarded, as her letter to Alan Jarvis shows, Paraskeva was feeling "not quite useless." However, she knew clearly what was happening to non-abstract painters. Taking a place in the "arrière-garde" did not come naturally to her in any "army" of artists. She was happiest on the front lines, but she was no longer there.

14

"Everything on
the Woman"

T he domestic arena, with its expectations of what women will do,
what they will be, what they will provide, is, more often than not,
anathema to the creative work women try to do. Because most women
cannot be in the family without taking care of it, and because being in
it in the traditional way is stultifying, it precludes any possibility of
finding their own safety in that realm. As caretakers for the ambitions,
creativity, and physical well being of others, women often have little
time, space and energy for themselves.[1]

Just as Paraskeva felt herself slipping into the "arrière-garde" of Toronto's art
world, the worst happened: Ben's mental health again deteriorated so much
that he needed hospitalization for a short time in 1957. Paraskeva was devastated. She "would tear her hair and say, Ben, Ben," and worry that he would
continue to need hospitalization.[2] She had come to realize that he would not

recover from his illness; all semblance of normalcy or recovery was gone, and she knew that in some ways she had lost this precious son.

As Clive Clark described it, other people who developed normally could follow a path from one stage to another and turn the pages of life. However, with Ben that was not possible; for him the pages were stuck together.[3] Ben had not grown up and left home, and it appeared Paraskeva would have to look after him for the rest of her life.[4] For many years, trying to find things for Ben to do became one of Paraskeva's major preoccupations. "I am perpetually worried about Ben — not working since December 4th 63," she wrote to A. Y. Jackson. "He's taking [a] course — evening classes in the College of Art on commercial art." She told Jackson that she asked other artists, her friends, to find work for him but it seemed any jobs he did land did not work out for very long. She ended her letter with "Painting is hell!"[5]

Looking back now, how Ben spent his time over the years is vague in the memory of family members. After his diagnosis of schizophrenia in 1943, he had attended classes at the Ontario College of Art off and on, and he managed to hold various jobs for short periods of time: at the National Film Board, Rapid Grip, and Batten, among other companies.[6] In the early sixties, Philip got Ben a job doing design and drafting work for the Ministry of Transportation. One of his biggest accomplishments was designing the pattern on the concrete retaining walls on Bayview Avenue at Lawrence Avenue, which is still in place. However, Ben did not have the ability to be consistently productive; he had problems with falling asleep at his drafting table. Apparently, this was the last time he held a position — he left this job the same year that Philip retired.

Paraskeva did not trust Ben to run his own life, and looked after him in the same way one would supervise an adolescent. When he went out, she gave him money to spend and told him when to be home. When he was out on his own, she feared he would get into situations he could not handle. "I think she gave him as much freedom as she felt she could, but he wouldn't be capable of having any real relationships with anybody on his own," Clive explained. His parents tried to do what they could to give him a normal life, but frequently things happened that made his inabilities obvious. Paraskeva simply stayed home with Ben.

Much of what the family could and couldn't do was determined by Ben's needs. "With Ben, the idea that there was any possibility of Mom and Dad going away and leaving Ben in someone else's care was absolutely beyond any possibility ... because Mother would be worried the whole time and she would not be able to enjoy herself."[7]

Ben determined Paraskeva's outlook on life, her attitude toward her painting. As he became increasingly silent and withdrawn, his presence became a heavy weight through interminable nights and days that must have felt as though they would multiply into the future and never end. However, she carried on with a stalwart constancy — characteristic of her Russian heritage — in her feeling that she had no choice: he was her son.

Her feeling of responsibility for Ben while trying to be an artist consolidated her feeling about the injustice of the order of things, that men have an enormous advantage. She believed that a woman could be a great actor, but not a great painter.[8] Women were short-changed when it came to painting; "god put everything on the woman — pregnancy, menstruation and what not." As she spoke about the place of women, Paraskeva's lower lip jutted out, and she flailed her arms — she spoke with her whole body, vibrating with frustration and anger, her voice emphatic.

"For women it's no good. They are not good painters. The lord made them to be mothers and that's all ... their heart always taken by anxiety or something while in painting you have to close the key on the door from everything."[9] She felt, if she were hard-hearted, she could lock her door, as men can do, and just paint, but she wasn't a man and she couldn't do it.

Upstairs from her perpetually unlocked studio door was her kitchen, which provided subject matter for work. She painted *Kitchen Still Life* (1957) (Plate 48) the same year that Ben's second breakdown occurred. In the painting, beets in a metal colander sit on her grey-blue tiled kitchen counter. Light from the window shines through the star-shaped perforations in the metal and throws a round shadow on the surface beside a cutting board and knife. Behind the colander, on the windowsill, stands a pitcher with "MILK" inscribed on it. However, it is filled with soil instead of milk, for a plant is growing in it, hanging down over the handle.

This painting is an image of what she faced in the kitchen where she was the cook, the one who nourished her family with these juicy, wine-red vegetables. And yet it was the hours given to preparing this wholesome food that prevented her from the amount of time she needed for painting, an activity that nourished her artist soul. It was an irresolvable conflict.

In her training with Petrov-Vodkin, she absorbed the point of view of artists after the Russian Revolution of honouring objects of everyday life, especially those in the domestic realm. Though this ideal might seem admirable, it was these very objects that symbolized the domestic trap in which Paraskeva found herself, creating an inherent contradiction in her artistic practice. Thus, her seemingly placid still lifes, appreciated by critics of the time as something normal for a housewife to paint, are politically charged statements — as were the paintings on social injustice in the thirties — in that their meaning represents a challenge to patriarchal order.

Above Paraskeva's kitchen sink were two beautiful, large windows, each one with twenty-five small panes. For more than forty years, Paraskeva spent hours on end looking through those windows onto the embankment behind the house as she washed the dishes and cooked meals for her family. What happened by the light of those windows never really changed all those years. Cooking is cooking.

It was inevitable that she would paint her windows, and she did it in somewhat of a cliché: a lone moth sitting in a corner of one of those many dark windowpanes, a departure from her usual subject matter, but also an experiment with acrylic paint rather than the oils she had used for years. It was her visual statement of the outbursts about women whose purpose was "just to produce more men ... It's nature. Everything male and female to produce more," she ranted, her voice tight, metallic sounding, full of scorn.[10] This window painting, *Summer Night* (1969) (Plate 58), can be seen as a self-portrait by an artist who sees how thwarted many women of her generation were in their attempts to break free.

Underlying her difficult personal experiences was also the social climate of the times. Women's domestic duties in the 1950s included responsibility for the morality of the family, what art historian Linda Nochlin called "the demands of atmosphere-making," as identified by the English writer Dorothy Richardson (1873–1957).

There is for a Dostoyevsky writing against time on the corner of a crowded kitchen table a greater possibility of detachment than for a woman artist no matter how placed. Neither motherhood nor the more continuously exacting and indefinitely expansive responsibilities of even the simplest housekeeping can so effectively hamper her as the human demands, besieging her wherever she is, for an inclusive awareness, from which men, for good or ill, are exempt.[11]

In the 1950s, married women were assigned the role of "tension manager," something that was emphasized by advertisements of the time: Ovaltine at bedtime for married couples, prepared by the wife of course, to sooth the day's tensions; Lysol as a disinfectant to keep the husband from leaving the house with his packed suitcase.[12] For Paraskeva, that "inclusive awareness" encompassed a schizophrenic son.

"But it's sad," she said about what happens to women.[13] And another time she observed, "Women cannot do the best work in comparison to men, but a whole lot of women are better than a whole lot of men. The talent is there — a lot of women are very good painters."[14] On another occasion she observed that even if women have equal talent, they have not "acquired the *power* of male painters" [emphasis in original][15] referring once more to the impact of society on women.

Other women Paraskeva knew experienced similar conflicts between domesticity and their painting. Her friend Pegi Nicol MacLeod, after her daughter Jane was born, discovered that the demands of motherhood and her role as a wife robbed her of her focus for painting and, like Paraskeva, "she complained constantly." A feeling of self-doubt also occasionally accompanied the conflict.[16]

That Paraskeva knew something of the strength of other women painters was a small piece of redemption for her in her otherwise bleak picture of female artists. And she also knew something of her own strength. According to Gail Singer, who spent many hours in conversation with Paraskeva and filming her, she was an "instinctive feminist in the sense that she experienced herself in a certain way to be capable of — if it weren't for the cultural shackles — to be capable of anything anybody else could do."[17] Even if the word "feminist" was not one Paraskeva used, one can find things she did throughout her life that make the description of her as an "instinctive feminist" ring true.

Here it is worth recalling Paraskeva's action at the 1941 artists' conference in Kingston. Of all the women present — and there were many — Paraskeva was the one who objected to an all-male resolutions committee. She spoke only two words: "No women?" Her question was significant. She dared to challenge the men in charge who hedged and put her off, thereby making her seem a nuisance in the proceedings. Nuisance or not, Paraskeva was committed to having a political voice.

The disappointment for Paraskeva at the Kingston conference would have been that all the other women were silent and did not support her. The biographies of the women who participated in the conference reveal that Paraskeva was the only "foreigner," the only one not native to North America or Britain; she had already been an outsider for ten years so perhaps she had less to lose in speaking out at a meeting in which men were totally in charge. One can only conclude that the proper order of the place of men and women — which Paraskeva could not accept — was so strong at the time that none of the other women had the courage to speak out. Paraskeva could feel at least some satisfaction that because of her interjection, in the end, one woman, the sculptor Frances Loring, sat on the continuation committee. That experience in Kingston confirmed her understanding of women's position in the art world of her era, something she had learned early in her career as an artist.[18]

Similarly, we know that during the war when she was asked to paint the drama of women's work, she pointed out that their jobs in the military were like those they did at home, working primarily as cooks or in clerical positions — not much drama there, and they had no positions of power. Even though she had the awareness of women's place in society, her own scope of understanding was limited, resulting in enormous contradictions. She was bothered that women had no authority in those positions, but she also believed women were physically less capable than men. She explained this point of view in a 1959 speech on women artists at Ridley College in St. Catharines, Ontario.[19] "When I came to the point — in my work — when frustration set in, long ago — I realised that the whole History of Painting is against the Women Painters. That her whole physical and mental make up is not suited to gather these forces — necessary to produce a really important work of Art — comparable to the World of Art — created by men."

Because painting is a plastic medium, one of the material arts, it requires physical effort, she said. "Man is more physical in all his impulses of life — hence — a greater ability to excell [*sic*] in Plastic Arts — which are in the realm of Material World." Here she was caught in the ideas of the time that women were weaker than men but was trying to refute it, saying that "Women Artist[s] realize that they have to stand up to this bad *world record* [emphasis in original] and tryed [*sic*] to combat it somehow — hence examples of Women Writers taking man's names such as George Sand in France and George Elliott [*sic*] [Eliot] in England."

Despite the "bad" history, Paraskeva singled out a number of female artists: among others, Marie Louise Elisabeth Vigée-LeBrun, Angelica Kauffmann, Constance Marie Charpentier, Rosa Bonheur, Paula Modersohn-Becker, Käthe Kollwitz, and Frances Hodgkins, one of Emily Carr's teachers. Paraskeva gave an overview of Emily Carr, the only Canadian artist she mentioned.

When it came to the French artist Suzanne Valadon (1865–1938), Paraskeva not only mentioned her but also went into detail about her life and her work. Among all the artists mentioned in the lecture, Valadon is the only one whose body of work included many still lifes, as well as portraits, nudes, and landscapes. As one art historian pointed out, Paraskeva "wanted to align herself with women artists,"[20] and Valadon would have been one of those.

It is highly possible that Paraskeva saw the two Valadon exhibitions in Paris in 1929 at the Galerie Bernier, a large retrospective of prints and drawings early in the year, and an exhibition of her recent works that summer, which would have included still lifes, nudes, and landscapes.[21] Paraskeva's *Overlooking a Garden* (1930), a tempera and watercolour piece she likely painted from her third-storey room in Chatou, has much in common with *Sacré Cœur*, a landscape Valadon painted the previous year.

In developing her lecture on female artists, it is not surprising that Paraskeva paid special attention to Valadon, a woman similar to herself; a vigorous, honest woman, who ignored the rules of society, was outspoken, and lived as she pleased. And Paraskeva would have admired Valadon for her daring in using the nude as one of the central themes in her work, as she cited in her lecture the "happy animal vitality" in Valadon's figures.

Valadon's paintings of nudes included many images of women at their bath, among them an oil called simply *Bathers*, an outdoor scene of women and girls bathing in a river. It is interesting to discover that one mother in this painting, leading her young daughter, resembles the mother and young daughter in Paraskeva's 1944 *Public Bath — Leningrad* (Plate 32.) Except for the paintings of the St. Petersburg bathhouse (the city's name when Paraskeva was a child was St. Petersburg, not Leningrad, but she insisted always on the use of "Leningrad"), Paraskeva did not paint nudes. However, more than once Paraskeva mentioned her desire to work on drawing the figure. In notes for an application for a Guggenheim Fellowship in the early forties, she stated that she wanted to study the figure, among other things. In the early fifties, she did take a life drawing class, and some of those pencil drawings of nudes still exist.[22]

As the conclusion of the section on Valadon in Paraskeva's lecture shows, the still lifes were what she admired most; she stated that Valadon reached the height of her art in the still lifes. And it was these paintings that fed into Paraskeva's many works in the same genre. However, Paraskeva did not necessarily choose the most beautiful objects for her still lifes, but she chose "things that are a little more symbolic, so she's pushing them in the direction that they have a meaning, an edge."[23] Valadon chose beautiful objects, and repeated them, for example a vase with a painted pattern and a certain piece of fabric. Her still lifes are rich with vibrant colour, many including the same patterned drapery. One of Paraskeva's still lifes in particular seems connected to Valadon's work: the formal aspects of her untitled watercolour of three pears with a patterned cloth behind them relates to Valadon's oil on canvas, *Still Life with Candle Holder* (1921), despite that the two works are in different media.

The parallels between Valadon and Paraskeva do not end with their painting; there were similarities in their personal lives. For both of them, early mother-hood was a time of struggle for survival; both married a man from a more well-to-do class; and each had a son who suffered from mental illness. Valadon's son, Maurice Utrillo, diagnosed when young by a psychiatrist as having "a schophrenic condition,"[24] was treated for "dipsomania" — an intense craving for alcohol — and spent time in asylums.[25] Valadon taught her son how to paint in an attempt to help him gain some stability, and eventually, unlike Paraskeva's son Ben, Utrillo achieved recognition and fame for his paintings. In the male-dominated art world, Valadon sometimes received more recognition for being Utrillo's mother than she did for her own painting. Of course, this did not happen to Paraskeva; she would have been overjoyed if Ben had recovered enough to have his work recognized.

Developing a lecture such as this one on women artists fed Paraskeva's spirit and bolstered her personal life. Her lectures are significant because they show us the extent to which she had educated herself on art history, and though she left behind little of her own writing, the handwritten lectures are dense with evidence of how well read she was in her areas of interest.

BY THE END of the 1950s, with the weight of her many losses and life disappointments, Paraskeva continued to find solace in her garden, which by then had become a passion. To the west of the house there was already an oak tree growing when the Clarks bought the house, and at the bottom of the hill a pine and an ash. Below the house, she covered the slope in trees — as many as seventy-five — because she loved trees, especially the birch trees she planted, and the Serbian Spruce.

Because of the hill, the Clarks' yard was the same level as the second floor of the house next door where the Miller family lived. Paraskeva's trees made a big impression on the boys. "Our bedroom window looked right into those spruce trees, thick, thick, thick," Gavin Miller recalled. Paraskeva, as she went up and down her stone steps, or along the path the mail carrier cut on the hill, often stopped to talk to the boys about her trees, saying they reminded her of Russia. "She waxed eloquent about their form," Eric Miller said; she liked trees with drooping boughs. He now feels that indirectly Paraskeva's love for growing things influenced his decision to become a botanist.[26]

Paraskeva made winding pathways on the hill among her trees. She also planted bushes and perennials in her garden around the house: monarda, rose mallow, Oriental poppies, veronica spicata. A few of her plantings, after the turn of the twenty-first century, were still growing: a Japanese tree peony, Solomon's Seal along a terraced area behind the house, and on the south and east sides of the house her climbing roses, with the trunk of the one on the east side at least four inches across at the ground.

Clematis Flower (1951) (Plate 51), one of Paraskeva's window paintings with a potted plant on a windowsill, pictures the hill outside her house in winter. The scene in oils in the subdued winter colours are broken only by the deep green of the indoor plant. The steep bank we see in this painting gave Paraskeva problems with soil erosion and she used all kinds of debris in an attempt to hold the soil in place — leftover building materials, like boards and pipes, to keep the embankment from washing away. She made war against the squirrels that chewed on her bulbs, calling them "rats with furry tails." They took the brunt of her frustration as Paraskeva squirted them with the hose.[27] This was her own territory, and no critters who worked against her were welcome. Needing the outlet for frustration and disappointment the digging and planting offered, she allowed no one else to help her with her work.

Paraskeva's way of being in the garden was completely different from that of the other Rosedale matrons, as she sometimes even worked in her bare feet. When Douglas Gibson came by one fall in his canvassing during a civic election in late October or early November, he found her in her garden, barefoot. When he told her it was too cold to be outdoors barefoot, she brushed him aside with "I am Russian" — she was far too tough to succumb to Toronto's damp, cold weather in her garden.[28]

Tidiness was the norm among Rosedale mothers, no matter what the task, and even in the garden, according to Geoffrey O'Brian who lived a few doors away from the Clarks when he was young. "When my mother worked in the garden she was very proper." But Paraskeva wore old grubby clothes when she worked outdoors. O'Brian would see her wearing old rubber boots and "old painter shirts and she would have mud and dirt all over her hands." She had dirt on her cheeks, too, and "looked like a Russian peasant who was embracing the soil."[29]

Paraskeva *was* bound to the soil. She asked O'Brian to bring her soil from Leningrad when he was a university student and travelled to Russia in the late sixties with his friend, the son of the deputy ambassador in Moscow. But those were the days when Westerners were monitored in where they went and what they did, and O'Brian would have been too nervous to dig up soil in Leningrad even if he had seen some. Instead, he brought Paraskeva a silver Leningrad pin.[30]

Paraskeva not only enjoyed the work of gardening, she enjoyed talking about her garden with people who were appreciative. Wentworth Walker, who loved looking at gardens, still recalls being in her garden with her one day in early spring. They discussed how a gardener nourishes plants and she told him one of the ways of doing that is by talking to the flowers, something she continued as long as she gardened.[31]

Paraskeva's garden became the opposite of the part of her world that veered outside her control; she created an "intimate landscape," a place that was safe, where she was fully in control. "While her career was moving away from her, her family and garden took its place."[32] She enjoyed sharing this space she created, and the Clarks' house on the hill became known for the summer garden parties, in which Paraskeva shone; she and Philip were welcoming hosts for these events, providing good food and drinks. Many artists, musicians, and others in the Clark circle of friends climbed the forty-three steps on a Sunday afternoon for a garden party with conversation, discussion of politics — sometimes arguments brought on by Paraskeva — and laughter. Always, by the late fifties and early sixties, Ben hovered quietly in the background, or disappeared into his room upstairs with his beer, cigarettes, and television.

In the spring of 1959, Paraskeva's family life entered a new phase with Clive's marriage to Mary Patterson. They had both graduated from the University of Toronto's School of Architecture the previous fall. Paraskeva was disappointed that they weren't graduating in the spring with the rest of their class. As Mary tells it, "Clive and I arrived on the doorstep and had to tell [Paraskeva] that we weren't going to graduate in May; we had some supplementals; we weren't going to have the spring Convocation. She turned on her heels and she grabbed her fork and she started digging, digging, digging and digging, and then she'd reach into her pocket like this and pull out her handkerchief and [wiped her eyes] and dig and dig and dig."[33] Paraskeva was upset because Clive and Mary weren't at the top of the class. Obviously, she was as demanding with her family as she was with herself in her painting. But the story is classic Paraskeva, and shows how she dealt with her frustration.

With her son's marriage came the prospect of grandchildren. Joel was born the year after Clive and Mary married, and two years later, Jennifer. Panya, named for Paraskeva, is the youngest of the three. Paraskeva loved being a grandmother and was soon presiding over a family dinner with Clive and Mary's family every other Sunday evening. These Sunday dinners at 56 Roxborough Drive became a tradition that none of Paraskeva's family would ever forget. Clive and Mary, with their young ones, would arrive in late afternoon in time for tea with petits fours and puff pastry "palm leaves." There was also liver pâté with crackers, and Philip served drinks. Paraskeva offered the children pop and candies, which Mary protested. Sometimes she and Paraskeva got into arguments over giving the children sweets before dinner and other times Mary "turned a blind eye."

There was a special drawer for the grandchildren in Paraskeva's kitchen, and they knew which one it was. With each visit, they found new little toys that their grandmother had bought, usually at Troyka, the Russian store. Paraskeva enjoyed clowning and joking around with the children and doing "wacky" things. Panya recalled that once her grandmother took out her dentures and pretended to put them in Panya's mouth. Or she might dance around and lift her skirt, any dramatics that would amuse the children.[34] They knew this was not a typical grandmother's behaviour; Mary's parents provided a stark contrast with their much more conventional ways.

Until dinnertime, Philip would sit in the living room reading the paper and Clive sat with him, reading, perhaps, *National Geographic*. Mary was here and there supervising the children and sometimes in the kitchen talking with Paraskeva. Meanwhile, Paraskeva had spent Sunday morning working in the garden or in the studio, while Philip was usually at the Arts & Letters Club. In the afternoon, she was in her well-equipped kitchen with its white enamel pastry table, pantry, and ample cupboards, making preparations for dinner. When everyone arrived, she was in and out of the kitchen cooking one of her big dinners: stroganoff, spaghetti with her own sauce — she called it "macaronis" — chicken with lemon and rice, or roast beef, the meats always with sauces or gravy.

But no Yorkshire pudding with the roast beef — too British. At the Clarks', mashed potatoes with lots of butter, lima beans, and turnip were all favourites. Her salads were plain, iceberg lettuce with vinegar and oil. For special occasions for dessert, she prepared *Kissel*, a puree of fruit — she had no blender in those days, so she had to mash the fruit through a sieve — mixed with sugar and corn flour to thicken it, something the uninitiated might call "fruit soup," but you could not call it that around Paraskeva. It was "KEE-ssel." Or she might make a chestnut-whipped cream dessert for guests.

Paraskeva did not bake pies or cakes; even for birthdays, she bought cakes at the patisserie. However, at Easter she prepared the elaborate traditional Russian rich cheese desert, Paskha. An article describing her as an artist in the kitchen as well as the studio was printed to coincide with her one-woman exhibition at the Laing Gallery in 1951, and reproduced her Paskha recipe.[35] Traditionally, to form the Paskha, Russians used pyramid- or mound-shaped moulds, for the cheese mixture had to sit under weights for several days and drain until it was compressed and firm. It was then decorated with nuts or candy in a pattern of the letters XB, which stands for "Christ is risen." Paraskeva sometimes put her cheese mixture in cheesecloth in clean, clay flowerpots so the excess liquid could drain through the bottom holes. She made these individual Paskhas and gave them to her friends and Clark family members.

Paraskeva must have been a careful, tidy cook, for her 1940 *The Modern Hostess Cookbook* is so used that the covers are loose, but on the inside, there are no spots whatsoever.[36] She claimed to be an advocate of plain, simple cooking, but it had to be delicious, which her family says her dishes always were. It was against her communist beliefs to be a gourmet cook or to have an interest "in food for the sake of food or fanciness. To get all excited about going to fancy restaurants and all these recipes and stuff was decadent," Clive said. What Paraskeva did in her kitchen, however, contradicted the doctrine she claimed to espouse. Her cooking would have been seen as gourmet.[37]

For the family dinners, Ben would set the table, and when everything was ready all the plates were taken to the kitchen and each plate was served there. Paraskeva did all this herself; she did not want anyone to help her. Philip was the kind of person who liked calm and order; the Clark family dinners were anything but that. Though Paraskeva's plate was filled like everyone else's, she never sat down to eat with the family. She was back and forth serving, doing innumerable tasks in the kitchen, in and out, and bringing dishes to the table.

The Clarks' television was on wheels, and Paraskeva occasionally wheeled it into the dining room so the kids could watch TV while they ate, something that threw their mother "over the top." Other times, when the grandchildren became too restless, she herself crawled under the table to play with them. Meanwhile, Philip, exasperated, and going "nuts," would say something like, "Paraskeva, sit down and eat your dinner ... Then she'd turn on her heel and go to the kitchen. She did not like being ordered." This was only one of the ways in which Paraskeva communicated that she would have nothing to do with the idea of Philip as "head" of the house, which was the custom in the family structure at the time. This scene was repeated over and over, each time the family gathered, so that it became predictable. Philip and Paraskeva then threw more words at each other, until at the end of the meal he got up, with Clive following, threw his napkin on the table, stomped off to the living room, slammed the door shut and turned on the television.

Meanwhile, Paraskeva and Mary, who also liked a good argument, took the opportunity to argue about art, life, and politics. "She would say no women could be Picasso," Mary recalled. "And then I would say, well, what about Barbara Hepworth? And she'd say, well, she's nobody and so on and it would go from there. There was always some kind of issue. But I mean, I enjoyed arguing with her. We sort of had fun doing it, but Philip couldn't stand it." Nor could Clive stand it. "It was always at high volume, and yelling. I wouldn't have any problem with a good discussion about art or politics. It was just this yelling that was unbelievable. I see no point in people yelling at each other, I just can't deal with it." Clive said. Ben, meanwhile, had gone to his room, the grandchildren were playing, and eventually Paraskeva and Mary had enough arguing. "The living room would open and they would come in nice and quiet and everything would be normal," Clive said.[38] But "normal" for Paraskeva was exactly what had been happening during the entire visit.

Her refusal to sit at the table for family dinners seems legendary, for it is something all the Clark family members talk about. More than that, it is perplexing. However, in certain cultures women who served the meal did not sit down to eat with the people they were serving. The art historian Linda Nochlin, in writing of the work of peasant women of the mid-nineteenth century, noted, "According to many witnesses, peasant-women never sat down to table with their menfolk, but stood, ready to serve those who ate at the table."[39] Was Paraskeva simply acting out her claim that she was a peasant even if she lived in Rosedale?

Michael Ignatieff, whose grandfather was Count Paul Ignatieff, the last minister of education in the Russian government of Nicholas II, gives an account of his grandmother Natasha at dinners when the family was in exile on a farm in England. Her origin was the noble class, the other end of the spectrum from peasant-Paraskeva; however Natasha Ignatieff, too, "served meal after meal, bringing in the dishes from the kitchen, wandering to and fro" and did not sit down to eat with everyone else.[40] These accounts give Paraskeva's behaviour some context and highlight the clash of cultures that were part of the fabric of the Clark family: Russian versus British-Canadian. For Paraskeva, this disparity was intensified by her devotion to the family in the face of her dedication to painting.

In many of her still lifes, she brought together her two worlds of family and art. When some of her choices of objects in her still lifes were questioned, as in the case of her 1935 *Rubber Gloves* (Plate 62), Paraskeva pointed out that rubber gloves are "formful" and "colourful."[41] This in itself was justification for using them in a still life, and in the same painting, she included a part of a watermelon for the same reasons. She attributed meaning to these objects beyond their everyday place. It might seem incongruous that in the still life a glove and a bowl of carrots in water are resting on a book, with riffled sheets of paper in the background, perhaps a magazine. However, she had her reasons: her chores, for which she needed rubber gloves, must take precedence over her book, which is closed, but her kitchen has not obliterated her love of reading.

She read widely, as shown by her collection of art magazines, books, and clippings on myriad subjects, which she left behind in her studio, most of them undated and unidentified: Nazi atrocities, clippings on health, schizo-phrenia, Einstein's theories, Soviet theatre and literature, European artists, her friends' exhibitions and awards, artist housing in New York City. Even as late as 1981, she was still saving clippings about the Communist Party.[42]

Reading was part of what she called her "three Bs": beer, book, bed. Her library at the end of her life included books on Russian art, Russian theatre, Canadian art, American art, as well as French and English magazines.[43] She read Russian novels all her life, in Russian, which she bought at Troyka, as well as anything she could find about Soviet art. She once told an inter-viewer, "I often dig into my family budget to get a book on art."[44]

As well she might. Philip, who supported her, was always well paid. He had been Assistant Controller of Revenue for Ontario after 1937 under three dif-ferent premiers until 1950 when he had moved up to Controller of Revenue under Leslie Frost who became premier the year before. Philip had developed a reputation as a tax expert, and was dubbed "Mr. Sales Tax" and "Mr. Three Per Cent" because he was the one who crafted the 1961 Ontario sales tax for the Leslie Frost government. Philip had spent the previous year working on the draft act, and since 1950 had studied taxes of other jurisdictions. He not only formulated the workings of the tax, but also hired and trained a staff of more than five hundred and became "a one-man answering service handling the thousands of questions directed to him."[45]

In 1937 when he began working for the Ontario government, Philip was paid $3,636.68, and by 1950, it was more than twice that, $7,999.92. By 1958, Philip's salary — $14,999.96 — was almost a thousand dollars more than the premier's. When Philip retired in 1963, his salary at $18,000 was two thousand more than that of Premier John P. Roberts, who was being paid $16,000.[46] That he was one of the highest paid senior civil servants was not something Philip would have divulged to his family or his friends, but it would have given him enormous satisfaction.

Just before he retired, he caught up on the vacation days owing him since 1961. His dedication to his work was evident during his holiday when he spent at least an hour of every day in the office, a five-minute walk from where he was born at 44 Willcocks Street. As a reminder of his origins, PTC4400 was his car license number.[47]

After Philip "retired," he set up his own business as a chartered accountant in an office in downtown Toronto. With his habit of working long hours every day, he knew he had to continue with some kind of work or it wouldn't be long before he would be "pushing up the daisies."[48] Furthermore, he and Paraskeva would have been asking for trouble if the two of them had been together at the house every day. Philip's clients included artists, who consulted him because they knew Paraskeva, and because he understood artists' situation. Philip also looked after the accounts for such arts groups as the Canadian Group of Painters, Canadian Society of Painters in Water Colour, and the Arts & Letters Club at no charge, demonstrating in a practical way his love for the arts, and his belief that those who were able should support the arts.

Artists appreciated Philip's support, but some detested his sales tax. A. Y. Jackson virtually ignored the business aspects of being an artist, and cursed bureaucrats such as Philip. O. J. Firestone, in his biography of Jackson, told a humorous story of visiting Jackson soon after agents from both the federal and provincial tax departments had visited him. These officials had pushed Jackson into a fury. In his visit, Firestone observed that a person selling something subject to sales tax in effect became "an agent acting for the Crown in collecting tax at the time of the sale." Jackson became furious all over again. "He was not going to be any damn Crown agent," he retorted, raising his voice (a rare happening).[49]

It would be interesting to know what Jackson's encounters were like with Philip at the garden parties at 56 Roxborough Drive. Certainly, the Clarks both considered Jackson a friend, and Philip must have known that he was one artist who could not be bothered with record keeping and accounts. Philip, of course, was a strong believer in a citizen's duty to pay taxes. "He really hated people who pulled all kinds of stunts to avoid paying taxes and then expected to get services and complained if they didn't."[50]

The year Philip retired, he and Paraskeva changed the way their house was registered.[51] The original registration was "Philip T. Clark and Paraskeva, his wife." At the end of 1963, the house was registered as "Philip T. Clark and Paraskeva Clark his wife as tenant in common." This legal transaction was significant because it meant that they each owned half the property and each had the right to possess the entire property. Philip would have known the ins-and-outs of tax laws, and by changing the designation the property would not be required to pass through probate, which would have been costly.

Paraskeva's own records of her income from her paintings are less than tidy. An old notebook lists her paintings and their prices from 1948 to 1967. Other financial records from 1957 to 1975 list both her expenses and sales. According to this list, she had no expenses after 1973, which means she painted very little after she was seventy-five.

Even though her own accounting records would not satisfy tax officials, Philip had set up an accounting system for her to the best advantage, a system he outlined in a 1969 letter to Charles Comfort in reply to a letter asking for advice for a fee on how to handle his finances when he had a sell-out exhibition.[52] Philip had meticulously "measured all her expenses, studio, canvases, boards, paints, glass, frames, travel expense" and anything else related to the production of her work in one calendar year to determine the percentage of the total value of her paintings. He discovered the expenses came to forty-five percent of the value of the paintings. If she sold nothing in a given year, she claimed no expenses. However, when she sold paintings, forty-five percent of the income was deducted as expenses. Philip recommended the same system to Comfort, and offered to prepare his income tax statement.

Financially, Paraskeva and Philip were secure. However, in her professional life Paraskeva was more insecure than ever because the art of the 1960s that she saw seemed not only foreign, but outright bizarre. Abstract canvases were one thing, but artists were exploring all kinds of other media: a variety of industrial materials including plastics, neon tubes, sheets of Mylar, and such found objects as charred barrel staves. Some artists played with colour in a way that tricked one's eyes, creating optical possibilities, or "op art." At the other end of the painting spectrum were the white paintings of Ronald Bloore.

All these changes in the art world were overwhelming. But through it all Paraskeva admired Harold Town and some of the other abstract artists of his generation. She even experimented with a few abstract paintings, but she knew herself well enough to realize that she could not reinvent herself to fit in with current trends. Other artists, some of Paraskeva's friends, shared her uneasiness with abstract painting. Pegi Nicol MacLeod was one, and unlike Paraskeva, she avoided the trend in her own work.[53] Carl Schaefer, too, agreed with her about abstraction, saying that her paintings, and his, held their own in comparison to the abstractionists he dubbed "space cadets and dribble boys."[54] Because he knew Paraskeva's point of view, the Montreal artist Henri Masson, with whom she had a show in December 1954, wrote to her staunchly defending figurative painting. He objected to artists' changing painting styles like new spring hats. Furthermore, he compared abstract art to the Tower of Babel; no one could comprehend the meaning, he said, and he could hardly stand the current Ontario Society of Artists (OSA) show in Toronto.[55]

Beginning in the early sixties, the number of exhibitions in which Paraskeva showed her work decreased dramatically, but not for lack of galleries; by the sixties interest in the arts swelled and Toronto had more than fifty galleries compared to three when she arrived thirty years earlier. Nor was the reason a lack of her submissions to the associations; it was because of rejections by the juries. The jury rejections hurt Paraskeva deeply. Her friend, the portraitist Irma Coucill visited Paraskeva in her studio, and recalls that she was upset and shocked. "She was so distraught. She said 'They've rejected my painting and I'm a member of the OSA and RCA — they reject my work.' It was quite a blow." She told Coucill that she could never paint like the non-objective artists because to her it was meaningless; she had to paint her own way and be true to her own beliefs.[56] Paraskeva unloaded her distress and criticism of the art world to Coucill more than once. As she held Coucill's hands Paraskeva spoke in a loud voice, no matter where they were. It did not bother her that everyone else on the street or the streetcar, for example, could hear what she was saying.

The fall of 1963, particularly, was for her "the season of troubles and blows from one jury to another," as she put it in a letter to the director of the Art Gallery of Hamilton. She felt so upset by the trends in art that her few attempts at abstraction confirmed for her the feeling that she was "too old to invent," and yet, like Chekov, she had a desire, she said, to "make the earth more beautiful."[57] However, in the midst of her feeling of being worn down and left behind, there was one bright spot: the Art Gallery of Hamilton bought her *Rain on the Window* (undated) (Plate 61) for $350. She was effusive in her thanks to the director because it gave "a shot in the arm for an old painter."[58]

15

More than a
Grain of Sand⤸

Art: to bring the joy to the eyes — to our hearts,
to banish sorrow and to express the joy of being alive,
and the thankfulness for the feeling of this joy.[1]

In 1965, the city of Toronto opened its new city hall on Queen Street, just west of the old city hall at the top of Bay Street. The two curved towers hugging the council chambers — a centre building shaped like an upside-down saucer — were designed by the Finnish architect, Viljo Revell. The wide concrete plaza in front of city hall, Nathan Phillips Square, with its pool and fountain in summer and ice rink in winter, would evolve into a popular gathering place.

And what about the old city hall? For a time it was threatened with demolition, but good sense and appreciation for Toronto's history prevailed and the red stone building, over a century old by then, with its clock tower overlooking Bay Street, was not torn down. Many Torontonians were fond of this old building. For Paraskeva, the old city hall held a special place in her memory; it was the vantage point of her painting *Pavlichenko and Her Comrades at City Hall* (Plate 28) from 1943.

In the thirty years since she had come to Toronto, the city's skyline had changed dramatically, something Paraskeva noticed as she walked the city's streets. Back then, the Royal York Hotel on Front Street was the tallest building. By Canada's Centennial year, 1967, the Toronto-Dominion Bank Tower designed by Mies van der Rohe, at fifty-six storeys, was the tallest building not only in Canada, but in all of the British Commonwealth. Its black tower, rectangular in contrast to the new city hall's white curved forms, dominated Toronto's skyline. For nearly ten years, the Toronto-Dominion Centre, joined by the matching forty-six storey Royal Trust Tower in 1969, stood as the highest point in Toronto until the seventy-two-storey First Canadian Place opened in 1975.

The make-up of the city — and the whole country — had also changed dramatically since World War II, with new immigrants from many countries. In the late fifties, the Canadian government's Department of Citizenship and Immigration published a booklet on immigrants and their contributions to the country. In this official government booklet, a paragraph on Paraskeva recognized her contribution as an artist. Her *Pink Cloud* (1937) (Plate 45) in the National Gallery of Canada collection was cited as an example of her delicate sense of colour: "In her use of colour to define form and render visible the solid shapes beneath the surface of things she is indebted to Cézanne and to a lesser degree Picasso."[2]

This cultural diversity brought energy and vitality to the fabric of Toronto. One third of the population was non-WASP, and a mix of languages was heard on city streets and in parks. Italian, Portuguese, Greek, and Chinese restaurants and cafés appeared in the sixties and seventies. Nevertheless, the city's sense of order, derived from the earlier immigrants from the British Isles, still held, but by the 1970s Paraskeva's complaints about Toronto as dour and boring were no longer justified. Toronto, now also Paraskeva's city, was burgeoning with the new, as was the city's art world.

The change in the city she could cope with; the change in art was something else, and Paraskeva continued to talk about her difficulty with being left behind:

There's something frightening about all this newness, it gives you a loss of aim. I follow the new shows, I'm aware of the new abstracts, but it puzzles me a bit because I am concerned with discipline. In the thirties and forties art had a place, I had a place and I was in all the shows — now it's painful. The new art goes into ideas and discovers techniques but forgets painting.[3]

Even though she thought the new kind of painting "frightening," she was influenced by the abstract work all around her in the 1960s and she was aware that her own work had become looser. She deliberately tried a number of abstracts, some that went "into ideas" as she put it, and some using a technique that "forgets painting." Her 1966 *Highway Still Life* (oil, metal, plastic, and woven wool on board) (Plate 46) is an example of the latter, a collage made up of highway debris in which she experimented with using found objects, a technique common in the sixties.[4]

Her *Baltic Deputy* pieces are two of her "into ideas" works. *Baltic Deputy* (1968) (Plate 60) is a watercolour of nine squares in red tones. "To Alice and Stewart with red salute," she inscribed for the Suttons on the back of it in 1969.[5] Like that painting, *Homage to a Soviet Film, Baltic Deputy* (Plate 59) is also made up of nine squares in tones of reds, but here they are placed against a yellow triangle surrounded with blue squares.[6] This painting is reminiscent of some of Lawren Harris's 1930s abstract works, *White Triangle* (1939), for example. These two works are completely different from anything else Paraskeva painted through-out her years as an artist.

The titles of these two abstract pieces came from a 1936 feature film *Baltic Deputy* by Russian filmmakers Alexander Zarkhi and Josef Heifitz about a scientist who was criticized by his colleagues for supporting the 1917 Russian Revolution. However, sailors of the Baltic fleet support him; they elect him their deputy for the Petrograd Soviet. This choice of subject for her paintings in 1968, along with her inscription to the Suttons, "with red salute," makes clear once again where her allegiance lay. While she stood with a foot in each of her two countries, it was still Russia that was wrapped around her heart.

Whether she had been in Canada for ten years or nearly forty, Paraskeva had the happy circumstance of looking in from the outside while she herself

Plate 43. *Alice Sutton* (1950–52), oil on canvas, 112 x 97 cm. Private collection, Shawville, Quebec. Photo credit: Heidi Ardern.

Plate 44. *Tom Thomson Memorial* (1950), oil on tempered hardboard, 60.0 x 32.9 cm. Inscribed "Parskeva to Murray, 28 March, 50." Art Gallery of Ontario, gift of Dorothea Larsen Adaskin, 2004.

Plate 45. *Pink Cloud* (1937), oil on canvas, 50.9 x 60.8 cm. National Gallery of Canada.

Plate 46. *Highway Still Life* (1966), oil, metal, plastic, and woven wool on board. Ottawa Art Gallery (FAC1553).

Plate 47. *Neighbouring Yards* (1954), oil on canvas, 50 x 60 cm. Private collection, Toronto. Photo credit: K. Ross Hookway.

Plate 48. *Kitchen Still Life* (1957), oil on masonite, 75 x 50 cm. Private collection, Toronto. Photo credit: Dean Palmer.

Plate 49. *Untitled (Still Life with Pears)* (c. 1941), watercolour on paper, 48.75 x 38.75 cm. Private collection, Victoria, B.C. Photo credit: Anthony Sam.

Plate 50. *Portrait of A. Y. Jackson* (1942–43), oil on canvas, 100 x 75 cm. The Power Corporation of Canada Art Collection.

Plate 51. *Clematis Flower* (a.k.a. *Through the Window*) (1951), oil on board, 61 x 50.5 cm. Private collection, Duntroon, Ontario. Photo credit: Bryan Davies Photography.

Plate 52. *Noon at Tadoussac* (1958), oil on canvas, 81.2 x 101.6 cm. Art Gallery of Windsor, gift of Mr. Jack Wildridge, the Roberts Gallery, Toronto, 1969 1969.0467.

Plate 53. *Self Portrait* (1937), watercolour on paper, 53.3 x 50.8 cm. Purchased with funds donated by Dalhousie University Alumni, Women's Division, 1954. Collection: Dalhousie Art Gallery, Halifax, Nova Scotia.

Plate 54. *Essentials of Life* (1947), oil on canvas, 61 x 50.8 cm. Private collection, Toronto. Photo credit: Dean Palmer.

Plate 55.
*Memories of
Leningrad*
(1955–56), oil
on canvas,
86 x 90.8 cm.
Private collec-
tion, Toronto.
Photo credit:
Dean Palmer.

Plate 56. *Kitchen Cupboard Aspect* (1956), oil on masonite, 50 x 60 cm. Private collection, Toronto. Photo credit: Dean Palmer.

Plate 57. *Sunlight in the Woods* (1966), oil on masonite, 79.8 x 70 cm. National Gallery of Canada, 15250.

Plate 58. *Summer Night* (1969), acrylic on masonite, 60.6 x 50.8 cm. Private collection, Toronto. Photo credit: Dean Palmer.

Plate 59. *Homage to a Soviet Film, Baltic Deputy* (1968), oil, graphite on masonite, 92.1 x 76.6 cm. Ottawa Art Gallery (FAC 1252).

Plate 60. *The Baltic Deputy* (1969), watercolour, 60 x 60 cm. Inscription on the back: "To Alice and Stewart with Red Salute. Paraskeva 1969." Private collection, Toronto. Photo credit: Dean Palmer.

Plate 61. *Rain on the Window* (nd), oil on board, 96.5 x 60.8 cm. Art Gallery of Hamilton, Gift of Richard Alway, 2001. Photo credit: Mike Lalich.

Plate 62. *Rubber Gloves* (1935), oil on canvas, 50 x 60.5 cm. Art Gallery of Hamilton, Patron's Purchase, 1964. Photo credit: Mike Lalich.

Plate 63. *Calla Lily* (1964–65), oil on masonite, 61.0 x 50.8 cm. Art Gallery of Windsor, gift from the Douglas M. Duncan Collection, 1970 1970.026.

Plate 64. *October Rose* (1941), oil on canvas, 40.3 x 54.2 cm. Robert McLaughlin Gallery, Oshawa, Ontario.

was inside, a Canadian. As we already know, Paraskeva never hesitated to say what she thought about Canadian painting, often lambasting it outright or taking subtle jabs. She used the subtle-jab approach in her *Portrait of A. Y. Jackson* (1942–1943) (Plate 50). We go back in time to look at this work for two reasons: it lays bare the contradictions Paraskeva saw in her world of art; and it sheds light on the divided person she was. A newspaper article and photograph featured her painting the oil in 1942 when it was nearly completed.[7] Curiously, five months later in a letter to his niece, Naomi Jackson Groves, Jackson said, "Paraskeva never finished the portrait of me."[8]

She *did* finish the portrait; however, he did not like it, and might have been relieved if she had not finished it. She painted him the way she perceived him, not the way he wanted to be seen, and he did not appreciate that. She once told him he "looked like a barrel."[9] Furthermore, even though she considered him a friend, she also thought he was something of a "fuddy-duddy."[10]

Not only does the angle from which she painted him make him look wide, but also she has him seated with his hands between his legs in a protective stance, an image of a balding, sober-faced man anxious about his manhood. Perhaps the position of his hands was related to her dislike of painting male nudes, for she once said, "Why should I bother painting males with all that stuff hanging out in front."[11] For Jackson, she covered — or replaced — the genitals with his hands, over-working them into a fleshy, soft form, perhaps suggesting that his potency lay in his hand — his art. We already know that Jackson, soon after Paraskeva's arrival in Toronto, had admitted to being afraid of her; it is likely that when he was sitting for his portrait in 1942 he might have felt at least a little uncomfortable as Paraskeva's subject.

One can imagine the sittings with the two of them arguing and talking, Paraskeva flinging her hands and punching the air with her paint brush as she made declarations about politics, the war, or what the Federation of Canadian Artists should do (Jackson was on the committee), or integrating art into Canadian culture.

While Jackson was sitting for his portrait, he could not have known that later on Paraskeva would add one of Picasso's paintings into the portrait (the Picasso picture was not in the July 1942 newspaper photo). In the lower left appears *Birdcage and Playing Cards* (1936-1937).[12] And here, again, we see

Paraskeva's contradictions spilling over into her painting: she portrayed Jackson as somewhat emasculated, but at the same time, she painted him as a sturdy figure wearing a three-piece suit and bathed in light — an enlightened man — telling us this is a leading light, a powerful man, which he was at the time.[13] She placed side-by-side two symbols of the art world: Picasso the icon of Modernism, whom she lionized; and Jackson, a leader in English Canada's art world. One can conjecture that she actually wanted to paint Picasso, but felt too intimidated and instead chose Jackson, the living painter who most symbolized Canadian art and landscape painting in which she dared to claim a place.

If Paraskeva wanted to include one of Picasso's images, she had many options. Why did she choose this particular painting of birds trapped in a cage? On the table in front of the cage lie five playing cards. A dove sits in the bottom of the cage, its tail and wing tips protruding from the side while a blackbird or crow pokes its wings and head through the top, its beak open as though it is squawking at its confinement. Was Jackson the white dove resting contentedly, and Paraskeva the black bird, both of them trapped in the cage of Canadian art? Was she saying something about her feeling about herself as the black bird discontent with her restrictions as a woman in comparison to Jackson, a satiated male artist free to go his own way and paint whenever and wherever he liked? Did the playing cards in the Picasso painting symbolize for Paraskeva, with tongue in cheek, that she and Jackson were caught in a game called Canadian Art?

Paraskeva knew Jackson well enough to think he might have mouthed appreciation for Picasso because of his stature in the art world, and because Paraskeva had such high regard for him, while in truth, it was likely that Jackson secretly did not like Picasso's work.[14] Nor would Jackson have liked the painting Paraskeva incorporated into the portrait. It was her way of taking a jab at her old friend, giving his nose a tweak. Including her source of inspiration — Picasso — was also an acknowledgment of Petrov-Vodkin, who himself included icons in his paintings as his source of inspiration. With the three references — Jackson, Picasso, Petrov-Vodkin — Paraskeva summarized her recognition of the three artists, all males, who held great importance in her painting career. One could also argue that Paraskeva was pointing forward to the latter years of the twentieth century when the practice of appropriation — using images from other artists' work — in a variety of art forms became common among artists.

By the late 1960s, Paraskeva and Jackson had weathered many storms and their feelings had mellowed toward each other. Just after New Year's in 1967, she wrote him a letter of thanks for a James Wilson Morrice book he sent her, and said she was sending him a Gabrielle Roy novel in French. She closed her letter with, "affectionately."[15] Paraskeva's feelings toward Jackson had mellowed, as is evident by her "Poem for Alex," which was perhaps a peace offering for her many complaints against the Group of Seven if not an acknowledgement of the belated respect she had for him and the Group — and for landscape:

When in 1931 I came
To Canada, the land of hope,
Heart full of pains
for lost Europe ...
First visit to the gallery
My mind moaned — such barren land ...
But — as time passed,
Thank Heaven
I discovered the group of Seven!
And ever since — I'm sitting pretty!
By the blazing flame
Of their hospitable hearth
I stopped being snooty
And thought "Tes m'aiment!"
A Maple Leaf — designed by Charles
Emblazoned my bosom soon after
Canadian group of Painters
I stand and die for thee! No laughter.
Although my mind and hope
Stay always set

On dazzling Heights of Art
of lost Europe, —
My "Maple Leaf" brand heart
For ever beats the gratitude
to Alex Jackson's Art.
For showing the plentitude
of vast and magic Canada, —
The Land of Hope — for him and me.[16]

Now that she accepted Canada as her land of hope in spite of herself, of significance for Paraskeva was that Canada accepted her. "This country was awfully good to me," she said. "It [her painting career] could only have happened in Canada."[17]

Being elected a full Academician of the Royal Canadian Academy (RCA) in 1966 was, for Paraskeva, a sign of her acceptance. Her diploma work was an oil, *Sunlight in the Woods* (1966) (Plate 57), which she deposited with the RCA. It automatically went into the National Gallery of Canada collection. Paraskeva had been an associate of the RCA since 1956, but the nomination by the RCA in 1966 was especially important because the Ontario Society of Artists jury had rejected the work she submitted the previous year, an indication she was being sidelined. She felt hurt and rejected and resigned from the OSA.

Grief came on a personal level as well. Douglas Duncan, who was still managing the Picture Loan Society, died in 1968, more than thirty years after the organization was formed. Ten days before his death, the Clarks had hosted a large June garden party and Duncan was there. Paraskeva had a clear memory of him telling her that he had just put a new frame on the first painting he bought from her, a landscape she had painted in Muskoka, probably in the summer of 1932. Not only had Duncan shown and sold her work, but he had shared with Paraskeva her interest in Europe and conversed with her in French. He had encouraged many artists, and bought their paintings, helping them survive, especially during the thirties and forties. "Many artists were orphaned!" Paraskeva said of Duncan's death.[18]

Gradually, in the following years, Paraskeva felt her physical energy was dwindling; her impetus for painting was also diminished and she became discouraged. Most days, she still followed her routine of walking downtown, but the time she left home became later and later, usually around one o'clock in the afternoon. After her shopping and tea or lunch, and perhaps gallery visits, she would arrive home around five o'clock in time to prepare dinner.[19] Her daily life seemed to have little to excite and inspire.

In late August of 1973, something happened that shook her loose from her doldrums in her house on the hill. She received a letter from Charles Hill, then Assistant Curator of Post-Confederation Art at the National Gallery of Canada in Ottawa telling her that he was preparing an exhibition of Canadian art of the 1930s. Hill said he wanted to include Paraskeva in the show, and asked to interview her that fall.[20] Even before the show was mounted, the National Gallery of Canada purchased her 1933 *Myself* for five thousand dollars.[21]

In the touring exhibition and the accompanying catalogue, *Canadian Painting in the Thirties*, Hill set out to explore the trends and themes of painting during that decade, and researched the key figures of the era. If the choice of paintings exhibited is representative, an analysis of the subject matter of those works would show the kind of painting produced during Paraskeva's early years in Canada when her career blossomed. More than half (sixty-five) of the one hundred and nine paintings, were landscapes and about a third of those included any signs of human presence. Surprisingly few political paintings were shown, only three that can be seen as overtly political; among those, of course, was Paraskeva's *Petroushka* (1937).

Considering the difficult times of the thirties, it would seem that more paintings of social comment would have been exhibited. Did they not exist? Barry Lord, author of *The History of Painting in Canada: Toward a People's Art*, claimed they did, but that Hill ignored many of them.[22] Lord pointed out that Nathan Petroff's *Modern Times* (1937), a watercolour of a young woman sitting in a posture of despair reading newspaper headlines about the Spanish Civil War, should have been included.[23] Lord characterized the decade as the first time when "our artists moved on from the resolution of the landscape to painting of our people, especially our working people." Lord is right if one looks at works in all media, but Hill's show did not include drawing, and focused primarily on works in oil on canvas or board, with some exceptions.[24] Although in the catalogue Hill mentioned the "demand for a social purpose for art," he did not emphasize the expression of that purpose as a major characteristic of the thirties.[25]

According to art historian Anna Hudson, however, the Toronto community of artists were socially engaged and their humanist aesthetic marked a distinct period. Furthermore, Paraskeva's 1937 articles, and those of other artists who entered into debate with her, are evidence of the exchange of ideas couched in an intense social awareness. These artists — Brooker, Comfort, Schaefer, and MacLeod, along with Paraskeva — built on the humanism in the Group of Seven's preoccupation with creating an art for the *people* of Canada. "A prevailing conviction that aesthetic experience was a positive and ultimately spiritually enlightening prospect precluded any interest in the portrayal of society's disastrous shortcomings."[26] This conclusion goes a long way to explaining why the socially aware artists in Toronto — who did move landscape painting away from scenes devoid of humans toward images depicting human activity — did not produce more political paintings; and it also offers a primary reason why Paraskeva turned to landscape painting. Despite her conviction that the artist is responsible to society for what she saw around her, she could not persist in the face of the prevailing persuasion to paint "positive" images.

Paraskeva was represented in *"Canadian Painting in the Thirties"* by four paintings: her 1933 *Myself, Wheat Field* (1936), *Petroushka* (1937), and *Trout* (1940). But the exhibition, and her work as part of it, did not excite her. In the spring of 1975 while the show was touring, she wrote a letter to Frances Adaskin, saying, "I hardly paint at all ... it is so hard — my era is gone and this show brought the amazing volume of publicity — but it is too late to excite me." And then she told Frances what else about the show was bothering her. "I am afraid of animosity of other painters — why me?"

She felt especially honoured, which she was, and worried about being singled out. Not only had the National Gallery bought her 1933 *Myself* the previous year, they chose it for the cover of the catalogue, reproduced it in full colour on their own page in the catalogue, and chose it for the official poster for the exhibition. She was also recognized for her contribution to

Canadian art in the catalogue text as well. But all this could not shake her out of her depression, as evidenced in her letter to the Adaskins: "the greatest sorrow is your having left Toronto — you were like family to me. I have no friends now." She also tells them she does not have the energy to cook, so they don't have parties anymore. Only her children and grandchildren, her "greatest pleasure," come to visit every two weeks, but that means a lot of work to cook dinner for them.[27] She was simply miserable about being old.

Other artists, too, were looking back at the events of their lives. Naturally, the exhibition brought on reminiscences of the hard times during the Depression; but there was also a sense that they had all been in it together. These artists, "united in poverty and obscurity," had struggled onward.[28]

Paraskeva was given yet another honour: in anticipation of the arrival of the National Gallery's 1930s show at the Art Gallery of Ontario, Marvin Gelber, president of the gallery, and Director William Withrow asked Paraskeva to open the exhibition in the spring of 1975. In his letter to her, Gelber said, "I can think of no person more suitable."[29] She and Philip were also invited to a dinner party at the Grange before the opening at the gallery. This honour brought to the surface emotions deep within Paraskeva, and drew her into musings about where she had come from and what she had achieved. She told Frances Adaskin: "I thought of my childhood — and my parents. Life!" Perhaps she recalled her father's comment when she had told him, years earlier, that she was planning to marry a Canadian and live in his country. Avdey's advice had been simple: Don't. There you will be little more than a grain of sand.[30] Now, in front of the podium at the Art Gallery of Ontario, she was proving her father wrong.

She must have conveyed her intense feelings about the course of her life, for she received responses to her two-minute speech in the mail: "Your remarks were so soulful, gleaned through experience and right from your heart."[31] Perhaps what also reached the audience was the tribute Paraskeva paid to the twenty-three artists in the exhibition who had died. She asked "the generations surrounding her to 'dip freely into our history. Our ideas, such as they were, may give a human quality to a neglected period of Canada's art history.'"[32] However, some of Paraskeva's old friends and colleagues *were* alive and attended the opening, among them Carl Schaefer, Louis Muhlstock, André Bieler, Yvonne McKague Housser, and Isabel McLaughlin. A photo of these six artists taken on 18 June 1975 shows Paraskeva with her typical intensity, her right arm and fist taut, stretched as high as she could reach in a salute of the Popular Front. Bieler and Schaefer, too, raised their fists into the air. The stance of the other three artists is more restrained.

Paraskeva received further recognition when Murray Adaskin wrote a new piece of music for strings and harpsichord called *In Praise of Canadian Paintings in the Thirties*. The work is in three movements named for three artist friends of Adaskin: "Paraskeva Clark," "Louis Muhlstock," "Charles Comfort."[33]

In a letter to Paraskeva, Murray told her: "Your works have given me almost a lifetime of joy, and all of you have been our personal friends and I wanted to add my voice to all those who have praised the exhibition in their own way." Murray said he was not trying to describe her, Muhlstock, and Comfort, but he believed that somehow his "affection and admiration" did come through in the music.[34] The movement titled "Paraskeva Clark" communicates a range of emotions. In parts, the music is intensely vivacious and bursting with energy and playfulness; but it is also sad and wistful at times. And this is how Murray sometimes thought of Paraskeva.

Murray was not the only friend who saw Paraskeva's many different sides. After not seeing Charles Comfort for many years, someone told him that he and his artist friends had become caricatures of their former selves. Comfort observed that certainly was true of Paraskeva, but she was "just a little bit more of everything she used to be."[35] In old age, the essence of a person often intensifies, as though distilled by years of experience. Paraskeva communicated that intensity. In her later years, she spoke with her whole body, thrashing about and making fists as she talked about her efforts to put on her canvas what she saw — she saw things as who *she* was, not what other people saw. "She had a running narration in her head," filmmaker Gail Singer recalled. It seemed her inner monologue was always spinning, and sometimes she opened it up like a door, and other times she closed it.[36] When she opened that door, her thoughts became transparent, spilling out onto her weathered face, her pursed lips — she no longer wore the bright red lipstick that offended Harold Clark in 1931 — and the lines on her cheeks and her crinkled forehead communicating her fervour. Her eyes were like her father's; fiery with passion, as though she had seen into hell. And her hands, always her hands, as expressive as her words, tensed and thrust out from her body. Then quickly, her face could change into an impish grin, or a look of scorn, or she might drop into a peaceful reverie, and a calm would wash over her as she slipped into a satisfying memory from years past, but her hands kept moving as she fiddled with her pencil on her drawing table. Calling herself a romantic, she claimed, "Men don't know anything about love," but her eyes became dreamy and the expression of her face seemed to mirror that of Pan the puppet hanging behind her, a gift from Bethune.[37]

The intense ferment of her personality was evident, too, in her relationship with Philip. When Charles Hill interviewed her for the 1930s show, she put on a great performance for his crew when they were filming *Some Canadian Paintings of the 1930s* in the Clarks' living room. "At one point Paraskeva stood akimbo, her hands on her hips and her elbows pointing out, singing a Spanish song from the days of the Spanish Civil War. And then "she started going on about 'haven't had sex in thirty years,' something like that, and poor Philip sitting there. He was just blithe, it didn't faze him. I'm sure he'd heard it before."[38] Of course, he had. We can be sure that if Paraskeva had no inhibitions when she was being filmed, she would also speak her mind when she and Philip were alone. But it is one of the unsolvable mysteries of this relationship that Paraskeva would take these pot shots at Philip and he would appear to let them slide off his back like rain on a rubber raincoat — unless, of course, they were in highly genteel company and he would take Paraskeva home like a naughty child.

In the 1970s, many second-generation Russians as well as recent Russian immigrants were afraid of the Soviet Union and were outspoken in their opposition to communism. Paraskeva became indignant when she met any of these people, and at least once Philip "bodily removed" her from a party when she insulted other guests whom she accused of abandoning Russia.[39] Paraskeva knew she caused Philip difficulty because she told someone that Philip is not a bad man since he put up with her all those years.[40]

He not only put up with her, he championed her. In the late seventies, he wrote close to twenty letters to other artists, Paraskeva's friends, and people respected in the area of arts and culture, asking them to write letters of nomination and endorsement in an effort to have her receive an appointment to the Order of Canada. At the time, Philip had heard rumours that George Ignatieff, the son of the Russian Minister of Education under the last czar, Nicholas II, might succeed Jules Leger as Governor General of Canada:

> Wouldn't it be wonderful if a 'New Canadian' governor general, born and raised in Russia but educated in England, were able to confer membership in The Order of Canada on another 'New Canadian,' born and raised in Russia, whose 'class' as shown by her Soviet Passport is 'PEASANT' and whose father was a factory worker in a shoe factory in Leningrad.[41]

This excerpt from Philip's letter to the Adaskins shows how genuine was his respect and affection for his wife. Even though he would have been "elated" if Paraskeva had received the honour, he also had reservations that her behaviour would not be appropriate to the ceremony at Rideau Hall.[42] But he needn't have worried, because she was not given the honour.[43] Nor did Ignatieff become governor general.

From his retirement until almost the end of his life, Philip spent five or six hours a day at his downtown office, and went home to a dinner Paraskeva cooked for him. As he told his friend Murray Adaskin in 1979, "I can count on poor old Paraskeva to look after me at dinner time, and then to spend the evening complaining, among other things, that I turned her into a capitalist, and holding forth about her bad luck in having come to Canada."

Philip had once written this little rhyme to her for her birthday: "Speaking of wives, some wives are clever, some wives are sexy, some wives are barrels of fun, and I've got some wife who happens to be all these things rolled into one."[44] He must have written this when he was still young, when she appeared tantalizing to him.

After many years, Philip described her as sometimes all "sweetness and light" but that within a short time she would be shouting that she wanted a separation and divorce. "So I carry on," he told the Adaskins. "She is so much better off than most of the women she meets, but she cannot be convinced. I've stopped trying."[45]

Although Clive feels certain of his parents' love for each other, he also says, "They had a pretty rough relationship. Dad would go to the end of the earth for her, but that didn't mean that he wouldn't love to see her change into a reasonable person that would sit down at dinner and not make nasty remarks to people about their religion." Apparently, there were times when Philip's ability to tolerate his wife's behaviour gave way. About a week before Philip died, he phoned Clive and said he couldn't take it anymore; he was divorcing Paraskeva. But Clive heard no more about it after that.[46]

Despite each threatening to end their relationship, these two were devoted to each other, but their relationship cannot be seen in isolation from their culture. In the social structure in which Philip's family lived — indeed a pattern that still exists in too many relationships between men and women today — men were in charge and had trouble seeing women as equals, frequently taking on the position of teachers, even to women in positions of authority.[47] This kind of male-female relationship did not work for Philip and Paraskeva because she refused him that kind of dominance and power. Yet they each knew that Philip *did* have power in that he supported Paraskeva. Symbolically, he was the bourgeois in the relationship because he was the wage earner; because Paraskeva did the unpaid work of housekeeping, symbolically she was the proletariat.[48] These symbolic categories are useful in understanding the Clarks' relationship, especially because they accurately describe their family origins, which affected the outlook of each.

Furthermore, Paraskeva came from a "world where a person like her would not consciously put her life together other than in terms of marriage and children."[49] All her life she had a fierce loyalty to the idea of family, which carried over into her daily life by faithfully taking care of Ben and Philip, including cooking dinner for them every evening, and also preparing dinner for Clive and his family every other Sunday. We know, despite all her comments about women's place in the world, that "questioning the bond of the family would have been inconceivable."[50] In other words, marriage was a container for the prescribed boundaries on her as a woman, the way she had chosen to live her life.

Despite Paraskeva's irascible nature, some of her friends, years later, still felt deeply and strongly about her. Wentworth Walker, the Clarks' neighbour, tried to articulate what she meant to him: "I cared for Paraskeva. She challenged me and charmed me at times." He liked her intolerance of hypocrisy, pretentiousness, and ostentation, regardless of her sometimes-offensive language. Unlike many people, she was not afraid to think things through, and she believed in challenging other people's points of view. Walker said that he still feels "in a relationship with her of some kind, which I can't put into words at all, but it tells me she was important to me when she was alive in a far more permanent way than any casual relationship."[51]

Another neighbour, the late George Miller, had similar feelings of appreciation for both Philip and Paraskeva. However, Miller also said that when he was with the two of them it was impossible to talk with Philip because Paraskeva took over. Miller liked to talk about politics, but he had to have that kind of conversation with Philip when Paraskeva was elsewhere.[52]

She needed people who could stand up to her, who were equally strong in their opinions and would yell back. Fellow artist, Joyce Wieland, whose painting Paraskeva probably did not like, met Paraskeva on the street from time to time: "I knew it was Paraskeva because she always comes up and boots me from behind. We had our usual conversation in front of Britnell's bookstore [at Yonge and Bloor Streets], wherein we yelled at each other about art. She was knocking the group [*sic*] of Seven as usual. She always thinks they were lazy painters."[53]

PARASKEVA HAD LITTLE reason to be glum, given her honours and the number of galleries showing her work. She participated in eight exhibitions in the 1970s and was part of rental programs at such galleries as the Art Gallery of Hamilton, the London Public Library and Art Museum, the Winnipeg Art Gallery and the Art Gallery of Greater Victoria. Financially, the rentals brought her little, sometimes sixty or seventy-five dollars a year.[54]

It is unclear exactly when Paraskeva stopped painting, but it was probably in the early to mid-seventies even though she told people she stopped when she was eighty, which was 1978. Most of the time she kept a painting on her easel (for a while it was *Pavlichenko and her Comrades at City Hall*, 1942) and frequently spent time in her studio surrounded by photos, among others, of J. S. McLean, David Milne, Paul-Emile Borduas, Harold Town, Frances Loring, and of course, Picasso.

It is somewhat ironic that her last major show in Toronto in the seventies was a two-person exhibition with her son, Ben, who frequently painted and drew over the years. She had so wanted him to succeed, but he could not fulfil her expectations; however, in this exhibition, he outnumbered her in his contributions.

In 1978, when Paraskeva was 80, she had a visit from Mary MacLachlan, then a curator at Dalhousie University Art Gallery in Halifax, Nova Scotia. MacLachlan had high regard for Paraskeva's work and wanted to mount a survey exhibition of Paraskeva's paintings and drawings. Paraskeva was surprised, but she agreed, and MacLachlan began working on the show in 1980.

What surprised Paraskeva even more was to learn that someone wanted to make a film about her. At the same time that MacLachlan was working on the exhibition, filmmaker Gail Singer began filming for *Portrait of the Artist as an Old Lady*.[55] By then Paraskeva tired very quickly during filming and some days her mind lapsed and her memory let her down. On those days, the film crew could not work. However, on her good days Paraskeva was "thrilled beyond words," and would exclaim, "I don't know how this happens," meaning she could hardly comprehend the attention she was getting, but she thought the film would be good for her grandchildren.[56] *Portrait of the Artist as an Old Lady* tells the story of Paraskeva's life and depicts her dramatic personality.

In 1982 and 1983, *Paraskeva Clark: Paintings and Drawings* opened in Halifax at the Dalhousie Art Gallery. From Halifax the show, including the film, went to Ottawa, then to Toronto and Victoria. Forty-six oils, watercolours, and pen and pencil drawings from 1925 to the mid-fifties, with a focus on the thirties and forties, were exhibited — political works, self-portraits, portraits of friends, still lifes, and landscapes.

Reviewers of the show hardly mentioned the still lifes, which comprised about a quarter of the exhibition, but pointed out the strengths of the self-portraits, one calling the self-portraits the "backbone" of her whole body of work.[57] Another review of the show said, "The evolution of Clark's self-image is one of the most compelling in Canadian art."[58] These observations are true: the self-portraits show this artist's evolution from the broad-faced, perplexed peasant into a self-assured, sophisticated woman of society; a Russian patriot anxious over the welfare of her native land; a mother worrying over her son.

AS I LOOK at paintings from the 1982–1983 exhibition many years later, I experience them as forceful. Their strength has not diminished over time; they depict the perceptive artist's eye, embody an energy and vitality consistent with who she was, and show her love of form and colour. The same can be said of her many paintings not included in the 1982–1983 survey exhibition, particularly her still lifes using the window motif and other architectural elements.

Window paintings are about space, interior and exterior space, symbolizing enclosure or expansion and looking out beyond the place where a person is at a given moment. Many artists have used the window and other architectural framing elements for centuries. Though they are not visible in the paintings, artists are present as observers in a specific moment in a particular space, which they portray to bring the viewer to the same spot. "The viewer becomes involved in the passage from one kind of space to another, from the literal to the figurative, and is offered the occasion to reflect upon the relationships between these two orders of space."[59]

This idiom of the window is one that was adopted by Canadian painters as an extension of the preoccupation with landscape. For Paraskeva, the window/framing metaphor comprised a happy synchronicity between Canadian still life painting and Petrov-Vodkin's work. Thus, she could allow herself to be influenced by these aspects of Canadian images compatible with her training.[60] After the first window Paraskeva painted in Canada — in the late thirties — she would return to this idiom every two or three years until 1969.

Some of Paraskeva's window paintings communicate enclosure and a preoccupation with the interior, whereas others express a more joyful side of her vision. Her early sketch for *Memories of Leningrad* (1923), for example, includes in the background a window at night, dark and closed in, as though the room where she sits is the only space that exists. On the other hand, *October Rose* (1941) (Plate 64) is a single rose with leaves in a blue glass on a windowsill, a painting glorious in itself, with no hint of exterior gloom. Sumac leaves in brilliant orange and pink press against the glass.

In another window painting, called *Self Portrait*, a 1937 watercolour (Plate 53), Paraskeva sits in front of a window with her head resting in her right hand. She wears her hat at a jaunty angle, partially covering her left eye; her one visible ear is pointed, making her pixy-like. To her right, part of a plant curves into the frame of the painting, the single leaf the same angle and form as her hat. Through the window, the shadowy houses and leafless trees tell us it is winter in the city. Her expression radiates confidence and energy similar to that in her 1933 *Myself*.

Neighbouring Yards (1954) (Plate 47) takes a broad view of her world, portraying what the artist saw from her balcony on Roxborough Drive in winter. It is a beautifully composed painting — animated through her use of diagonal lines — taking the viewer from the edge of her second floor outward to the far side of the ravine. Like a window that provides the architectural framework in some of Paraskeva's still lifes, here the railings give us her point of reference, with the fence in the mid-distance echoing the angle of the railings. Winter's colours, predominately white and blue-grey, are punctuated by the red berries — perhaps bittersweet — running along the rail; at the corner, the red is interlaced with the green of the pines in the mid-distance. The tree trunks slope slightly to the right, in the same direction of the angles of the fence and railing. The whole painting would be skewed in that direction, except that the roof, the only "quiet" area in the scene, anchors the picture and your eye comes back to rest at the lower edge of the canvas

The calla lily is a sensuous, waxy flower, which has a strikingly elegant form. However, this is not what Paraskeva's *Calla Lily* (1964–1965) (Plate 63) portrays. It is a somewhat depressing painting for its lack of energy. She depicts the lily as scrawny — even smaller than the single drooping leaf — sitting in a globe-shaped glass vase on a windowsill. Beyond the window, we see only trees, as though they are pressing against the window, communicating a feeling of being closed in even if the top of the picture suggests a vista. One can read this painting as a metaphor for her personal life in the mid-sixties when her energy and enthusiasm had begun to diminish.

Rain on the Window (undated) (Plate 61) is one of Paraskeva's strongest statements about enclosure: the feeling of being stuck indoors on a day of heavy rain. Large drops of water trail down the windowpane. In the near distance the black leafless trees seem like bars outside the window, while farther away houses sit along the upper and lower edges of the painting surrounded by a deep golden glow, as though autumn leaves were covering the ground. The window paintings speak of Paraskeva's ability to transform her environment of "ordinary" scenes — even when she was housebound with family obligations — into images that stimulate the senses and evoke in the viewer memories of similar experiences.

Also in these window paintings, indeed in all of her work, we learn about what she saw through her eyes as a formalist, and how she thought about what she saw. As a humanist, she had a unique ability to fuse history and aesthetics in her work, but at the same time, she moved in a circle of like-minded artists, among whom she was a catalyst "in the shift from a wilderness to a civilized landscape in the thirties."[61]

Paraskeva knew in her Russian-Canadian soul, with a bedrock certainty, that art is the heart of society, and she articulated that belief at every opportunity. She spoke out for artists' organizations and government support for the arts, as well as challenging artists to paint about social issues. In the late thirties, she published key contributions that are still quoted today in any dialogue about Canadian art during that era.

Not only is she quoted, but today her paintings hang in art galleries across the country. In the National Gallery of Canada, more than century after her birth in Russia, Paraskeva Avdeyevna Plistik Allegri Clark rubs shoulders with her Canadian-born colleagues Emily Carr, A.Y. Jackson, Tom Thomson, Carl Schaefer, and Charles Comfort. Instead of hearing her voice booming above all of theirs, we look at *Myself* and *Petroushka*, and each time we see something new.

Epilogue ⤳

But we have all entered the cage of time and
have been changed by the lives we haven't lived
and by the one life we have lived. [1]

In Toronto's 205-acre Mount Pleasant cemetery, stretching from Yonge Street to Bayview Avenue, stands a four-foot-high stone monument with daisies carved in relief arching over a bronze plaque engraved with the names of Clark family members. An inscription reads, "When spring comes and the flowers start to appear, I just talk to them." [2] These were Paraskeva Clark's own words near the end of her life and this bit of land is where she was laid to rest after her long journey that began in St. Petersburg, Russia, on 28 October 1898 and ended in Toronto, Canada, on 10 August 1986.

Paraskeva's ashes were interred in this beautiful park-like cemetery about a kilometre north of her Roxborough Drive home. She would be pleased that trees and bushes grow near her final resting place. When I visited her grave in early spring, in front of her tombstone, yellow crocuses and purple scilla bloomed, and a Shasta daisy was waiting for summer's warmth. As in her garden, the black and grey squirrels she hated populate the cemetery, running over her grave. Here, she can no long swear at them and run them out with her garden hose.

The last six years of Paraskeva's life were not happy ones. Her health and mental condition deteriorated rapidly after Philip's death from a cerebral hemorrhage in 1980. He had been suffering from myasthenia gravis, a muscular disability that affected his neck. In Singer's film, it is obvious that Philip was not well, but nevertheless he participated in the filming within that year before he died.

At first Paraskeva refused to believe he had died.[3] He lived his last days in hospital and she did not see his body because it was taken directly from the hospital to the medical faculty of the University of Toronto; Philip had stated in his will that he wanted no funeral and his body was to be donated for research. However, later on a commemoration for him was held at the Arts & Letters Club.

With Philip gone, Paraskeva and Ben continued living at the Clarks' house on Roxborough Drive. It soon became clear, though, that Paraskeva was having difficulty with daily life, even with Clive and Mary close by and checking in on her. They would receive phone calls from Ben saying Paraskeva had fallen. They also discovered Paraskeva was not eating properly, and they hired a live-in nursing aide to look after both Ben and Paraskeva; she was unhappy with this arrangement and it did not last long.

Paraskeva had to be hospitalized several times for a twisted bowel, and she became depressed and spent some time in the psychiatric ward of the Toronto General Hospital. While she was in hospital, Clive and Mary realized that Paraskeva could not look after herself, and they also knew that having her live with them would not work. She was frequently confused, and her short-term memory often did not function. It was impossible to have a coherent conversation with her about where she might live; she needed round-the-clock supervision. Clive and Mary finally discussed with her the possibility of a nursing home, which Paraskeva did not like. However, they felt it was the only option, and tried to find the best care possible. Joel, Clive and Mary's son, offered to live with Ben and care for him, an arrangement that continued until Ben's death in January 2006.

Paraskeva began living at the Heritage Nursing Home at the east end of Toronto in 1981. For a time she was allowed to come and go. One day she showed up at 56 Roxborough Drive and fell down on the landing before she even got into the house. A roofer working across the street responded when she called to him for help and took her into the house.

As is characteristic of dementia, Paraskeva was sometimes confused and sometimes lucid. By the fall of 1981, at least some of the time she was sedated.[4] She was in a wheelchair when the film on her was completed and the retrospective of her work opened at the Art Gallery of Ontario in early 1983. Clive and Mary picked her up and took her to the opening and, for that event, Paraskeva was able to rally her strength and talk to her guests at the gallery.

Increasingly her strength failed, and looking back at the last few years of her life we see a sad story.[5] The clear-eyed, expressive woman was gone; she was now "pudgy" faced and seemed disoriented, even unsure of how old she was. Paraskeva had put on weight, was puffy from medication, and fretted about how she looked. She did not like people to see her like this and seemed uncomfortable in her body.[6] That this dynamic artist, so full of contradictions, so fierce and irascible, should live her final years in this dispirited state is incongruous; it seems yet another addition to her accounts of a difficult life with its "400 Blows."

Her last blow came when she was a few months short of her eighty-eighth birthday. She died of stroke. Her ashes were placed with Philip's family, without Philip. The remains of Harold Clark, Philip's father, and Marguerite Green, Harold's first wife whom Paraskeva had never known, and his brother Ralph are buried there. The irony is that her ashes were placed with her in-laws, who were never quite able to accept her.

At her funeral, tributes referred to her dedication to her family and to the causes in which she believed. Her friends talked about her "acerbic tongue" and her questions that challenged those around her. They spoke of what this artist gave to Canada, her political works, her portraits, her landscapes, and her still lifes. These paintings live on as a "tangible, visible record of insight, opinion and hope ..."[7]

There is no question that Paraskeva's work has left an imprint on Canadian art. And her life has affected many people and remains strong in the memory of those who knew her. Over the years, many writers, including this biographer, have tried to describe her; but as Gail Singer concluded, Paraskeva carried her own artistic dream, was "a bundle of contradictions," and still defies definition, which is "perhaps the price of originality."[8]

Paraskeva had a good response for people like Singer and me who try to describe her: "Now, if you consider me an artist — asking how it was done — is similar to asking what facts went into making a rose or an iris. Just accept the fact of my being so — and let it go at that."[9]

Notes ⁊

Paraskeva Clark's personal papers are housed at the Library and Archives Canada (LAC) in the Paraskeva and Philip T. Clark fonds, MG30 D398. I also consulted other files in LAC: Carl Fellman Schaefer fonds, MG30 D171; Charles Fraser Comfort fonds, MG30 D81; Norman Bethune fonds, MG30 B55; and the A.Y. Jackson fonds, MG30 D259 and MG30 D351. I consulted, as well, the National Gallery of Canada Archives (particularly the Charles Hill Files); the Edward P. Taylor Library and Archives, Art Gallery of Ontario (particularly the Douglas Duncan fonds, SC905); the Robertson Davies Library, Massey College, University of Toronto (particularly the Graham McInnes files); and the Toronto Arts & Letters Club Archives.

I conducted many taped interviews with people for this biography. Paraskeva Clark's family was extremely helpful and I interviewed them as follows: Clive Clark, 11 December 2001 and 12 February 2002; Clive and Mary Clark, 2 January 2001, 8 February 2001, 15 February 2001, 10 April 2001, 8 January 2002, 30 October 2002, 13 November 2002, 4 March 2003, and 16 February

2004; Ben and Joel Clark (Milton, Ontario), 3 May 2001 and 29 November 2001; Joel Clark, 3 May 2001 and 11 January 2002; Panya Clark Espinal, 13 February 2001, 22 January 2004, and 22 June 2004; and Jennifer Clark Mazurkiewicz, 5 April 2001.

As well, the following friends (and relatives of friends), neighbours, and experts shared their memories and their insight. All interviews took place in Toronto, unless otherwise noted: Dorothea Larsen Adaskin, 19–20 April 2004 (Victoria); Susan Adaskin, 25 April 2004 (Surrey, British Columbia); Anna Sutton Anderson, 16 September 2003 (Shawville, Quebec); Barry Appleton, 25 September 2003; Bay Cardy, 5 September 2002; Francis and Penny Chapman, 24 April 2002; Howard and Valerie Chapman, 12 April 2001; Irma Coucill, 4 December 2001; Dora de Pédery-Hunt, 31 May 2001; Ann Duff, 30 April 2002; Naomi Jackson Groves, 14 November 2001 (Ottawa); Sandy Miller Harris, 13 April 2005; Charles Hill, 8 April 2002, (Ottawa); Jean Horne, 30 May 2001; Anna Hudson, 23 January 2001, 13 March 2003, 24 March 2003, 13 September 2004, and 28 February 2005; Marguerite Hunt, 13 February 2001; Murray Laufer and Marie Day, 16 April 2002; Maja Miller Lees, 8 June 2005; John Libby, 28 February 2002; Mary MacLachlan, 9 July 2003 (Halifax); Gordon MacNamara, 23 October 2001; Doris McCarthy, 1 February 2001; Simon and Heather McInnes, 16 September 2003 (Ottawa); June McLean, 9 April 2003; June McLean and Mike Stewart, 2 April 2003; Gavin Miller, 25 May 2005; the late George Miller, 11 January 2001; Joan Murray, 25 May 2001 (Oshawa); Tamar Nelson, 19 April 2001; Ann O'Brian, 5 April 2001; Geoffrey O'Brian, 8 April 2002 (Ottawa); Michael Pantazzi, 21 November 2002 (Ottawa); Donald Patterson, 6 January 2001; Adam Rayco, 23 January 2001; Nancy Reynolds, 14 May 2002; Claire Shoniker, 11 October 2001; Gail Singer, 1 February 2001; Bill Stapleton 5 December 2000; Janina Stensson, 22 October 2001; Rod Stewart, 26 June 2003; Alice Sutton, 19 February 2001 (Markham, Ontario); Christopher Varley, 4 March 2003; Francine Volker, 24 February 2003; Wentworth Walker, 19 April 2001; Lela Wilson, 30 July 2001.

I also conducted the following phone interviews: Paul Duval, 15 May 2002; Margaret Evans, RCMP Archives, April 2002 (Ottawa); Frances Gage, June 2001 (Coburg, Ontario); Charlotte Townsend-Galt, 4 December 2002 (Vancouver); Avrom Isaacs, 7 May 2002; Mary MacLachlan, 4 September, 2003

(Halifax); Eric Miller, 25 May 2005; Penny Pepperell, 18 April 2002; Audrey Pratt, 9 May 2001; Rebecca Sisler, 10 September 2002 (Calgary); Christopher Varley, 27 November 2002.

Among the public/published sources I consulted are the following:

John Alford, "Trends in Canadian Art," *University of Toronto Quarterly* Vol. XIV, No. 2 (January 1945), pp. 168–180.

———, "The Development of Painting in Canada," *Canadian Art* Vol. 11, No. 3 (March 1945), pp. 95–103.

Robert Ayre, "The Canadian Group of Painters," *Canadian Art* Vol. VI, No. 3 (Spring 1949), pp. 98–102.

Andrew Bell, "The Art of Paraskeva Clark," *Canadian Art* Vol. VII, No. 2 (Christmas 1949), pp. 43–46.

———, "Canadian Painting and the Cosmopolitan Trend," *The Studio* Vol. CL, No. 751 (October 1955), pp. 97–105.

Bertram Brooker, ed., *Yearbook of the Arts in Canada* (Toronto: Macmillan, 1936).

Norman Bryson, *Looking at the Overlooked: Four Essays on Still Life Painting* (London: Reaktion Books, 1990).

Donald W. Buchanan, "Contemporary Painting in Canada," *The Studio* Vol. CXXIX, No. 625 (April 1945), pp. 99–117.

Vivian Cameron, "The Useful and the Human Paraskeva Clark," *Vanguard* Vol. 12, No. 3 (April 1983), pp. 6–9.

Paraskeva Clark, "Come Out From Behind the Pre-Cambrian Shield," *New Frontier* Vol. 1, No. 12 (April 1937), pp. 16–17.

———, "Travelling Exhibitions: Is the Public's Gain the Artist's Loss?" *Canadian Art* Vol. VII, No. 1 (Autumn 1949), pp. 21–23.

———, "Thoughts on Canadian Painting," *World Affairs* (February 1943), pp. 17–18.

———, "The Artist Speaks: A Statement by Paraskeva Clark," *Canadian Review of Music and Art* Vol. III, Nos. 9, 10 (1944), pp. 18–19.

Barker Fairley, "Canadian Art: Man vs. Landscape," *The Canadian Forum* Vol. XIX, No. 227 (December 1939), pp. 284–285.

Orlando Figes, *A People's Tragedy: A History of the Russian Revolution* (New York: Penguin Books, 1996).

Adele Freedman, "In the Shadow of the '30s: The Winter of Paraskeva Clark," *Toronto Life* (February 1979).

Camilla Gray, *The Russian Experiment in Art 1863–1922* (New York: Harry N. Abrams, 1971).

Josephine Hambleton, "A Painter of Sylvan Canada," *Ottawa Citizen*, 17 January 1948.

Charles S. Hill, *Canadian Painting in the Thirties* (exhibition catalogue) (Ottawa: The National Gallery of Canada, 1975).

———, *The Group of Seven: Art for a Nation* (Toronto and Ottawa: McClelland & Stewart and The National Gallery of Canada, 1995).

Anna Hudson, "Art and Social Progress: The Toronto Community of Painters, 1933–1950," unpublished PhD thesis, University of Toronto, 1997.

———, *A Collector's Vision: J.S. McLean and Modern Painting in Canada* (Toronto: Art Gallery of Ontario, 1999).

Kay Kritzwiser, "Paraskeva in the Looking Glass," *Globe and Mail*, 16 February 1983, p. 13.

Mary E. MacLachlan, *Paraskeva Clark: Paintings and Drawings* (Halifax: Dalhousie Art Gallery, 1982).

Pearl McCarthy, "Artist Paints Artist," *Globe and Mail*, 11 July 1942.

Anne McDougall, "Paraskeva Clark, un peintre exotique," *Vie des Arts*, March/April 1983.

Graham Campbell McInnes, "Art," *Saturday Night* (16 November 1935), p. 10.

———, "Canadian Critic Proclaims Independence of the Dominion's Art," *The Art Digest* (March 1936), pp. 10–11.

———, "World of Art: Water Colors," *Saturday Night* (18 April 1936), p. 8.

———, "New Horizons in Canadian Art," *New Frontier* Vol. 2, No. 2 (June 1937), pp. 19–20.

———, "Contemporary Canadian Artists: No. 7 — Paraskeva Clark," *The Canadian Forum* Vol. XVII, No. 199 (August 1937), pp. 166–167.

———, *A Short History of Canadian Art* (Toronto: Macmillan, 1939).

———, "Street Scenes: Toronto, Drawings by Paraskeva Clark," *New World Illustrated* Vol. II, No. 7 (September 1941), pp. 12–14.

Marsha Meskimmon, *The Art of Reflection* (New York: Columbia University Press, 1996).

Kathryn O'Rourke, "Labours and Love: Issues of Domesticity and Marginalization in the Works of Paraskeva Clark," unpublished MA thesis, Department of Art History, Concordia University, Montreal, March 1995.

Yury Rusakov, *Kuzma Petrov-Vodkin* (Leningrad: Aurora Art Publishers, 1986).

Lawrence Sabbath, "Paraskeva Clark — Artist in Action Series #3," *Canadian Art* Vol. XVII, No. 5, September (1960).

Gail Singer, *Portrait of the Artist as an Old Lady*, National Film Board of Canada, 1982.

Roderick Stewart, *Bethune* (Toronto: New Press, 1973).

Maria Tippett, *Making Culture* (Toronto: University of Toronto Press, 1990).

Frank H. Underhill, "The Canadian as Artist," *The Canadian Forum* Vol. xvi, No. 191 (December 1936), p. 28.

Elizabeth Wyn Wood "Art and the Pre-Cambrian Shield," *The Canadian Forum* Vol. xvi, No. 193 (February 1937), pp. 13–15.

Taped interviews with Paraskeva include the following:

"Andrew Bell Interviews Paraskeva Clark," 11 April 1948. MG30 D398, Volume 6 File 27.

Charles Hill, interview with Paraskeva Clark, 18 October 1973, National Gallery of Canada Archives.

Marguerite Hunt, interview with Paraskeva Clark, c. 1979, personal collection of Marguerite Hunt.

Joan Murray, "Joan Murray Talking to Paraskeva Clark," 29 May 1979, Joan Murray Artist Files, the Robert McLaughlan Gallery, Oshawa, Ontario.

INTRODUCTION

1   Quoted in William Kilbourn, ed., *The Toronto Book* (Toronto: Macmillan of Canada, 1976), p. 192.

2   Gail Singer, *Portrait of the Artist as an Old Lady, National Film Board of Canada, 1982.*

3   Ibid.

4   MG30 D398, Volume 5 File 4.

5   The Paraskeva Clark papers (MG30 D398) are housed in Library and Archives Canada in Ottawa.

6   *Sor Juana* (Cambridge: Belknap Press, 1988), p. 197. A biographer of Katherine Mansfield said of her work, "In a biography, the problem is one of documentation; it is not possible to prove every detail of the story I propose to trace, but it does fit all the facts we know, and has an inner logic which makes sense of everything else that happened ..." Claire Tomlin, *Katherine Mansfield: A Secret Life* (Toronto: Penguin Books, 1987), p. 71.

CHAPTER 1

1   Marina Tsvetaeva, *Stikhotyoreniya I poemy v pyati tomakh* (Lyric and narrative poetry in five volumes), ed. Alexander Sumerkin and Viktoria Schweitzer

(New York: Russica, 1980–1990), Volume I, p. 219. Quoted in Lily Feiler, *Marina Tsyetaeva, The Double Beat of Heaven and Hell* (Durham: Duke University Press, 1994), p. 7.

2   See http://www.belarusguide.com/culturel/religion/icons/XVI-4.html, www.belarusguide.com/culture1/religion/icons/XVI-4 and www.antiochian. org/martyr_paraskeva. Paraskeva was born on Friday 15 October 1898 (Julian calendar) as given on the register of vital statistics in the possession of Clive and Mary Clark. The Old Style Julian calendar, which was thirteen days behind the Gregorian calendar, was used in Russia until February 1918. According to the New Style Gregorian calendar, Paraskeva's birthday was 28 October 1898. Paraskeva gave a bit of information about her name in an interview with Joan Murray ("Joan Murray Talking to Paraskeva Clark," 29 May 1979).

3   "Fedorovna" was her patronymic name; her family name is unknown.

4   Notes taken by Mary Clark from a conversation with Paraskeva Clark sometime between 1983–1986. MG30 D398, Volume 6 File 27.

5   The first medical school for women had opened in St. Petersburg in 1897. Linda Harriet Edmondson, *Feminism in Russia, 1900–17* (London: Heinemann, 1984), pp. 21, 22.

6   "Joan Murray Talking to Paraskeva Clark," 29 May 1979, Tape 1.

7   According to *Russia* by Karl Baedeker (New York: Charles Scribner's Sons, 1914), the name "White Russians" originated from the characteristic light colour of their clothing, p. XLI. See also Henri Troyat's *Catherine the Great* (New York: Penguin, 1994), p. 194.

8   Hunt, interview with Paraskeva Clark, c. 1979.

9   Troyat, pp. 56, 202.

10   Michael Ignatieff, *The Russian Album* (New York: Viking, 1987) p. 36.

11   Skorokhods are light summer shoes. The factory, originally called the Association of Mechanical Footwear Production when it was founded in 1882, was officially named Skorokhod in 1910. The factory is still in production today. See www.encspb.rulen/index.

12   Dates on the copy (in Russian) of the register of vital statistics for Paraskeva in the possession of Clive and Mary Clark.

13   W. Bruce Lincoln, *Between Heaven and Hell: The Story of a Thousand Years of Artistic Life in Russia* (New York/Toronto: Penguin Books, 1998), p. 228.

14   George Woodcock, *Strange Bedfellows: The State of the Arts in Canada* (Vancouver: Douglas & McIntyre, 1985), p. 27.

15   Orlando Figes, *A People's Tragedy: A History of the Russian Revolution* (New York: Penguin, 1996), p. 129.

16   Camilla Gray, *The Russian Experiment in Art: 1862–1922* (New York: Harry N. Abrams, 1971), p. 48.

17   Figes, fn. p. 149.

18   See www.marxists.org/archive/cliff/works/1972/xx/circle.htm. Tony Cliff, "From Marxist Circle to Agitation," in *International Socialism* (1st series), No. 52, July–September 1972, p. 9.

19   Ibid., p. 2.

20   This painting is now on display in the National Gallery of Canada.

21   A photograph on the inside back cover of James H. Bater's *St. Petersburg Industrialization and Change* (London: Edward Arnold, 1976) shows a metal-working factory in the background, and in the foreground apartment buildings and the owner's mansion surrounded by trees and gardens. This photo validates Paraskeva's description of the type of situation in which they lived. See also Bater, p. 133, for a discussion of why owners lived at the factories.

22   Bater, p. 111.

23   Francine Du Plessix Gray, *Soviet Women: Walking the Tightrope* (New York: Doubleday, 1990), p. 2.

24   Bater, pp. 43, 112.

25   Joel Clark, 11 January 2002.

26   A legend relating to the construction says that the marsh swallowed all the stones as the city was being constructed. Peter the Great told his people "You don't know how to do anything," and with that he lifted stones, assembled them in mid-air to construct the city and then let them fall to the earth.

27   This figure was derived from the census of December 1897, cited in the 1906 edition of the *Encyclopaedia Britannica* (New York: Saalfield Publishing, 1906), p. 5190.

28   http://wolfieluc.tripod.com/russ.stpete.html.

29   Bater, p. 270. The number of electric streetcars went from zero in 1900 to 525 in 1910.

30   Ibid.

31   Figes, p. 126.

32   Alexandre Benois, *Memoirs* (London: Columbus Books, 1988), p. 19.

33   Quoted in Modris Eksteins, *Rites of Spring: The Great War and the Birth of the Modern Age* (Toronto: Lester & Orpen Dennys, 1989), p. 39.

34   *Portrait of the Artist as an Old Lady.*

35   Suzanne Massie, *Land of the Firebird: The Beauty of Old Russia* (New York: Simon & Schuster, 1980), p. 371. See also MacLachlan, p. 9.

36 Notes taken by Mary Clark in the early 1980s from the interview with Paraskeva Clark taped by Hunt c. 1979. MG30 D398, Volume 6 File 27. In the history of art, because achieving a satisfactory shade of red was difficult, the term "perfect red" came to have special significance.

37 "Joan Murray Talking to Paraskeva Clark," 29 May 1979.

38 Hunt, interview with Paraskeva Clark, c. 1979.

39 Vasily Romanovich Nossenkov to Clive Clark in 1992. From the files of Clive and Mary Clark.

40 Hunt, interview with Paraskeva Clark, c. 1979.

41 Ibid.

42 Mary Clark's undated notes after Paraskeva was in a nursing home, sometime between 1983–1986. MG30 D398, Volume 6 File 27.

43 "Icons," by Robert Steele in *The Soul of Russia*, Winifred Stephens, ed. (London: Macmillan, 1916), p. 64. Steele describes the Russian icon as "a panel picture of any dimensions from a few square inches to life size, painted in oil or tempera (oil painting does not become usual till the eighteenth century), generally on a gold ground, now covered in great measure by a gilt metal sheet leaving apertures for the face and hands, and containing any number of figures from one to thousands." p. 64.

44 Suzanne Massie, p. 53.

45 Figes, opposite p. 194.

46 Clive and Mary Clark, 15 February 2001.

47 Figes, p. 89.

48 Figes, p. 178.

49 "Joan Murray Talking to Paraskeva Clark," 29 May 1979.

CHAPTER 2

1 From "A June Night in Russia," by Maurice Baring, in Winifred Stephens, ed., *The Soul of Russia* (London: Macmillan, 1916), one of Paraskeva Clark's books in MG30 D398, Volume 15 File 1.

2 John Reed, *Ten Days that Shook the World* (New York: Random House, 1935), pp. 315–316.

3 Robert K. Massie, *Nicholas and Alexandra* (New York: Atheneum, 1967), p. 398.

4 Maja Miller Lees, 8 June 2005. It's interesting that Clive Clark did not recall ever seeing this wooden box with the fabrics, but I have no reason to doubt Lees's memory. From her conversations in the artist's studio, Lees got the

impression that Paraskeva wished she had daughters with whom she could share an interest in such "feminine" things as fabrics and flower-making.

5   E. M. Almedingen, *Tomorrow Will Come* (Boston: Little, Brown, 1941), pp. 97, 210.

6   "Plissie" is a derivation from Plistik, and Paraskeva's friends in those days often called her "Plissa" or "Plissie."

7   Hunt, interview with Paraskeva Clark, c. 1979.

8   MacLachlan, p. 10.

9   Paraskeva Clark's undated written notes for an application for a Guggenheim Fellowship, probably in 1941. MG30 D398, Volume 6 File 21.

10 Hunt, interview with Paraskeva Clark, c. 1979.

11 MG30 D398, Volume 4 File 5.

12 Guggenheim application notes, MG30 D398, Volume 6 File 24.

13 Camilla Gray, pp. 214–217.

14 Figes, p. 192.

15 Figes, p. 300.

16 Figes, p. 310.

17 The revolution is dated 25 October 1917 on the Julian calendar and 7 November 1917 on the Gregorian calendar. Geraldine Norman, *The Hermitage: The Biography of a Great Museum* (London: Pimlico, 1999), p. 137.

18 Camilla Gray, pp. 231–232.

19 MacLachlan, p. 11.

20 "Joan Murray Talking to Paraskeva Clark," 29 May 1979.

21 Mikhail Guerman, *Art of the October Revolution* (New York: Harry N. Abrams, 1979).

22 The Academy is also described in Alexandre Benois, *Reminiscences of the Russian Ballet* (London: Wyman & Sons, 1947), p. 103.

23 It is possible that another artist, Nikolay Akimov, who studied with Shukhayev sometime between 1915 and 1919 (see www.artnet.com/library), would have been in the same group with Paraskeva. Akimov, who became a stage designer, director, and painter, would have been yet another contact for Paraskeva in the world of stage design and set painting.

24 Guggenheim application notes, MG30 D398, Volume 6 File 24.

25 Sabbath, p. 293.

26 Guerman, p. 17; Yury Rusakov, *Kuzma Petrov-Vodkin* (Leningrad: Aurora Art Publishers, 1986), p. 250. Unless otherwise noted, Rusakov is the source for the quotations and information on Petrov-Vodkin in this section.

27 MacLachlan, p. 43, fn. 19.

28   Rusakov, p. 6.

29   Rusakov, p. 74. See also Lev Mochalov, *Kuzma Petrov-Vodkin* (Leningrad: Aurora Publishers, 1980), p. 10.

30   Guggenheim application, MG30 D398, Volume 6 File 24. Unless otherwise noted, this is the source for the material on Paraskeva's art school experience in this chapter.

31   MacLachlan, p. 12.

32   MG30 D398, Volume 6 File 24.

33   Paraskeva remembered a group of eight students who were Petrov-Vodkin's disciples. However, the Rusakov (p. 249) photo includes seventeen of his students with their teacher. If Paraskeva is right about his "disciples," it is possible that some of them had been studying with him for up to ten years since he returned to St. Petersburg in 1908 and began teaching there in 1909–1910. (See Rusakov, p. 246).

34   MG30 D398, Volume 6 File 24.

35   See MacLachlan, p. 12 for a discussion of Petrov-Vodkin's work and his teaching.

36   See MacLachlan, pp. 28, 45 n. 68.

37   Roberta Reeder, *Anna Akhmatova: Poet and Prophet* (New York: St. Martin's Press, 1994), p. 124.

38   Michael Pantazzi, 21 November 2002.

39   Figes, pp. 727, 759.

40   Benois, *Reminiscences of the Russian Ballet*, p. 243.

41   Paraskeva apparently told Adele Freedman ("In the Shadow of the '30s: The Winter of Paraskeva Clark," *Toronto Life* (February 1979), pp. 127–129) that they were married within two weeks. However, in all other contexts, she said they were married in 1922, which means several months would have passed before they married.

42   MG30 D398, Volume 6 File 27. Handwritten notes by Mary Clark from Hunt, interview with Paraskeva Clark, c. 1979.

43   These photos are in Library and Archives Canada, Acc No. 1995-019, Bar Code #2000761359.

44   Hunt, interview with Paraskeva Clark, c. 1979.

45   Notes written by Mary Clark. MG30 D398, Volume 6 File 27.

46   Murray Laufer and Marie Day, 16 April 2002.

CHAPTER 3

1   Paraskeva Clark in *Portrait of the Artist as an Old Lady*.

2   Clive and Mary Clark, 13 November 2002.

3   Reeder, p. 212.

4   Maxim Gorky, *My Childhood*, Ronald Wilks, trans. (New York: Penguin, 1966), p. 172.

5   I had several conversations with Clive and Mary Clark about Paraskeva's reasons for leaving Russia, and they firmly accept that it was for practical reasons, as Paraskeva claimed.

6   MG30 D398, Volume 3 File 1, a photocopy of a document (Moscow, 6 August 1923) written in Italian, which cites the Soviet decree #263 art. 103, 7 December 1921.

7   According to MacLachlan (p. 13), *Tomb of Allegri* was the only painting to have survived from that period. However, Clive and Mary Clark have the sketch for *Memories of Leningrad* that Paraskeva painted in 1923 (Clive and Mary Clark, 4 March 2003). Paraskeva must have taken this sketch with her when she left for Paris.

8   Paraskeva would have learned some French in school, and she would have learned more in her association with the Allegris. According to a 1916 publication (N. I. Karêev, "How Far Russia Knows England," in *The Soul of Russia*, Winifred Stephens, ed., (London: Macmillan) French and German were more widely known in Russia than was English.

9   Hunt, interview with Paraskeva Clark, c. 1979.

10   MacLachlan, p. 13.

11   MG30 D398, Volume 3 File 44, Avdey Plistik, Petrograd, to Paraskeva Allegri, Paris, 12 March 1924.

12   Paraskeva insisted the city of her birth was Leningrad, disregarding the other names — St. Petersburg and Petrograd — during different time periods.

13   In an interview with Charles Hill (18 October 1973), Paraskeva said she painted this in 1924 while she was feeling lonely. She painted the scene again in 1941 (MacLachlan, p. 63).

14   MG30 D398, Volume 3 File 44, letter dated 19 June 1925.

15   The group was Franklin Brownell, F. S. Challener, Clarence A. Gagnon, E. Wyly Grier, Randolph S. Hewton, Arthur Lismer, Horatio Walker, and Florence Wyle. (*A Portfolio of Pictures from the Canadian Section of Fine Arts*, British Empire Exhibition, 1924, London).

16   See Rebecca Sisler, *Passionate Spirits* (Toronto: Clarke, Irwin, 1980), pp. 108–109.

17   Pages from Paraskeva Clark's photo albums in Library and Archives Canada, Acc No 1995-019, Bar Code #2000761359.

18   Morley Callaghan, *That Summer in Paris* (Toronto: Macmillan, 1976), pp. 114, 116.

19   Janet Flanner, *Paris was Yesterday 1925–1939* (New York: Harcourt Brace Jovanovich, 1988).

20   William Wiser, *The Crazy Years: Paris in the Twenties* (London: Thames & Hudson, 1983), p. 154.

21   Ibid., pp. 83, 95 and du Plessix Gray, *Them*, p. 29.

22   Alexandre Benois, *Memoirs* Volume II (London: Shatto & Windus, 1964), p. 258.

23   Hunt, interview with Paraskeva Clark, c. 1979.

24   MG30 D398, Volume 3 File 5.

25   Clive and Mary Clark, 13 November 2002.

26   Wiser, p. 182.

27   Handwritten notes in MG30 D398, Volume 6 File 24.

28   *Portrait of the Artist as an Old Lady*.

29   O'Rourke, "Labours and Love," p. 54.

30   Hunt, interview with Paraskeva Clark, c. 1979.

31   MG30 D398, Volume 1 File 39.

32   These magazines, along with some of Paraskeva's books, were deposited in the Art Gallery of Ontario Edward P. Taylor Library and Archives in 2003 by Clive and Mary Clark.

CHAPTER 4

1   Lines from *Piers Plowman* by William Langland (c. 1330–1387) found among Paraskeva's clippings in MG30 D398, Volume 14 File 7.

2   Much of the information for this part of Philip's story comes from the unpublished memoirs Philip Clark wrote in 1979, "Memoires of Philip Thompson Clark, Elder son of Harold Clark, Doctor of Dental Surgery and Marguerite Cleveland Greene," in the possession of Clive and Mary Clark.

3   "Murray Adaskin, March 28, 1906–May 6, 2002," unpublished autobiography, p. 3. My thanks to Dorothea Larsens Adaskin for making this document available to me.

4   Kathleen Niwa, *For Frances and Murray: The Adaskin Art Collection* (Victoria: The Maltwood Art Museum and Gallery, 1988).

5   The details of the work Philip did vary in Murray's and Philip's accounts. According to Murray's memoirs, Philip completed a paper of complex accounting problems each week and mailed it to McGill University in Montreal. In his "Memoires," Philip makes no mention of this, only that he was studying for exams.

6   Clark, "Memoires."

7   In fact, Paraskeva was not as tall as Murray indicates in his memoirs.

8   Clark, "Memoires."

9   O'Rourke, "Labours and Love," p. 27.

10   Adaskin, memoirs, p. 31.

11   Ibid.

12   Clive and Mary Clark, 15 February 2001.

13   Freedman, p. 127.

14   MG30 D398, Volume 21 File 6.

15   John Herries McCulloch, "The Luxury of Ocean Travel," *Toronto Daily Star*, 23 June 1931.

16   MG30 D398, Volume 2 File 31.

17   MG30 D398, Volume 4 File 5, 5 May 1931.

18   Hunt, interview with Paraskeva Clark, c. 1979.

19   Clark "Memoires," Chapter III.

20   MG30 D398, Volume 3 File 1, letter from the Minister of Immigration and Colonization, 8 April 1931, addressed to G. B. Nicholson, House of Commons, Ottawa.

21   Library and Archives Canada, Canadian Immigration Service records, Vol. 6, p. 194, Sheet No. 8, 1931.

22   Ben and Joel Clark, 3 May 2001.

23   *Self Portrait* (1929–1930), watercolour on paper, 24 cm x 24 cm, in the collection of Clive and Mary Clark.

CHAPTER 5

1   Wyndham Lewis to Naomi Mitchison, 31 May 1943, quoted in Kilbourn, p. 192.

2   Hunt, interview with Paraskeva Clark, c. 1979.

3   Mount Pleasant Road cut across Roxborough Street, creating two separate streets. East of Mount Pleasant the name was changed to Roxborough Drive in 1952. The Clarks' address was then changed from 256 Roxborough Street to 56 Roxborough Drive.

4   According to Clive Clark, the Clark family belonged to the United Church of Canada, but did not attend church. The United Church of Canada was formed in 1925 when Canadian Methodists, Congregationalists, and most Presbyterians joined to become the largest Protestant body in the country.

5   Clive and Mary Clark, 15 February 2001.

6   "Clark Family History 1830–1913," by Philip T. Clark, unpublished document, courtesy of Clive and Mary Clark.

7   Clive and Mary Clark, 15 February 2001.

8   MG30 D398, Volume 21 File 6.

9   Ibid.

10 Ibid.

11 *Portrait of the Artist as an Old Lady*.

12 Hunt, interview with Paraskeva Clark, c. 1979.

13 Marguerite Hunt, 13 February 2001.

14 Clive and Mary Clark, 15 February 2001.

15 Ibid.

16 Virginia Clark Moogk to Paraskeva Clark, 14 December 1980, Toronto. MG30 D398, Volume 3 File 24.

17 Marian Fowler, *The Embroidered Tent* (Toronto: House of Anansi Press, 1982), p. 150.

18 G. P. de T. Glazebrook, *The Story of Toronto* (Toronto: University of Toronto Press, 1971) pp. 168–169.

19 Introductory phrase of section 91 of the *British North America Act* that formed Canada in 1867.

20 Emma Goldman, *Living My Life* (Salt Lake City: Peregrine Smith, 1982), p. 991.

21 The books in question would have been imports from the United States and/or Great Britain, as the Canadian editors at the Methodist Book and Publishing House would never let such works pass their desks. See two articles: "Books Classed Unfit for Public: Two Works of Light Literature Published by the Methodist Book Room Have Been Excluded From Library as Unfit for Public Reading — Consternation Follows," *Toronto World*, 10 April 1912, p. 1; "A Fuss Over Two Books Withdrawn from Library: Dr. William Briggs Reticent — Dr. George H. Locke Would Not Discuss Report," *Toronto Evening Telegram*, 10 April 1912, p. 25.

22 Glazebrook, pp. 189, 190.

23 Sharon Anne Cook, Lorna R. McLean, and Kate O'Rourke, eds., *Framing Our Past: Canadian Women's History in the Women's History in the Twentieth Century*

(Montreal & Kingston: McGill-Queen's University Press, 2001), p. 474, n. 5.

24   Statistics Canada, 2006 census.

25   "Fire Where There's Smoke," *Globe and Mail*, 25 February 1937.

26   The Arts & Letters Club was men-only until 1985, with the occasional excep-
     tion, such as in 1921 when women were allowed in as guests for the first time
     to hear the speaker, Nellie McClung. The club had many famous members,
     including the Group of Seven. See http://www.pc.gc.ca/culture/proj/urbain/
     cartes-maps/index_e.asp?mapid=1&buildingid=27 for more information.

27   Maria Tippett, *Making Culture* (Toronto: University of Toronto Press, 1990),
     p. 9.

28   Kilbourn, p. 63.

29   *Portrait of the Artist as an Old Lady.*

30   George Miller, 11 January 2001. My thanks to Mr. Miller, who was the Clarks'
     neighbour for many years, for his insights about Philip's personality.

31   12 August 1931.

32   Undated in MG30 D398, Volume 3 File 34.

CHAPTER 6

1   Paraskeva Clark in undated handwritten notes. MG30 D398, Volume 6 File 24.

2   See Rusakov, p. 117.

3   Rusakov, p. 115.

4   Hunt, interview with Paraskeva Clark, c. 1979.

5   MG30 D398, Volume 2 File 26.

6   Clive and Mary Clark, 30 October 2002.

7   MG30 D398, Volume 2 File 26.

8   Alan Jarvis, ed., *Douglas Duncan: A Memorial Portrait* (Toronto: University of
     Toronto Press, 1974), p. 61.

9   The catalogue of the exhibition (Toronto: The Art Gallery of Toronto, 1931)
     is housed in the Edward P. Taylor Library and Archives, Art Gallery of
     Ontario.

10   *By Woman's Hand*, National Film Board of Canada, 1995. This is a film about
     Prudence Heward, Sarah Robertson, and Anne Savage, painters who were
     part of the Beaver Hall Group in Montreal in the 1920s and 1930s.

11   MacLachlan, p. 17.

12   "Trends in Canadian Art," *University of Toronto Quarterly* Vol. XIV, No. 2
     (January 1945), p. 171.

13   Hill, interview with Paraskeva Clark, 18 October 1973.

14   Charles Hill, *The Group of Seven: Art for a Nation* (Toronto: McClelland & Stewart/National Gallery of Canada, 1995), pp. 287–288.

15   "When We Awake," *Yearbook of the Arts in Canada 1928–1929* (Toronto: Macmillan, 1929), pp. 5, 6.

16   Hill, *The Group of Seven*, p. 285.

17   John Alford, "The Development of Painting in Canada," *Canadian Art* Vol. 11, No. 3 (March 1945) p. 100.

18   *Portrait of the Artist as an Old Lady.*

19   Hudson, "Art and Social Progress," p. 30.

20   George Russell, "The Thirties: A Crash Course in the Facts of Life and Art," *Globe and Mail Weekend Magazine*, 25 January 1975, p. 18. This is a reference to Rasputin who, through Alexandra, the wife of Nicholas, was given incredible political power because she believed he had healing power over their hemophiliac son, Alexis Nicolaievich.

21   See Oscar Ryan, *Tim Buck: A Conscience for Canada* (Toronto: Progress Books, 1975), and Morris Wolfe, "The party owes him more," *Globe and Mail*, 29 March 1975, p. 23.

22   *Portrait of the Artist as an Old Lady.*

23   Tippett, *Making Culture*, p. 29.

24   See Appendix II and III of the catalogue by the late Natalie Luckyj, *Visions and Victories: 10 Canadian Women Artists 1914(1945* (London, Ontario: London Regional Art Gallery, 1983) for lists of female artists in major exhibitions during those years.

25   Dorothy Farr and Natalie Luckyj, *From Women's Eyes: Women Painters in Canada* (Kingston: Agnes Etherington Art Centre, Queen's University, 1975), p. 3.

26   Emily Carr, *Hundreds and Thousands: The Journals of Emily Carr* (Toronto: Clarke Irwin, 1966), p. 78.

27   Hunt, interview with Paraskeva Clark, c. 1979.

28   Hudson, "Art and Social Progress," p. 3.

29   Mary MacLachlan, 4 September 2003.

30   Anna Hudson, 23 January 2001; Hudson, "Art and Social Progress," p. 4.

31   Hudson, "Art and Social Progress," p. 20.

32   Anne McDougall, "Paraskeva Clark, un peintre exotique," *Vie des Arts*, March/April 1983.

33   Jehanne Bietry Salinger, "One More Exhibition," *The Canadian Forum*, 11 (April 1931), p. 261.

34   Paul Duval, *Four Decades: The Canadian Group of Painters and their Contemporaries* (Toronto: Clarke, Irwin, 1972), pp. 12–13.

35   A. Y. Jackson, "Lawren Harris, A biographical Sketch," in *Lawren Harris:*
      Paintings, exhibition catalogue (Toronto: Art Gallery of Toronto, 1948); quoted
      in Douglas Ord, *The National Gallery of Canada: Ideas, Art and Architecture*
      (Montreal & Kingston: McGill-Queen's University Press, 2003), p. 39. Ord's
      book is a well-researched and fascinating history and his sense of humour
      and ability to portray the personalities of the institution make his book a
      delight to read.

36   The founding members of the Canadian Group of Painters (CGP) were:
      Bertram Brooker, Frank Carmichael, Emily Carr, A. J. Casson, Charles Comfort,
      LeMoine L. Fitzgerald, Lawren Harris, Prudence Heward, Randolph S.
      Hewton, Edwin Holgate, Bess Housser, A. Y. Jackson, Arthur Lismer,
      J. W. G. (Jock) MacDonald, Thoreau MacDonald, Yvonne McKague, Mabel
      H. May, Isabel McLaughlin, Lilias Torrance Newton, Will Ogilvie, George
      Pepper, Sarah Robertson, Albert Robinson, Anne Savage, Charles H. Scott,
      Frederick Varley, W. P. Weston, W. J. Wood. See Duval, *Four Decades*, p. 14; and
      Joan Murray, *Pilgrims in the Wilderness: The Struggle of the Canadian Group of*
      Painters, 1933–1969 (Oshawa: The Robert McLaughlin Gallery, 1993).

37   Hudson, "Art and Social Progress," p. 74.

38   "Orienting the True North," in Michael Tooby, ed., *The True North 1896–1939*
      (London: Barbican Art Gallery, 1991), p. 16.

39   "Joan Murray Talking to Paraskeva Clark," 29 May 1979.

40   Quoted in Maria Tippett, *By a Lady: Three Centuries of Art by Canadian Women*
      (Toronto: Penguin Books, 1992), p. 75.

41   Charles C. Hill, *Canadian Painting in the Thirties* (Ottawa: National Gallery of
      Canada, 1975), p. 11.

42   Handwritten notes of conversation of Charles Hill with Paraskeva Clark,
      30 January 1974. Charles Hill Files, "Paraskeva Clark"; also Wentworth Walker,
      19 April 2001.

43   MacLachlan, p. 52.

44   The reason for the exhibition in Ocean City was that Bertram Brooker
      worked for J. J. Gibbons Ltd., which handled the Heinz advertising account.
      It was Brooker's connection that resulted in the invitation to the Canadian
      Group of Painters to hold an exhibition in Ocean City. See Hill, *Canadian*
      Painting in the Thirties, p. 30, n. 40.

45   In the CGP exhibition of 1933, Paraskeva also showed her *View from*
      Huckleberry Rock, Muskoka (1933).

46   Veronica Strong-Boag, *The New Day Recalled: Lives of Girls and Women in English*
      Canada, 1919–1939 (Toronto: Copp Clark Pitman, 1988), p. 152.

47   16 June 1933 in MG30 D398, Volume 3 File 2.

48   Strong-Boag, *The New Day Recalled*, p. 161.

49   Murray Adaskin quoted in Niwa, *For Frances and Murray*. A 29 March 1975 letter (MG30 D398, Volume 3 File 14) from Frances and Murray to Paraskeva described the gown as having "the opening on your Middle."

50   Source unidentified in MG30 D398.

51   Mary MacLachlan, 9 July 2003.

52   Marsha Meskimmon, *The Art of Reflection* (New York: Columbia University Press, 1996), p. xvi.

53   Hill, interview with Paraskeva Clark, 18 October 1973.

54   Derek May, director, *Pictures from the 1930's*, National Film Board of Canada, 1977.

55   Meskimmon, *The Art of Reflection*, p. 156.

56   MacLachlan, p. 18.

57   MG30 D398, Volume 6 File 24.

58   Tamar Nelson, 19 April 2001; Susan Adaskin, 25 April 2004. My thanks to Susan Adaskin for taking time to show me the portrait.

59   See Stewart Hoffman, "What's old is Carlu again," *Toronto Star*, 27 April 2003, p. B6. Although the building is now a centre for shops, the seventh floor was restored and reopened in 2003 after almost thirty years of neglect, thanks to the efforts of Eleanor Koldofsky and Friends of Eaton Auditorium.

60   Joan Murray, ed., *Daffodils in Winter: The Life and Letters of Pegi Nicol MacLeod, 1904–1949* (Moonbeam, Ontario: Penumbra Press, 1984), p. 31.

61   For more about Eaton's, see the Archives on Ontario web pages http://www.archives.gov.on.ca/english/on-line-exhibits/eatons-windows/curatorial.aspx and http://www.archives.gov.on.ca/english/on-line-exhibits/eatons/eatons-christmas-memories-01.aspx.

62   Guggenheim notes, MG30 D398, Volume 6 File 24.

63   Ibid.

64   MacLachlan, p. 21. See also Hill, *Canadian Painting in the Thirties*, p. 95. Other artists who worked for Cera were Charles Comfort, Carl Schaefer, and Cavin Atkins. In 1969, Cera, a friend of media guru Marshall McLuhan, painted a mural for him, *Pied Pipers All*. This mural, taken down and stored for a number of years, now hangs again at the McLuhan Centre at the University of Toronto. Cera was one friend who understood McLuhan's ideas before many others did, and from that understanding painted this mural.

65   Murray, *Daffodils in Winter*, p. 31.

66   "Joan Murray Talking to Paraskeva Clark," 29 May 1979.

67 Graham McInnes, "Art," *Saturday Night*, 16 November 1935, p. 10.

68 Graham McInnes, "World of Art," *Saturday Night*, 20 April 1935.

69 Francine du Plessix Gray, *Them: A Memoir of Parents* (New York: The Penguin Press, 2005), p. 2.

70 Gordon MacNamara, 23 October 2001.

71 This sketchbook includes sketches, photos, and signatures by many Toronto artists and other prominent people, among them, Norman Bethune, Will Ogilvie, Barker Fairley, Douglas Duncan, Carl Schaefer, Graham Campbell McInnes, Peter Haworth, Harry and Frances Adaskin, and Elizabeth Wyn Wood.

CHAPTER 7

1 Frank H. Underhill, "The Canadian as Artist," *The Canadian Forum* Vol. XVI, No. 191 (December 1936), p. 28.

2 McInnes, "The World of Art," Saturday Night, 18 January 1936.

3 The paintings McInnes cited are *Sail Boat, View in a Gorge*, and *Daffodils* (all undated). I was not able to trace the whereabouts of any of these paintings.

4 "New Horizons in Canadian Art," *New Frontier*, June 1937, pp. 19–20.

5 "Women Throng Docks Pleading for Workers," *Toronto Daily Star*, 24 June 1931.

6 Paraskeva Clark, "Come Out from Behind the Pre-Cambrian Shield," *New Frontier* Vol. 1, No. 12 (April 1937) pp. 16–17.

7 Pino Cacucci, *Tina Modotti: A Life*, Patricia J. Duncan, trans. (New York: St. Martin's Press, 1999), p. 146. Modotti, a well-known photographer, was associated with Edward Weston and Diego Rivera. She joined the Mexican Communist Party and moved to Spain in 1936. There she worked as a medical volunteer with Red Aid during the Spanish Civil War, and at one point met Norman Bethune and offered to help him with performing transfusions. However, the Soviet Comintern drafted her to work in their propaganda department. Modotti returned to Mexico in 1939 and died there in 1942. Cacucci's biography of this remarkable woman provides yet another glimpse of the political aspects of the Spanish Civil War.

8 See Reeder, p. 235.

9 MG30 D398, Volume 4 File 16.

10 Murray, *Daffodils in Winter*, p. 111.

11 Author's conversation with Anna Hudson, 30 January 2006, Toronto.

12 Murray, p. 123.

13   Rod Stewart, 26 June 2003; MacLachlan, p. 22.

14   Niwa, *For Frances and Murray.*

15   Murray, *Daffodils in Winter*, p. 123.

16   "Joan Murray Talking to Paraskeva Clark," 29 May 1979.

17   Rod Stewart, 26 June 2003; Libbie Park, "Bethune as I Knew Him," in Wendell MacLeod, Libbie Park; Stanley Ryerson, *Bethune: The Montreal Years* (Toronto: James Lorimer, 1978), p. 119; *Portrait of the Artist as an Old Lady.*

18   Larry Hannant, *The Politics of Passion: Norman Bethune's Writing and Art* (Toronto: University of Toronto Press, 1998), p. 164.

19   Ibid., p. 163.

20   *Portrait of the Artist as an Old Lady.*

21   Philip Clark to Murray and Frances Adaskin, 17 October 1977, courtesy of Murray and Dorothea Adaskin.

22   Ibid.

23   Gail Singer, 1 February 2001.

24   Ibid.

25   "Contemporary Canadian Artists," *The Canadian Forum*, August 1937, p. 166.

26   Hudson, "Art and Social Progress," p. 118. As Hudson pointed out, these paintings were shown together in the Canadian Group of Painters show in 1937.

27   Unfortunately, this painting has disappeared.

28   See O'Rourke, "Labours and Love," p. 55.

29   "World of Art," *Saturday Night*, 23 April 1938. This watercolour, according to MacLachlan (p. 28), is untraced.

30   In 1975, Paraskeva donated to the Bethune Memorial House in Gravenhurst, Ontario, this notebook, along with the items that appear in *Presents from Madrid* and other gifts Bethune sent. The items are listed in a document in MG30 D398, Volume 4 File 13. My thanks to Site Manager Scott Davidson for talking with me about Bethune, and for showing me the set of Russian playing cards in a red burnished wooden box that apparently Bethune brought back with him from the Soviet Union and later gave to Paraskeva.

31   Hannant, *The Politics of Passion*, p. 88.

32   Florence Boyard Bird to Douglas Duncan, 2 April 1940, D2. F1 Vol. 2, Letters and lists, Picture Loan Society, Frances Barwick and Douglas Duncan fonds, National Gallery of Canada Archives.

33   Frances Gage, June 2001.

34   Elizabeth Wyn Wood, "Art and the Pre-Cambrian Shield," *The Canadian Forum* Vol. XVI, No. 193 (February 1937), pp. 13, 14.

35   Ibid., p. 14.

36   Frank Underhill, "The Season's New Books," *The Canadian Forum*, December 1936 (Volume XVI, No. 191), p. 28.

37   Wood, "Art and the Pre-Cambrian Shield," p. 13.

38   MacLachlan (p. 28) gives the date of this exhibit in error as 1936, but see *Montreal Gazette* 18 May 1935, "Russian Paintings on Exhibit in City" and Robert Ayre, "Soviet Art Comes to Canada," in *The Canadian Forum* Vol. XV No. 77, August 1935.

39   Clark, "Come Out From Behind the Pre-Cambrian Shield," pp. 16–17.

40   Pablo Picasso, quoted in Russell Martin, *Picasso's War* (New York: Penguin Putnam, 2002), frontispiece.

41   Clark, "Come Out from Behind the Pre-Cambrian Shield," p. 16.

42   MG30 D398, Volume 14 File 20.

43   George V. Plekhanov, *Art and Society: A Marxist Analysis* (New York: Critics Group, 1937), p. 33.

44   Ibid., p. 48.

45   Letter dated 21 August 1938, National Gallery of Canada Archives, file 7.1-c.

46   MacLachlan, pp. 28, 74. Although MacLachlan attributed six shows to Paraskeva that year, a count revealed five.

47   Anna Hudson, 28 February 2005.

48   Unless otherwise noted, my source on Petrushka was Catriona Kelly, *Petrushka: The Russian Carnival Puppet Theatre* (Cambridge: Cambridge University Press, 1990).

49   Hill, interview with Paraskeva Clark, 18 October 1973. In MacLeod, Park, and Ryerson, *Bethune*, Park says Bethune painted the colour of the puppet stand blue, covering Paraskeva's red. However, I think Paraskeva's memory can be trusted for this detail.

50   Wood, "Art and the Pre-Cambrian Shield," p. 14.

51   *Portrait of the Artist as an Old Lady*.

52   Reeder, p. 114.

53   Mary MacLachlan, 9 July 2003.

54   See Richard Guy Wilson, *The Machine Age in America, 1918–1941* (New York: The Brooklyn Museum/Harry N. Abrams, 1986), p. 240; and Willim Henning, www.huntermuseum.org/philipevergood.html.

55   See Martin, *Picasso's War*, for the story of *Guernica*. "Gernika" is the Basque spelling.

56   Paraskeva Clark to Douglas Duncan, 26 August 1937, MG30 D398, Volume 4 File 18.

57   Martin, *Picasso's War*, pp. 148–155.

58   MG30 D398, Volume 4 File 16. Evelyn Ahrend to a "Miss Lane," received at the Art Gallery of Ontario, 17 August 1939.

59   Martin, *Picasso's War*, p. 178.

60   It was disquieting that in 2003 during the sessions of the United Nations Security Council when the United States attempted to convince the world body of the necessity for bombing Iraq, the reproduction of *Guernica* hanging at the United Nations was draped over and covered.

61   The Toronto Heliconian Club is one of the oldest associations of its kind in Canada. Founded in 1909 to give women in the arts and letters an opportunity to meet socially and intellectually, 2009 marks the 100th anniversary. See http://www.heliconianclub.org/ for more information.

62   "Art and Society," *Toronto Telegram*, 8 February 1939.

63   MG30 D398, Volume 4 File 16.

64   Ibid.

CHAPTER 8

1   MG30 D398, Volume 6 File 24, Paraskeva Clark notes for an application for a Guggenheim Fellowship.

2   "Joan Murray Talking to Paraskeva Clark," 29 May 1979.

3   Anna Hudson, *A Collector's Vision: J. S. McLean and Modern Painting in Canada* (Toronto: Art Gallery of Ontario, 1999), p. 10.

4   MG30 D398, Volume 6 File 8. Unfortunately, McLean gives no details in his 24 January 1938 letter so we don't know for sure which painting this was. However, two 1938 paintings were in his collection: *The Bush* and *On Hahn's Island*, the earliest Clarks he owned.

5   Hudson, *A Collector's Vision*, p. 18.

6   Wentworth Walker, 19 April 2001.

7   "Joan Murray Talking to Paraskeva Clark," 29 May 1979.

8   In MG30 D398, Volume 2 File 27. Unfortunately, Paraskeva's letter to which McLean refers has not survived because McLean destroyed most of his papers, according to June McLean, his daughter-in-law (June McLean and Mike Stewart, 2 April 2003).

9   J. S. McLean, "On the Pleasures of Collecting Paintings," *Canadian Art* Vol. X, Autumn 1952.

10   Hudson, *A Collector's Vision*, p. 19.

11   J. S. McLean to Paraskeva Clark, Toronto, 12 April 1938, MG30 D398, Volume

6 File 8.

12 Sabbath, pp. 291, 292.

13 MacLachlan, p. 29.

14 Clark, "Come Out From Behind the Pre-Cambrian Shield," p. 16. See also MacLachlan, p. 30.

15 MacLachlan, p. 28 and n. 68, p. 45.

16 Family letters in MG30 D398, Volume 4 File 5.

17 Adrienne Clarkson, *Norman Bethune* (Toronto: Penguin Canada, 2009). In 2005, Tim Brady wrote an opera about Bethune but could find no one to produce it. See "Is Norman Bethune's legacy too big for opera?" *Globe and Mail*, 22 January 2005, R4.

18 Geoffrey York "China revives Bethune's spirit in SARS fight," *Globe and Mail*, 13 May 2003, p. A3.

19 Ibid.

20 For more information on Norman Bethune, see the Parks Canada website: http://www.pc.gc.ca/eng/lhn-nhs/on/bethune/natcul/natcul1.aspx.

21 MacLachlan, p. 31.

22 MacLachlan, p. 31. The drawing is listed on a 1 November 1979 record of works in MG30 D398, Volume 6 File 07.

23 Hill, interview with Paraskeva Clark, 18 October 1973.

24 Paraskeva Clark to H. O. McCurry, 10 January 1938, Charles Hill Files, "Paraskeva Clark: Correspondence."

25 Paraskeva Clark to H. O. McCurry, 25 July 1939, ibid.; also H. O. McCurry to Paraskeva Clark, 24 July 1939, National Gallery of Canada Archives, 5.41S Southern Dominions.

26 Paraskeva Clark's handwritten notes in MG30 D398, Volume 8 File 16.

27 In Roald Nasgaard, *The Mystic North: Symbolist Landscape Painting in Northern Europe and North America 1890–1940* (Toronto: University of Toronto Press, 1984), p. 168.

28 "Art of the Modern Europeans," *Saturday Night*, 18 December 1939.

29 Paraskeva Clark, Toronto, to Carl and Lillian Schaefer, Vermont, 21 December 1940, MG30 D398, Volume 1 File 5.

30 "Contemporary Canadian Artists No. 10: Marian Scott," *Canadian Forum* Vol. 17, No. 202 (November 1937), p. 274.

31 Simon and Heather McInnes, 16 September 2003.

32 Graham McInnes papers in Robertson Davies Library, Massey College, University of Toronto.

33 "Joan Murray Talking to Paraskeva Clark," 29 May 1979.

34 Gail Singer, 1 February 2001.

35 MG30 D398, Volume 1 File 40.

36 "Public Accounts of the Province of Ontario for the Fiscal Year ended 31st March, 1941" (Toronto: Baptist Johnston printer to the Queen's Most Excellent Majesty, 1941), p. QII.

37 16 March 1941, Carl and Lillian Schaefer fonds, MG30 D171, Volume 1 File 5, National Library and Archives Canada, Ottawa.

38 Wentworth Walker, 19 April 2001.

39 Paraskeva Clark to Carl and Lillian Schaefer in Vermont, 21 December 1940. MG30 D171, Volume 1 File 5.

40 MG30 D398, Volume 6 File 24.

41 "Plans for work," notes for Guggenheim application, MG30 D398, Volume 6 File 24. There is no evidence Paraskeva ever sent in an application.

42 Amédée Ozenfant (1886–1966) was educated in Paris. He, with Édouard Jeanneret (known as the architect Le Corbusier) invented "Purism," an approach to making art void of decoration and fantasy with detail eliminated. He taught at the Ozenfant School of Fine Arts in New York from 1939 to 1955 and lectured widely in the States.

CHAPTER 9

1 Käthe Kollwitz in Mina C. Klein and H. Arthur Klein, *Käthe Kollwitz: Life in Art* (New York: Schocken Books, 1975), p. 160.

2 Reprint of *The Kingston Conference Proceedings* (Kingston: Agnes Etherington Art Centre, 1991), fn. 19, p. xxiii.

3 Ibid., p. vi.

4 *Maritime Art* was the first regional art magazine in Canada, and in 1943 was moved to Ottawa under the auspices of the National Gallery and renamed *Canadian Art*. This magazine became an important voice for the arts in Canada.

5 Walter Abell to Paraskeva Clark, 21 August 1938, National Gallery of Canada Archives, File 7.1-C.

6 *The Kingston Conference Proceedings*, pp. 23–28.

7 "Art and Artists," *The Globe and Mail* , 11 July 1942.

8 *The Kingston Conference Proceedings*, p. 121.

9 Program in MG30 D398, Volume 4 File 17.

10 *The Kingston Conference Proceedings*, pp. 21, 107.

11 Murray, *Daffodils in Winter*, p. 157.

12   Perhaps of even greater consequence was that the FCA organized a committee that recommended the federal government establish the Canadian Arts Council, which eventually became part of the process leading to the formation of the current-day Canada Council for the Arts.

13   Other members were A. Y. Jackson, Jack Nichols, Carl Schaefer, Charles Comfort, Isabel McLaughlin, Lowrie Warrener, Eric Aldwinckle, Charles Goldhamer, Yvonne McKague Housser, George Pepper, Caven Atkins, Rody Kenny Courtice, Peter Haworth, Bobs Coghill Haworth, Graham McInnes, John Alford, and Barker Fairley. See Hudson, "Art and Social Progress," p. 245.

14   Tippett, *Making Culture*, p. 166.

15   See Camilla Gray, p. 105.

16   *New World Illustrated*, September 1941.

17   O'Rourke, "Labours and Love," p. 32.

18   Dora de Pédery-Hunt, 31 May 2001.

19   Harrison Salisbury, *The 900 Days: The Siege of Leningrad* (New York: Avon Books, 1969), p. 101.

20   Salisbury, *The 900 Days*, pp. 167, 168.

21   Norman, p. 241.

22   Sabbath, p. 293.

23   O'Rourke, "Labours and Love," pp. 39, 40.

24   *Globe and Mail*, 22 September 1942.

25   A.Y. Jackson fonds, MG30 D351, Volume 1 File 8.

26   *Globe and Mail*, 22 September 1941, front page.

27   Merrily Weisbord, *The Strangest Dream: Canadian Communists, the Spy Trials, and the Cold War* (Toronto: Lester & Orpen Dennys, 1983), p. 119.

28   22 September 1941, front page.

29   A list of the other incorporators and organizers of the fund is given in a document about the organization (MG28 165 Vol. 13 National Archives, Ottawa): J. E. Atkinson (*Toronto Daily Star*), George McCullagh (*Globe and Mail*), R. M. Fowler (McCarthy & McCarthy Barristers & Solicitors), Clifford Sifton, Harrison Gilmour, Margaret Gould (editorial writer, *Toronto Daily Star*), Mrs. W. L. Grant (former Dean of Women, McGill University).

30   June McLean, the daughter-in-law of J. S. McLean, feels that much of his interest in Russia was because of Paraskeva (June McLean, 9 April 2003).

31   "Address by Mr. J. S. McLean Canadian Aid to Russia Fund Toronto, 25th November, 1942," p. 3, MG28 165, Volume 13 in Library and Archives Canada.

32   "Canadian Aid to Russia Fund," last page (unpaginated) MG28 165,Volume 13.

33   Maria Shkapskaya, "Soviet Women on All Fronts," *Soviet Russia Today*, October 1942, p. 17, and William Mandel, "Leningrad Under Siege," *Soviet Russia Today*, February 1943, pp. 17–18.

34   "The Russian View," The Essays of Virginia Woolf II, 1912–1918, Andrew McNeillie (New York: Harcourt Brace Jovanovich Publishers, 1987), p. 343. In another essay, "The Russian Point of View," Woolf calls this core the "soul" and claims the passionate Russian soul to be the most common character in Russian literature. See "Collected Essays I" (London: Hogarth Press, 1966), pp. 238–246.

35   *Toronto Daily Star*, 4 December 1942.

36   Hill, interview with Paraskeva Clark, 18 October 1973.

37   See Chapter 7.

38   Although a Picture Loan Society statement in Library and Archives Canada (MG30 D398,Volume 4 File 19) gives the total sales as $444.50, a *Toronto Daily Star* article (17 December 1942) gives the gross amount as more than $500.

39   20 February 1943 in MG30 D398,Volume 4 File 19.

40   MG30 D398, Volume 4 File 19.

41   MG30 D398, Volume 2 File 28.

42   This painting is now in the collection of the Art Gallery of Ontario.

43   Pantazzi, 21 November 2002.

44   Anna Hudson, 23 January 2001 and 13 March 2003.

45   Wilson, *The Machine Age in America*, pp. 230, 240.

46   In *World Affairs* Vol. 8, No. 6 (February 1943) pp. 17, 18.

Chapter 10

1   Käthe Kollwitz, *The Diary and Letters of Käthe Kollwitz*, Hans Kollwitz, ed. (Evanston, Illinois: Northwestern University Press, 1995), p. 144.

2   In the 1990s, Clive Clark enlisted the help of the Consulate General of Canada in St. Petersburg to send a letter to his cousin Vasilly Nossenkov. The cousin replied in December 1992 and gave these details about the tragic ending of the lives of these relatives. He quoted this proverb in his letter.

3   Paraskeva Clark to Douglas Duncan. Douglas Duncan fonds, SC905, Edward P. Taylor Library and Archives, Art Gallery of Ontario. This letter is undated, but a Canadian Committee to Aid Spanish Refugees receipt, dated 30 June 1939, was attached to the letter in which she said she had had the receipt for

a while and forgot to give it to Duncan. According to George Vernadsky, *A History of Russia* (New Haven: Yale University Press, 1961) Red Army troops crossed the Polish frontier 17 September 1939 (p. 422), which tells us approximately when Paraskeva wrote this letter.

4   Letter from Paraskeva Clark to Carl and Lillian Schaefer, 21 December 1940. MG30 D398, Volume 1 File 5.

5   Ben and Joel Clark, 29 November 2001.

6   Djuwe Joe Blom and Sam Sussman, *Pioneers of Mental Health and Social Change* (London, Ontario: Third Eye Publications, 1989), p. 73.

7   Ben once explained what he remembered about that period. He was going to the armoury every day with the other boys who were drafted, doing the drills, and one day Paraskeva told him there's something wrong with him, he's not going back there anymore, that she's taking him to see a doctor. There's a question about how much one can trust Ben's memory after all these years of trauma and illness, but his comments lead one to wonder about the circumstances of his breakdown. We will never know the details of what happened. Ben said he was rejected from going overseas because he was ill and was glad he was turned down because he would have had to leave home. Ben and Joel Clark, 29 November 2001.

8   Clive Clark, 11 December 2001.

9   Ibid.

10   Ibid. After these many years, family members do not remember the timing of events in Ben's life, such as when he joined the Reserves. Ben remembered that he joined the Signal Corp and went to a building on Spadina Avenue regularly, going through drills. Though Ben's memory is not always reliable, in this case it seems his recounting of these events is accurate. Joel and Ben Clark, 3 May 2001.

11   Clive Clark, 11 December 2001.

12   Murray Laufer and Marie Day, 16 April 2002; Rebecca Sisler, 10 September 2002.

13   Hunt, interview with Paraskeva Clark, c. 1979.

14   J. S. Tyhurst, MD, et al., *More for the Mind* (Toronto: The Canadian Mental Health Association, 1963), p. 1.

15   Harvey G. Simmons, *Unbalanced Mental Health Policy in Ontario 1930–1989* (Toronto: Wall & Thompson, 1990), pp. 15–29. From 1938–1943, metrazol, a convulsion-inducing drug was used for treating schizophrenia but was abandoned because of its severe side effects. Because so little was known about

treating mental illness, a great deal of experimentation took place. When insulin was first used, the experimentation was limited to females. The reason for selecting females is unclear, but one doctor thought perhaps it was because women "were more tractable than men," fn. 39, pp. 28, 29.

16 Clive Clark, 11 December 2001, Toronto.

17 Ibid.

18 See Salisbury, *The 900 Days*, pp. 626 ff. for this stage of the war.

19 This document, sent to H. O. McCurry, is in 7.4W Writers', Broadcasters', and Artists' War Council (Outside Activities/Organizations) National Gallery of Canada Archives.

20 *Toronto Daily Star*, 18 June 1943, and *The Evening Telegram*, 19 June 1943, p. 5.

21 18 October 1944 in MG30 D398, Volume 4 File 31.

22 Despite my best efforts, including sending inquiries to the city of St. Petersburg and to the Hermitage Museum in St. Petersburg, I was unable to find out where the artworks that were sent to that city during World War II are now.

23 *Toronto Daily Star*, 22 June 1943.

24 Letters from J. Ellsworth Flavelle, Chair of the Council to H. O. McCurry, 10 August 1943; and Malcolm Ross to H. O. McCurry, 26 April, 1944; and Paraskeva Clark to H. O. McCurry, 19 September 1944 in 7.4N National Council for Soviet Friendship (Outside Activities/Organizations), National Gallery of Canada Archives.

25 See *Toronto Daily Star*, 10 November 1943, p. 4. Paraskeva's lists are found in MG30 D398, Volume 4 File 22.

26 Unfortunately, a reproduction of this painting could not be included because the owner declined having it photographed.

27 MacLachlan, p. 35.

28 The Allegri letters are in MG30 D398, Volume 2 File 26, Volume 3 Files 5 and 6.

29 Paraskeva described her family life this way in a letter dated 20 January 1947 to H. O. McCurry, but it seems clear from other comments that she felt this way about her family situation long before that.

30 Carol Becker, *Zones of Contention: Essays on Art, Institutions, Gender and Anxiety* (Albany: State University of New York Press, 1996), p. 191.

31 O'Rourke, "Labours and Love," p. 83.

CHAPTER 11

1   Käthe Kollwitz in *The Diary and Letters of Käthe Kollwitz*, pp. 62–63.

2   Salisbury, *The 900 Days*, p. 651.

3   This working drawing is in the collection of the Ottawa Art Gallery.

4   MacLachlan, p. 35, from an interview between Mary MacLachlan and Paraskeva Clark, November 1980.

5   MacLachlan, p. 36.

6   H. O. McCurry to Paraskeva Clark, 2 March 1944, Charles Hill Files, "Paraskeva Clark: Correspondence."

7   Paraskeva Clark to H. O. McCurry, 17 May 1944, ibid.

8   Niwa, *For Frances and Murray.*

9   H. O. McCurry to Paraskeva Clark, 8 May 1944 in MG30 D398, Volume 4 File 32.

10   Paraskeva Clark to H. O. McCurry, 17 May 1944, Charles Hill Files, "Paraskeva Clark: Correspondence."

11   See Christine Boyanski, *The 1940s: A Decade of Painting in Ontario* (Toronto: Art Gallery of Ontario, 1984), p. 9.

12   Joyce Zemans, "Establishing the Canon: Nationhood, Identity and the National Gallery's First Reproduction Program of Canadian Art," *The Journal of Canadian Art History* Vol. XVI, No. 2, 1995, p. 22.

13   Ibid., p. 25.

14   Joyce Zemans, "Envisioning Nation: Nationhood, Identity and the Sampson-Matthews Silkscreen Project: The Wartime Prints," *The Journal of Canadian Art History* Vol. XIX, No. 1, 1998, p. 13.

15   Ibid., p. 15.

16   Boyanski, *The 1940s*, p. 28.

17   H. O. McCurry to Paraskeva Clark, 8 May 1944. MG30 D398, Volume 4 File 32.

18   Paraskeva Clark to H. O. McCurry, 17 May 1944, Charles Hill Files, "Paraskeva Clark: Correspondence, 5.42c."

19   See Joan Murray, *Canadian Artists of the Second World War* (Oshawa: Robert McLaughlin Gallery, 1981).

20   H. O. McCurry to Paraskeva Clark, 9 December 1944. MG30 D398, Volume 4 File 32.

21   See Alison Prentice et al. *Canadian Women: A History* (Toronto: Harcourt Brace Jovanovich, 1988), pp. 301–303.

22   H. O. McCurry to Paraskeva Clark, 20 December 1944. MG30 D398, Volume 4 File 23.

23   Paraskeva Clark to H. O. McCurry, 22 January 1945, Library and Archives, National Gallery of Canada, Clark 5.42c. "Quaicker" was a term "derived from the clicking sound of a telegraph key, although this was not a common air force expression" (MacLachlan, p. 68).

24   Ibid.

25   Paraskeva Clark to H. O. McCurry, 20 February 1945, National Gallery of Canada Archives, Clark 5.42c.

26   Paraskeva Clark to H. O. McCurry, 22 March 1945, ibid.

27   Ibid.

28   Paraskeva Clark to H. O. McCurry, 24 March 1945, National Gallery of Canada Archives, 5.42c.

29   *Portrait of the Artist as an Old Lady.*

30   National Gallery of Canada Archives, 5.42c; MG30 D398, Volume 4 File 32.

31   Clive and Mary Clark, 8 February 2001.

32   Paraskeva Clark to H. O. McCurry, 11 May 1945, National Gallery of Canada Archives, Clark 5.42c.

33   Paraskeva Clark to H. O. McCurry, 9 August 1945, ibid.

34   MacLachlan, pp. 37, 38. Among the other landscapes from that holiday is *Little Lake in Tadoussac* (1945). An undated painting, *Tadoussac*, is also probably from the same holiday.

35   Paraskeva Clark to H. O. McCurry, 13 November 1945, National Gallery of Canada Archives, Clark 5.42c.

36   MacLachlan, p. 37.

37   Paraskeva Clark to H.O. McCurry, 20 January 1947, National Gallery of Canada Archives, 5.42c.

CHAPTER 12

1   Paraskeva Clark to H. O. McCurry, 25 August 1947, Charles Hill Files, "Paraskeva Clark: Correspondence, 5.42c."

2   Clive and Mary Clark, 2 January 2001.

3   This is how Geoffrey O'Brian described people on his street, though he said there were some exceptions (8 April 2002).

4   Nancy Reynolds, 14 May 2002.

5   Ann O'Brian, 5 April 2001; Audrey Pratt, 9 May 2001, Toronto.

6   Penny Pepperell, 18 April 2002.

7   Geoffrey O'Brian, 8 April 2002.

8   Ann O'Brian, 5 April 2001.

9   Bay Cardy, 5 September 2002.

10   Geoffrey O'Brian, 8 April 2002.

11   *The North Star*, Parry Sound, 25 January 1945.

12   A collection of 23,000 vintage photographs, taken by Soviet Union photog-
        raphers during the Stalinist period, from about 1935 until 1953 when Stalin
        died, is now in the holdings of the MacLaren Art Centre in Barrie, Ontario.
        These photos, originally owned by the SovFoto/Eastfoto agency, clearly show
        the extent to which the authorities tried to present a positive image of the
        Soviet Union during that time. My thanks to Sarah Chate for guiding me
        through "Broken Promises: Soviet Photography in the Age of Stalin," a selec-
        tion of the SovFoto images on exhibit at the gallery in October 2007.

13   Adam Rayco, 23 January 2001.

14   By 1949, the number of members had dropped to 2,709, and by the late 1980s
        there were fewer than 800 members. *Vestnik* stopped publication in 1994. See
        www.thecanadianencyclopedia.com.

15   MG30 D398, Volume 5 Files 7, 8.

16   *Toronto Daily Star*, 28 November 1944. Paraskeva also gave a lecture at the
        Heliconian Club luncheon in April 1945. *The Globe and Mail* , 13 April 1945.

17   Typed lecture "Russian Art" in MG30 D398, Volume 4 File 44, p. 1. The infor-
        mation in this section about her lecture comes from this file.

18   Weisbord, *The Strangest Dream*, p. 159.

19   Lela Wilson, 30 July 2001; Jean Horne, 30 May 2001.

20   Weisbord, *The Strangest Dream*, p. 152.

21   Jay Myers, *Canadian Facts and Figures* (Markham, Ontario: Fitzhenry &
        Whiteside, 1986), p. 191; Weisbord, *The Strangest Dream*, p. 145, 157.

22   Clive and Mary Clark, 15 February 2001.

23   Weisbord, *The Strangest Dream*, p. 161.

24   Clive and Mary Clark, 15 February 2001.

25   Adam Rayco, 23 January 2001.

26   Letter to the author from J. Christian Picard, Supt. Departmental Privacy and
        Access to Information Coordinator, 23 March 2004; and telephone interview
        with Margaret Evans, RCMP Archives, April 2002. Neither Library and Archives
        Canada, nor CSIS had any records on an investigation of Paraskeva. I did
        find, however, that she was listed in the "R.C.M.P. Security Bulletins: The
        War Series, Part II, 1942–45," edited by Gregory S. Kealey and Reg Whitaker
        (St. John's, Newfoundland: Canadian Committee on Labour History, 1993)

p. 23. Her name was listed as "P. Clark, Toronto (lady) well known Russian artist" among the names of people who attended the Congress of the Federation of Russian Canadians.

27 Ibid.

28 National Gallery of Canada Archives, 5.5R Russian Art Exhibition (Proposed).

29 MG30 D398, Volume 5 File 11. These notes are undated, but references to thirty years "since the establishment of Soviet Power" and correspondence with VOKS in Moscow means we can be quite sure these notes were made for the lectures she gave in 1947, or possibly 1948.

30 My thanks to Barry Appleton for giving me the opportunity of seeing this work.

31 Sabbath, p. 292.

32 Ira B. Nadel, *The Cambridge Companion to Ezra Pound* (Cambridge: Cambridge University Press, 1999), p. 81.

33 Ibid., pp. xxi, xxv, 11. Pound's *A Draft of the Cantos 17–27* was published in London in 1928 (p. xxiii), and *Eleven New Cantos XXI–XLI* in New York in 1934 (p. xxiv).

34 David Mawr, "Artist Buys Few Groceries on Traveling Show Income," *Windsor Star*, 25 June 1949. A search through Toronto newspapers around that time did not yield any articles about this meeting of "museum people," which Mawr mentions in his article. Nor did the E. P. Taylor Research Library and Archives at the Art Gallery of Ontario have any records of that meeting (email from Randall Speller to Jane Lind, 24 March 2004).

35 Typed manuscript in MG30 D398, Volume 5 File 22; and Paraskeva Clark, *Canadian Art* Vol. VII, No. 1 (Autumn 1949), pp. 21–23.

36 Andrew Bell, "The Art of Paraskeva Clark," Vol. VII, No. 2 (Christmas 1949).

37 My thanks to Mary MacLachlan for a conversation (taped 9 July 2003 in Halifax) that contributed to my thinking about this part of Paraskeva's life.

38 Bell, "The Art of Paraskeva Clark," p. 46.

39 Andrew Bell, "Toronto as an Art Centre," *Canadian Art* Vol. VI, No. 2 (Christmas 1948), p. 75.

40 Josephine Hambleton, "A Painter of Sylvan Canada," *Ottawa Citizen*, 17 January 1948; Sabbath, p. 291.

41 See note 3, chapter 5.

42 MacLachlan, p. 38.

43 I'm thinking particularly of two Petrov-Vodkin paintings: *Fantasy 1925* and *Spring 1935*, both in the Russian Museum in St. Petersburg.

44 *Globe and Mail*, 12 July 1949.

45 MG30 D398,Volume 4 File 10.

46 Sergei N. Kournakoff, "The Nineteenth Month," *Soviet Russia Today*, February 1943, p. 11.This article includes a map showing the developments in the war at that time.

47 Telephone conversation between Zoja Vladimirivna Plistik, Paraskeva's cousin by marriage in St. Petersburg, and translator Elina Zavgorodny, Guelph, Ontario, 3 November 2002.This family has a copy of the death certificate for Zakhar with the date of his death.

CHAPTER 13

1   Becker, *Zones of Contention*, p. 42.

2   Paraskeva Clark, "Thoughts on Canadian Painting," *World Affairs*, February 1943, p. 18.

3   The first show of abstract art in Canada was held at the Art Gallery of Toronto twenty-two years earlier 1–24 April 1927, International Exhibition of Modern Art, Assembled by the Société Anonyme. Lawren Harris was the only Canadian in this exhibition, and made sure that the press covered the show (Dennis Reid, *Bertram Brooker*, 1885–1955, Ottawa: National Gallery of Canada, 1973, pp. 13, 14).

4   My thanks to Anna Hudson for a conversation about this aspect of Paraskeva's life (taped 24 March 2003). Although Paraskeva had painted many landscapes before this time, after 1950 she did no more work with human subjects and painted only still lifes and landscapes.

5   Sabbath, p. 292.

6   Handwritten copy of lecture in MG30 D398,Volume 5 File 17.

7   Quoted in Ord, *The National Gallery of Canada*, p. 65.

8   The sense of the importance of art in Russian culture was demonstrated during the World War II Nazi siege of Leningrad. When the staff of the Hermitage was packing up the paintings in the collection, people from all over the city poured in to help, including a "team of students from the Academy of the Arts who had copied paintings in the Hermitage before the war." More than a million objects were packed up and transported to the Urals by train until the war was over. See Norman, pp. 241, 245.

9   Quoted in Ord, *The National Gallery of Canada*, p. 41.

10 "Joan Murray Talking to Paraskeva Clark," 29 May 1979.

11 MG30 D398,Volume 5 File 17.

12   James T. Lemon, *Toronto Since 1918* (Toronto and Ottawa: James Lorimer and National Museums of Canada, 1985), p. 113.

13   Ibid., p. 134.

14   These were Leaside, Mimico, New Toronto, Weston, Forest Hill, Long Branch, Swansea, East York, Etobicoke, North York, Scarborough, and York. See Bruce West, *Toronto* (Toronto: Doubleday Canada, 1967), p. 229.

15   Letter from Philip Clark to Murray and Frances Adaskin, 21 July 1950, courtesy of Dorothea and Murray Adaskin. The Suttons had a cottage near Honey Harbour at that time.

16   Alice Sutton, 19 February 2001.

17   Anna Sutton Anderson, 16 September 2003.

18   Alice Sutton, 19 February 2001.

19   Alice Sutton, 19 February 2001; Anna Sutton Anderson, 16 September 2003.

20   Ibid., Anderson.

21   Niwa, *For Frances and Murray*.

22   MG30 D398, Vol. 5 File 19; Russell Harper, *Canadian Paintings in Hart House* (Toronto: University of Toronto, 1955) p. 59.

23   MG30 D398, Vol. 5 File 19.

24   Adaskin, memoirs, p. 67.

25   Dated 14 January 1961. My thanks to June McLean for sending me a copy of this card and note. Since the date on the painting Paraskeva gave to Murray was March 1950, she must have visited the memorial the summer of 1949, for it is not likely she would have gone North in March even though she says in the note that she painted it in 1950.

26   Sherrill Grace, *Inventing Tom Thomson* (Montreal and Kingston: McGill-Queen's University Press, 2004), p. 5.

27   O'Rourke, "Labours and Love," p. 37.

28   Andrew Bell, "Contemporary Canadian Water-Colours," *The Studio*, April 1952, p. 110.

29   Letter in the McInnes Papers, Robertson Davies Library.

30   See Donald W. Buchanan, *The Growth of Canadian Painting* (London: Collins, 1950) pp. 54–56.

31   Hambleton, "A Painter of Sylvan Canada."

32   The title "Melancholy on a Winters Day" is lettered on the back of this painting, but it is not Paraskeva's hand. The 1951 reviews of this show give the title as "Melancholy of a Winter Day," as does Paraskeva's handwritten list for her show at Victoria College in 1952.

33   Painting list for the Victoria College show in MG30 D398, Volume 5 File 23.

Myself was purchased by the National Gallery of Canada in 1974 and *Petroushka* in 1976.

34 Yvonne Housser to Paraskeva Clark, undated, and Carl Schaefer to Paraskeva Clark, 2 February 1952. MG30 D398, Volume 5 File 33.

35 Paraskeva Clark to H. O. McCurry, 19 February 1954, Charles Hill Files, "Paraskeva Clark: Correspondence."

36 Becker, *Zones of Contention*, pp. 213, 216.

37 Paraskeva Clark to H. O. McCurry, 24 June 1954, Charles Hill Files, "Paraskeva Clark: Correspondence."

38 Ord, *The National Gallery of Canada*, p. 152.

39 26 May 1956.

40 June McLean, 9 April 2003.

41 Gordon MacNamara, 23 October 2001.

42 Letter to Charles and Louise Comfort from the Publication Offices of *Canadian Art* in Ottawa, 6 March 1956. Charles Fraser Comfort fonds, MG30 D81, Volume 31 File 18.

43 MG30 D398, Volume 1 File 41.

44 Clive and Mary Clark, 8 January 2002.

45 O'Rourke, "Labours and Love," p. 86.

46 John A. Becker to Paraskeva Clark, 19 June 1956. MG30 D398, Volume 5 File 37.

47 Paraskeva Clark to Alan Jarvis, Director of the National Gallery of Canada, 25 October 1956, Charles Hill Files, "Paraskeva Clark: Correspondence."

CHAPTER 14

1 Becker, *Zones of Contention*, p. 191.

2 Gordon MacNamara, 23 October 2001.

3 Clive and Mary Clark, 11 April 2001.

4 Joel Clark, who took responsibility for Ben from the early eighties until his death on 10 January 2006, questions Ben's original diagnosis of schizophrenia. Joel believes, from what he has observed and heard from Ben during more than twenty years of living with him, that Ben was somewhat smothered in his youth and increasingly isolated over the years. Nor was Ben expected to take responsibility for the day-to-day details of adult life. However, when Joel assumed Ben's care, he made it clear to Ben that he was expected to function like an adult. In the mid-nineties, Joel took Ben to see a psychiatrist at the Toronto General Hospital who concluded he was not schizophrenic

(Joel Clark, 3 May 2001). Of course, after so much time, I do not believe it is possible to be sure exactly what Ben experienced in 1943 when he was diagnosed — and the circumstances of his illness then — though some of his symptoms did point to schizophrenia at that time. However, isolation, which Ben did experience, would certainly affect his ability to relate to other people.

5   Paraskeva Clark to Alex Jackson, 5 January 1966, Naomi Jackson Groves, Personal Archives.

6   Clive and Mary Clark, 11 December 2001 and 30 October 2002. These many years later, the length of time Ben held his jobs and the places he worked are somewhat vague in the Clarks' memories.

7   Clive Clark, 11 December 2001.

8   "Joan Murray Talking to Paraskeva Clark," 29 May 1979.

9   *Portrait of the Artist as an Old Lady*. It's interesting that Paraskeva clipped an article quoting American painter Mary Cassatt who said, "After all a woman's vocation in life is to have children." The article also said that in her later years she often stamped her cane at younger artists (unidentified, undated clipping, MG30 D398, Volume 2 File 6).

10 Ibid.

11 Dorothy Richardson quoted in Linda Nochlin, *Representing Women* (New York: Thames & Hudson, 1999), p. 184.

12 See Prentice, *Canadian Women*, Chapter 12, especially p. 308.

13 *Portrait of the Artist as an Old Lady*.

14 Hill, interview with Paraskeva Clark, 18 October 1973.

15 James Purdie, *Globe and Mail*, 29 January 1977.

16 Laura Brandon, *Pegi By Herself* (Montreal and Kingston: McGill-Queen's University Press, 2005) pp. 157, 160, 166.

17 Gail Singer, 1 February 2001.

18 See *The Kingston Conference Proceedings*, especially page 21.

19 Paraskeva's handwritten speech is in MG30 D398, Volume 5 File 15. A letter of thanks in MG30 D398 from Headmaster J. S. Guest, dated 7 January 1959, mentions some details about her speech that led me to conclude this hand-written copy was the one she gave there even though the copy does not specify so. I contacted the archivist at Ridley College, Paul Lewis, and he could find no record of Paraskeva's speech. Further, he said that Ridley College did not become co-ed until 1972 (phone 15 January 2004). This is puzzling, because the J. S. Guest letter mentions having "pounded" into "the girls" what Paraskeva said about Frances Hodgkins. "But it [is] so hard to keep their minds on such study when the mental clockwork is saying — Loblaws loblaws

loblaws dominion dominion dominion Aan'P Aan'P Aan'P Aan'P Baby Baaby Baby lunch lunch lunch. I have so many sad cases of arrested development here & elsewhere of the girls imitating so beautifully but boggling when the inner processes are required." Clearly, he was unusual for his time, a man who agreed with Paraskeva.

20   Anna Hudson, 13 September 2004.

21   Thérèsa Diamand Rosinsky, *Suzanne Valadon*, Universe Series on Women Artists (New York: Universe Publishing, 1994) p. 123.

22   Many of these are in private collections. Others are in the collection of Libby's of Toronto.

23   Anna Hudson, 13 September 2004.

24   The term "schizophrenia" was coined in 1908 and this diagnosis preceded that. The term "schophrenic" is still used in certain situations.

25   June Rose, *Suzanne Valadon: The Mistress of Montmartre* (New York: St. Martin's Press, 1998), p. 129.

26   Eric Miller, 25 May 2005; Gavin Miller, 25 May 2005.

27   Francine Volker, 24 February 2003; email from Mary Clark to the author, 24 March 2005.

28   Letter from Douglas Gibson to the author, 8 August 2007.

29   Geoffrey O'Brian, 8 April 2002.

30   Ann O'Brian, 5 April 2001.

31   Wentworth Walker, 19 April 2001.

32   O'Rourke, "Labours and Love," p. 46.

33   Clive and Mary Clark, 10 April 2001.

34   Panya Clark, 13 February 2001.

35   MG30 D398, Volume 11 File 11.

36   MG30 D398, Volume 1 File 46.

37   The source for the information on Paraskeva's cooking is Clive and Mary Clark, 10 April 2001.

38   Jennifer Clark Mazurkiewicz, 5 April 2001; Clive and Mary Clark, 15 February 2001.

39   Meskimmon, *The Art of Reflection*, p. 94.

40   Ignatieff, p. 154.

41   Pearl McCarthy, "Art and Artists," *The Globe and Mail* , 14 July 1942, p. 7.

42   MG30 D398, Volume 14 File 28. A variety of Paraskeva's books, magazines, and clippings are found in MG30 D398 in a number of files.

43   Some of Paraskeva's books and magazines from her library are now archived at the E. P. Taylor Research Library and Archives, Art Gallery of Ontario.

44   "Andrew Bell Interviews Paraskeva Clark," 11 April 1948. MG30 D398, Volume 6 File 27.

45   Ralph Hyman, "Ontario's Mr. Three Per Cent," *Globe Magazine*, 26 August 1961, p. 23.

46   Salaries of Ontario government employees are listed in the *Public Accounts of the Province of Ontario* (Toronto: Baptist Johnston Printer to the Queen's Most Excellent Majesty, 1937, 1950, 1959, 1964) for any given fiscal year.

47   Clive and Mary Clark, 10 April 2001.

48   Hyman, p. 23.

49   O. J. Firestone, *The Other A. Y. Jackson* (Toronto: McClelland & Stewart, 1979), p. 211.

50   Clive and Mary Clark, 15 February 2001.

51   Information on properties in the city is recorded in the Land Registry Office of the City of Toronto.

52   MG30 D398, Volume 22 File 1. March 13, 1969.

53   See Brandon, *Pegi By Herself*, p. 161.

54   Carl Schaefer to Paraskeva Clark, 6 January 1954. MG30 D398, Volume 3 File 7.

55   Henri Masson to Paraskeva Clark, 2 April 1959. MG30 D398, Volume 3 File 9.

56   Irma Coucill, 4 December 2001.

57   Sabbath, p. 293.

58   Paraskeva Clark to T. R. MacDonald, Director of the Art Gallery of Hamilton, 27 January 1964. Art Gallery of Hamilton.

CHAPTER 15

1   Paraskeva Clark, lecture at the Art Gallery of Hamilton, 11 May 1950. MG30 D398, Volume 5 File 17.

2   MG30 D398, Volume 7 File 29. Alan Jarvis, then director of the National Gallery, was a consultant for this booklet.

3   Sabbath, p. 293.

4   This work is in the collection of the Ottawa Art Gallery, donated by the Ontario Heritage Foundation to the City of Ottawa.

5   This painting is in the collection of Jenny Sutton, Toronto.

6   Firestone Art Collection: The Ottawa Art Gallery.

7   Pearl McCarthy, "Artist Paints Artist," *Globe and Mail*, 11 July 1942.

8   Dated 18 December 1942. MG30 D351, Volume 1 File 8.

9   A. Y. Jackson to Paraskeva Clark, 16 June 1949, National Gallery of Canada Archives File 7.1-C.

10   Christopher Varley, 27 November 2002.

11   Wentworth Walker, 19 April 2001.

12   I am indebted to Christopher Varley for identifying the small image in Paraskeva's Jackson portrait. The painting, *Birdcage and Playing Cards* is reproduced in Alfred H. Barr, *Picasso: Fifty Years of His Art* (New York: Museum of Modern Art, 1966), p. 208.

13   I am indebted to Anna Hudson for her reading of the portrait (28 February 2005).

14   Christopher Varley, 27 November 2002.

15   Paraskeva Clark to A. Y. Jackson, 10 January 1967, Naomi Jackson Groves, personal archives.

16   Undated, handwritten in MG30 D398, Volume 1 File 41.

17   *Portrait of the Artist as an Old Lady.*

18   Jarvis, *Douglas Duncan*, p. 39.

19   Email from Clive and Mary Clark to the author, 24 March 2005.

20   22 August 1973 in MG30 D398, Volume 5 File 45.

21   Charles Hill to Paraskeva Clark, 26 September 1974. MG30 D398, Volume 6 File 12.

22   See Barry Lord, "Canadian Painting in the Thirties at the National Gallery of Canada," *Art Magazine* (Spring 1975), Volume 6, No. 21, p. 8.

23   Ibid., p. 13.

24   Ten of the 109 paintings were in another medium such as watercolour or ink.

25   Hill, *Canadian Painting in the Thirties*, p. 15.

26   Hudson, "Art and Social Progress," pp. 61, 299.

27   17 April 1975, courtesy of Dorothea Adaskin.

28   James Purdie, "The survivors of the harsh decade look back," *Globe and Mail*, 3 June 1975, p. 15.

29   Marvin B. Gelber to Paraskeva Clark, 20 March 1975. MG30 D398, Volume 5 File 61.

30   Adele Freedman, pp. 127–129.

31   Margaret Walters to Paraskeva Clark, 4 June 1975. MG30 D398, Volume 3 File 14.

32   Purdie, "The survivors of the harsh decade look back," p. 15.

33   Compact disc, the Canadian Music Centre, Toronto.

34   14 October 1975 in MG30 D398, Volume 3 File 15.

35   Audio Tape, Charles Hill Interview with Charles and Louise Comfort, 3 October 1973, National Gallery of Canada Archives.

36   Gail Singer, 1 February 2001.

37   *Portrait of the Artist as an Old Lady*.

38   Charles Hill, 8 April 2002, Ottawa.

39   O'Rourke, "Labours and Love," p. 72, note 162.

40   Donald Patterson, 6 January 2001.

41   Philip Clark letter, Toronto, to Murray and Frances Adaskin, Victoria, B.C., 17 October 1977, courtesy of Dorothea Adaskin.

42   Ibid. Also, see letters in MG30 D398, Volume 22 Files 5, 6 and Volume 21 File 18.

43   Clive Clark has speculated that the reason for rejecting Paraskeva was that through some glitch the Government of Canada had no record of her being a Canadian citizen. After she died, and Clive and Mary Clark made application for government services for Ben, to their surprise and dismay, they were told there was no record of her citizenship (Clive Clark, 11 December 2001).

44   Undated birthday card in MG30 D398, Volume 3 File 34.

45   5 September 1979 in MG30 D398, Volume 21 File 18.

46   9 August 1979 in MG30 D398, Volume 21 File 18.

47   Clive and Mary Clark, 10 April 2001.

48   See Becker, *Zones of Contention*, p. 236, for an analysis of this aspect of the relationship of men and women.

49   See O'Rourke, "Labours and Love," p. 77.

50   Gail Singer, 1 February 2001.

51   O'Rourke, "Labours and Love," p. 73.

52   Wentworth Walker, 19 April 2001; "Funeral Service for Paraskeva Clark," MG30 D398, Volume 3 File 31.

53   George Miller, 11 January 2001.

54   Joyce Wieland fonds in Clara Thomas Archives and Special Collections, York University, W633/91-014, Box 2, File 38.

55   MG30 D398, Volume 6 File 20.

56   The National Film Board contracted with Paraskeva to pay her five hundred dollars for her part in the film. MG30 D398, Volume 6 file 10.

57   Gail Singer, 1 February 2001.

58   Kay Kritzwiser, "Paraskeva in the Looking Glass," *Globe and Mail*, 16 February 1983, p. 13.

59   Christopher Hume, "Painting is not a woman's job," *Toronto Star*, 29 January 1983.

60   Philip Fry, *Charles Gagnon*, (Montreal: The Montreal Museum of Fine Arts, 1978), p. 81.

61　Paraskeva would have seen Fred Varley's classic *Open Window* (c. 1933) and Isabel McLaughlin's *Budding Hyacinths* of the same year before she painted her own window still lifes. She would also have been familiar with Pegi Nicol McLeod's *Cold Window* (c. 1935).

62　Anna Hudson, 23 January 2001. My thanks also to Charles Hill for a conversation (8 April 2002) that stimulated my thinking.

Epilogue

1　Mary Meigs, *In the Company of Strangers* (Vancouver: Talonbooks, 1991), p. 76.

2　*Portrait of the Artist as an Old Lady.*

3　Much of the information in this epilogue is drawn from the interview I had with Clive and Mary Clark, 10 April 2001.

4　Mary MacLachlan, Halifax, Nova Scotia, to Murray and Frances Adaskin, Victoria, British Columbia, 21 September 1981.

5　Judy Stoffman, "The Rediscovery of Paraskeva Clark," *Chatelaine*, August 1983.

6　Sandy Miller Harris, 13 April 2005 (former neighbour).

7　Wentworth Walker and Mary MacLachlan in a transcript of funeral notes. MG30 D398, Volume 3 File 31.

8　*Portrait of the Artist as an Old Lady.*

9　Paraskeva Clark, in "Andrew Bell Interviews Paraskeva Clark," 11 April 1948. MG30 D398, Vol. 6 File 17.

Acknowledgements ❧

This book on the life and work of Paraskeva Clark would not have been possible without the help of many people.

I am most indebted to Paraskeva's family. Clive and Mary Clark's generosity was outstanding. They gave me many hours of conversation and answered myriad questions; and they spent even more time looking through photos of family and friends for use in the book. The late Ben Clark, too, told me as much as he was able. Paraskeva's grandchildren, Joel Clark, Jennifer Mazurkiewicz, and Panya Clark Espinal, recounted memories of their grandmother. Marguerite Hunt, Philip Clark's niece, generously provided access to her taped interview with Paraskeva and gave of her time.

Fortunately, Clive and Mary Clark took care of Paraskeva's papers and records extant at her death in 1986. In 1994, they deposited these papers and some of her books and magazines in Library and Archives Canada in Ottawa, along with pertinent records from Philip's life. This archival material, made available with the generous help from the staff at Library and Archives Canada, was invaluable in writing about Paraskeva. The Clarks also deposited part of her library in the Edward P. Taylor Library and Archives at the Art Gallery of Ontario in Toronto. I appreciate the help of the staff at the Edward P. Taylor Library and Archives: Randall Speller, Larry Pfaff, and Amy Marshall. Registrar Barry Simpson took time to show me Paraskeva's paintings and drawings in the Art Gallery of Ontario collection.

I wish to thank, too, Cyndie Campbell and Michael Williams at the National Gallery of Canada Library and Archives. Shawn D. Boisvert, Documentation Officer, showed me drawings in the National Gallery collection and Sharon Odell, Documentation Assistant, went to great lengths to make the paintings in the vaults available to me.

Mary E. MacLachlan's extensive research and interviews with Paraskeva in her later years resulted in an exhibition and fine catalogue *Paraskeva Clark: Paintings and Drawings*. Until now, this 1982 volume was the only substantial published material available about this important artist. MacLachlan's catalogue, and my conversation with her, formed an integral part of my exploration of Paraskeva's life and work.

Anna Hudson, a curator at the Art Gallery of Ontario when I began my research, and now on the Faculty of Fine Arts at York University in Toronto, spent many hours talking with me about Paraskeva and the other artists of her era. Anna also generously loaned me her 1997 doctoral thesis, *Art and Social Progress: The Toronto Community of Painters, 1933–1950*. I am indebted to Anna for taking time to read an earlier draft of my manuscript and for her helpful comments. She inspired me, and our mutual pleasure in talking about Paraskeva, and the artists of her era, evolved into a friendship that I treasure.

I am grateful to Kate O'Rourke for loaning me her 1995 Masters thesis, *Labours and Love: Issues of Domesticity and Marginalization in the Works of Paraskeva Clark*. Her astute and intelligent writing on Paraskeva's life from a feminist perspective was extremely helpful.

Diane Young read an early draft of the first third of the book; her comments on my approach sent me back to my computer to rework this draft again and again. Eva Major-Marothy, curator of the National Portrait Gallery, went out of her way to help, and cheered me on from the day we first met.

Dorothea Adaskin offered me extraordinary hospitality in Victoria, British Columbia, and allowed me to sit surrounded by the Paraskeva Clark paintings in the collection she shared with her late husband, Murray Adaskin. She also sent me invaluable letters, clippings, and photos from Murray's files. I am so grateful for her generosity and for her endless encouragement.

Joan Murray provided access to the Robert McLaughlin Gallery Archives in Oshawa and gave me a copy of her transcripts of interviews with Paraskeva. Ray Peringer opened the Arts & Letters Club archives for me in Toronto. John Libby, of Libby's art gallery of Toronto, took time on several occasions to show me his Paraskeva Clark drawings and paintings. His assistant, Maria Hazel, also took time to help me. Barry Appleton made time in his schedule and went to some inconvenience to show me his collection of Clark's work.

The following people helped me trace some of Clark's drawings and paintings: Christopher Varley, Toronto; Kapil Harnal of Roberts Gallery, Toronto; Hughene Acheson of Heffel Gallery, Toronto. My thanks to the owners of Clark's works for their kind permission to use reproductions in the book, and to those who helped in obtaining reproductions: Janet Lauthon-Mackay; Sara and Eric Jackman of Toronto; and Patrick Stewart of Victoria and Rod Green of Masters Gallery in Calgary both of whom not only arranged for photography but also subsidized it. Albert Rain went to great lengths to have a painting in his collection photographed and sent to me at his own expense.

A number of people of Guelph, Ontario, helped me with translation. Elina Zavgorodny translated Russian documents and phoned some of Paraskeva's remaining cousins in St. Petersburg, helping me verify information about Paraskeva's family. I wish to thank others who helped with translation: Maren Kasulke, Lise Otis, George Renninger, and Armando Carere.

I interviewed many people who talked to me about Paraskeva and her work. Thank you all for your help.

I deeply appreciate the generous support of the Canada Council for the Arts and its program, "Grants for Professional Writers — Creative Writing, Non-Fiction." I am also indebted to the Ontario Arts Council for grants from the Writers' Reserve program. This kind of government support on both levels is so essential for the continued flourishing of Canadian culture.

My thanks to my friends and family for their continued interest; and for listening to my frustrations, my stories, and my excitement about Paraskeva, who, for me, lives on.

Eleanor Johnston, manager of Mirvish Books in Toronto, deserves thanks for introducing me to Marc Côté, publisher of Cormorant Books. His enthusiasm for the book from the beginning gave me the encouragement I needed. I also wish to thank the Cormorant staff for their hard work.

This book benefitted more than I can say from the thoughtful work of my editor, Ruth Bradley-St-Cyr. Any errors or oversights are mine.

List of Colour Plates ⁓

Plate 9. *Fruit* (1931), oil on paper board, 45 x 58.3 cm. Private collection. Photo credit: Dean Palmer.

Plate 10. Waterfalls painting on the back side of *Fruit*. Photo credit: Dean Palmer.

Plate 11. *Myself* (1933), oil on canvas, 101.6 x 76.2 cm. National Gallery of Canada, 18311.

Plate 12. *Portrait of Naomi Yanova* (1934), 100 x 75.5 cm. Private collection, Vancouver, B.C. Photo credit: Cameron Heryet.

Plate 13. Working Drawing for Eaton's Windows (c. 1935) (deer leaping), gouache, ink, graphite on paper. Ottawa Art Gallery.

Plate 14. *Untitled (Trout)* (1936), watercolour on paper, 61 x 50.8 cm. A.G. Rain Family Collection, Toronto. Photo credit: Dean Palmer.

Plate 15. *Presents from Madrid* (1937), watercolour over graphite on wove paper, 51.5 x 62 cm. National Gallery of Canada, 23666.

Plate 16. *Wheat Field* (1936), oil on canvas, 63.6 x 76.5 cm. National Gallery of Canada, 16452.

Plate 17. *Image of the Thirties* (nd), pencil on paper, 35 x 24 cm. Private collection. Photo credit: Richard Goldthorpe.

Plate 18. *Evening Walk on Yonge Street* (1938), watercolour on paper, 40 x 34.5 cm. Private collection, Toronto. Photo credit: Dean Palmer.

Plate 19. *Petroushka* (1937), oil on canvas, 122.4 x 81.9 cm. National Gallery of Canada, 18624.

Plate 20. *Pen Drawing for Petroushka*, pen and pencil on paper, 41 x 27 cm. Libby's of Toronto. Photo credit: Dean Palmer.

Plate 21. *The Bush* (1938), oil on canvas, 76.3 x 68.5 cm. Art Gallery of Ontario, gift from the J.S. McLean Collection, Ontario Heritage Foundation.

Plate 22. *In the Woods* (1939), oil on canvas, 77.5 x 69 cm. Hart House Permanent Collection, University of Toronto.

Plate 23. *Swamp* (1939), oil on canvas, 76.2 x 50.8 cm. Art Gallery of Ontario, gift from the Albert H. Robson Memorial Subscription Foundation, 1939.

Plate 24. Drawings for *New World Illustrated*.

Plate 25. *Memories of Leningrad* (1941), watercolour on paper, 41.1 x 50.4 cm. Winchester Galleries, Victoria, B.C. Photo credit: Anthony Sam.

Plate 26. *Self Portrait* (aka. *Self Portrait with Concert Program*) (1942), oil on canvas, 76.6 x 69.8 cm. National Gallery of Canada, 4592.

Plate 27. *It's 10 Below Outside* (1940), wax crayon, ink, graphite on paper, 28.5 x 30.2 cm. Ottawa Art Gallery.

Plate 28. *Pavlichenko and Her Comrades at the Toronto City Hall* (1943), oil on canvas,

127.7 x 128.3 cm. Art Gallery of Ontario.

Plate 29. *Evening After Rain* (1946), oil on canvas, 45.8 x 40.6 cm. Private collection, Victoria, B.C. Photo credit: Anthony Sam.

Plate 30. *Ben* (1945), pencil and watercolour on paper, 43 x 48 cm. Libby's of Toronto. Photo credit: Dean Palmer.

Plate 31. *Portrait of Murray Adaskin* (1944–45), oil on canvas, 98.7 x 75.0 cm. Library and Archives Canada, C51465K.

Plate 32. *Public Bath — Leningrad* (1944), watercolour, pastel on paper, 29 x 59 cm. Private collection, Toronto. Photo Credit: Dean Palmer.

Plate 33. *Percée* (1945), oil on canvas, 51 x 61 cm. Art Gallery of Ontario, gift of Dorothea Larsen Adaskin.

Plate 34. *Quaicker Girls* (1946), oil on canvas, 73.8 x 89 cm. Accession Number 19710261-5680, Beaverbrook Collection of War Art, Canadian War Museum.

Plate 35. *Maintenance Jobs in the Hangar* (1945), oil on canvas, 81.6 x 101.6 cm. Accession Number 19710261, Beaverbrook Collection of War Art, Canadian War Museum.

Plate 36. *Parachute Riggers* (1946–1947), oil on canvas, 101.7 x 81.4 cm. Accession Number 19710261-5679, Beaverbrook Collection of War Art, Canadian War Museum.

Plate 37. *View on the St. Lawrence Shore* (1945), oil on canvas, 80 x 100 cm. Private collection. Courtesy of Masters Gallery, Calgary. Photo credit: John Dean.

Plate 38. *Road Builders* (1948), oil, 50 x 60 cm. Private collection, Toronto. Photo credit: Dean Palmer.

Plate 39. *Diana Hunting in Caledon* (1948–1951), watercolour on paper, 52.1 x 83.8 cm. Private collection. Photo credit: Dean Palmer.

Plate 40. *Boathouse, Still Life* (1954), oil on canvas, 76.2 x 68.6 cm. Private collection, Toronto. Photo credit: Dean Palmer.

Plate 41. *Portrait of Frances James* (1950–1952), oil on canvas, 121 x 85.4 cm. Library and Archives Canada, C151469K.

Plate 42. *Melancholy of a Winter Day* (1951), oil on board, 60 x 50 cm. Private collection, Markham, Ontario. Photo credit: Dean Palmer.

Plate 43. *Alice Sutton* (1950–52), oil on canvas, 112 x 97 cm. Private collection, Shawville, Quebec. Photo credit: Heidi Ardern.

Plate 44. *Tom Thomson Memorial* (1950), oil on tempered hardboard, 60.0 x 32.9 cm. Inscribed "Parskeva to Murray, 28 March, 50." Art Gallery of Ontario, gift of Dorothea Larsen Adaskin, 2004.

Plate 45. *Pink Cloud* (1937), oil on canvas, 50.9 x 60.8 cm. National Gallery of Canada.

Plate 46. *Highway Still Life* (1966), oil, metal, plastic, and woven wool on board. Ottawa Art Gallery (FAC1553).

Plate 47. *Neighbouring Yards* (1954), oil on canvas, 50 x 60 cm. Private collection, Toronto Photo credit: K.Ross Hookway.

Plate 48. *Kitchen Still Life* (1957), oil on masonite, 1957, 75 x 50 cm. Private collection, Toronto. Photo credit: Dean Palmer.

Plate 49. *Untitled (Still Life with Pears)* (c. 1941), watercolour on paper, 48.75 x 38.75 cm. Private collection, Victoria, B.C. Photo credit: Anthony Sam.

Plate 50. *Portrait of A.Y. Jackson* (1942–43), oil on canvas, 100 x 75 cm. The Power Corporation of Canada Art Collection.

Plate 51. *Clematis Flower* (a.k.a. *Through the Window*) (1951), oil on board, 61 x 50.5 cm   Private collection, Duntroon, Ontario. Photo credit: Bryan Davies Photography.

Plate 52. *Noon at Tadoussac* (1958), oil on canvas, 81.2 x 101.6 cm. Art Gallery of Windsor, gift of Mr. Jack Wildridge, the Roberts Gallery, Toronto, 1969, 1969.0467.

Plate 53. *Self Portrait* (1937), watercolour on paper, 53.3 x 50.8 cm. Purchased with funds donated by Dalhousie University Alumni, Women's Division, 1954. Collection: Dalhousie Art Gallery, Halifax.

Plate 54. *Essentials of Life* (1947), oil on canvas, 61 x 50.8 cm. Private collection, Toronto. Photo credit: Dean Palmer.

Plate 55. *Memories of Leningrad* (1955–56), oil on canvas, 86 x 90.8 cm. Private collection, Toronto. Photo credit: Dean Palmer.

Plate 56. *Kitchen Cupboard Aspect* (1956), oil on masonite, 50 x 60 cm. Private collection, Toronto. Photo credit: Dean Palmer.

Plate 57. *Sunlight in the Woods* (1966), oil on masonite, 79.8 x 70 cm. National Gallery of Canada, Ottawa.

Plate 58. *Summer Night* (1969), acrylic on masonite, 60.6 x 50.8 cm. Private collection, Toronto. Photo credit: Dean Palmer.

Plate 59. *Homage to a Soviet Film, Baltic Deputy* (1968), oil, graphite on masonite, 92.1 x 76.6 cm. Ottawa Art Gallery (FAC 1252).

Plate 60. *The Baltic Deputy* (1969), watercolour, 60 x 60 cm. Inscription on the back: "To Alice and Stewart with Red Salute. Paraskeva 1969." Private collection, Toronto. Photo credit: Dean Palmer.

Plate 61. *Rain on the Window* (nd), oil on board, 96.5 x 60.8 cm. Art Gallery of Hamilton, gift of Richard Alway, 2001. Photo credit: Mike Lalich.

Plate 62. *Rubber Gloves* (1935), oil on canvas, 50 x 60.5 cm. Art Gallery of Hamilton, Patron's Purchase, 1964. Photo credit: Mike Lalich.

Plate 63. *Calla Lily* (1964–65), oil on masonite, 61.0 x 50.8 cm. Art Gallery of
  Windsor, gift from the Douglas M. Duncan Collection, 1970, 1970.026.
Plate 64. *October Rose* (1941), oil on canvas, 40.3 x 54.2 cm. Robert McLaughlin
  Gallery, Oshawa, Ontario.

Index

ENVIRONMENTAL BENEFITS STATEMENT

Cormorant Books saved the following resources by printing the pages of this book on chlorine free paper made with 100% post-consumer waste.

TREES	WATER	SOLID WASTE	GREENHOUSE GASES
29	**13,245**	**804**	**2,750**
FULLY GROWN	GALLONS	POUNDS	POUNDS

Calculations based on research by Environmental Defense and the Paper Task Force.
Manufactured at Friesens Corporation